KYLA -

A FEW EXCELLENT AND
SELECTED STORIES FOR
YOU AND A LITTLE
INSPIRARATION AS
WELL

UNCLE BEN

A Sailor's History
of the U.S. Navy

Other Titles in the Blue & Gold Series

The U.S. Naval Institute
Blue & Gold Professional Library

For more than a hundred years, U.S. Navy professionals have counted on specialized books published by the Naval Institute Press to prepare them for their responsibilities as they advance in their careers and to serve as ready references and refreshers when needed. From the days of coal-fired battleships to the era of unmanned aerial vehicles and laser weaponry, such perennials as *The Bluejacket's Manual* and the *Watch Officer's Guide* have guided generations of Sailors through the complex challenges of naval service. As these books are updated and new ones are added to the list, they will carry the distinctive mark of the Blue & Gold Professional Library series to remind and reassure their users that they have been prepared by naval professionals and they meet the exacting standards that Sailors have long expected from the U.S. Naval Institute.

BLUE & GOLD
PROFESSIONAL LIBRARY

A Sailor's History of the U.S. Navy

Thomas J. Cutler

A Co-publication of the U.S. Naval Institute and
the Naval History & Heritage Command

NAVAL INSTITUTE PRESS
Annapolis, Maryland

Naval Institute Press
291 Wood Road
Annapolis, MD 21402

Lyrics to the ballad "Brave Yankee Boys" appear here courtesy of the American Antiquarian Society in Worcester, Massachusetts.

ISBN-10: 1-59114-151-6
ISBN-13: 978-1-59114-151-8

Library of Congress Cataloging-in-Publication Data

Cutler, Thomas J., 1947–
   A sailor's history of the U.S. Navy / Thomas J. Cutler.
      p. cm. — (U.S. Naval Institute blue & gold professional library)
   1. United States. Navy—History. 2. Sailors—United States—History. I.
Title. II. Series.
   VA58.4.C88 2004
   359'.00973—dc22

                                                    2004023713

Printed in the United States of America on acid-free paper ∞

12   9 8 7 6 5

To all who serve—
yesterday, today, tomorrow

Contents

A Sailor's Preface

More than half a century ago, Theodore Roscoe wrote a book called *This Is Your Navy,* an informal history written specifically for Sailors. On the first page he asked: "What's the good of going back to the old days, or even yesterday, when you've got your hands full with affairs in the present? You're kept jumping by what's going on around you here and now. You're busy with what you're doing here today." His comments are still true today.

Roscoe's answer to his own question was, "What you do today depends largely on what was done yesterday"; that "the things you're doing now result from, and are a continuation of, things done in the past." He quoted American patriot Patrick Henry (who is best known for his stirring words, "Give me liberty or give me death") as saying: "I have but one lamp by which my feet are guided, and that is the lamp of experience. I know no way of judging the future but by the past."

This is a good answer. But for me, there has always been an even better reason. Perhaps it's a little selfish in its origin, but it has served me well. In my many years of service in the U.S. Navy, I sometimes felt like quitting. Although I loved many things about the Navy, it was a tough life in a lot of ways, making demands on me that other people my age—those who had chosen an easier life in the civilian world—did not face. Sometimes the hardships of life at sea, the separation from my family and friends, or the multitude of dangers that were never very far away would cause me to long for a quieter life, a more "normal" life, a less demanding life. But then I would stand before a mirror, getting ready to shave, look at the face staring back at me, and say, "You work for the Acme Soap Company." And I did not like what I saw. I would try again. "You work for Smith & Johnson, Inc." And I still did not like what I saw. Then I would say, "You are a Sailor in the United States Navy." And I very much liked what I saw.

The reason that the last statement worked when the others did not was that I knew I was part of something special. And what made it special—far different from anything else I might do—were the great things that had been done in the past by Sailors just like me. The uniform I wore with such pride—that made me instantly identifiable as someone special—meant little without the knowledge that other people wore that same uniform, or some form of it, when they fought the Barbary States of North Africa, charged into hostile Confederate fire at Mobile Bay, and destroyed Nazi submarines and Japanese aircraft carriers when evil men were hell-bent on dominating the world.

Another thing that made being a Sailor special for me was using terms like "galley" and "starboard" and "scuttlebutt," a language that connected me with "iron men who sailed wooden ships," that made me part of a "club" that has been around for a very long time and whose initiation requirements were that I give my own "honor, courage, and commitment."

The lather-covered face I saw each morning in the mirror was not unusual in any particular way. Yet it was special because it had felt the sting of salt spray and had seen the wonders of a starry night at sea just as Sailors had done for many centuries before. It had been darkened by the sun while patrolling the waters of Vietnam and weathered by heavy gales in the Mediterranean during the Yom Kippur War. It had known the bitter cold of patrols in the North Atlantic during the Cold War and been streaked with tears of pride the first time I heard "Anchor's Aweigh" played at the Navy Memorial in Washington, D.C.

No doubt, I would have been proud of my service even if I had never known any of the history that had preceded me. But the more I learned about those Sailors who had gone before me, the more special I felt, the more determined I became to measure up to the standards they had set. I could have served the Navy well without knowing its history, *but I sure wouldn't want to.*

In the pages that follow, I have tried to capture some of the magic I myself experienced as I served in the Navy and discovered the exciting past that made my "club" so special. I have done so in an unconventional way. Even though this book can be called an "informal history" of the Navy, just as Roscoe's book was, I have tried to make it a *heritage book* instead of a history book. To me, history is the stuff that scholars study for the good of the world. Heritage is the stuff that makes me stand a little taller and walk with a hint of a swagger.

Most history books start at the beginning and move forward through time. This book charts a different course. I have chosen to explore our heritage by way of themes rather than by chronology. It may be a little confusing at times, because we may jump from the recent war in Afghanistan to a battle in the American Revolution, but the goal here is not to make us historians, but to share in the heritage that makes us different and special. In case you occasionally need a road map to figure out where we are, I have included a chronological account of the major parts of our history in the appendix, titled "Battle Streamers." You may also want to refer to the date-by-date chronology that is Appendix B in your *Bluejacket's Manual*, which includes other major historical events besides the battles. For the most part, however, we will be traveling through time with few concerns about dates and chronologies, focusing instead on the Sailors who gave us reasons to be proud.

The word *sailor* has many meanings, ranging from the "iron men in wooden ships" of yesteryear to highly trained technicians running nuclear power plants in submerged submarines, from a young girl plying the waters of her hometown lake in a tiny sloop to a merchant marine captain carrying oil from the Middle East to Japan. The word has even had different meanings within the Navy; there was a time when it was used to differentiate enlisted personnel from officers. Today, however, *sailor* has come to have a special meaning, with a bit of mystique to it—so much so that it is now capitalized to make it clear that "Sailor" means a man or a woman who is a part of the greatest Navy the world has ever seen, one who carries on the heritage we will sample in this book. It refers to officer and enlisted alike: to seamen, airmen, firemen, and corpsmen; to those who stand watches on decks and those who man the ramparts of a five-sided building near the nation's capital; to those who stay for thirty years and those who move on after a single hitch; to those whose names are distinguished by USN or USNR.

Unlike most other histories of the Navy, this one focuses on all Sailors, in all their varied roles, from seaman to admiral. You will come to know Vernon Highfill, a fireman in the forward engine room of USS *Lexington* in World War II, as well as Commodore George Dewey, commander of the squadron that defeated the Spanish fleet at Manila Bay. You will meet Lieutenant John Worden, who commanded USS *Monitor* in her epic battle with CSS *Virginia*, and Quartermaster Peter Williams, who steered that ironclad into history. You will fly with Petty Officer Alvin Kernan, submerge with "Doctor" Wheeler Lipes, and sail with Ordinary Seaman John Kilby.

Although this is a proud celebration of the greatness of our Navy and how it came to be great, it is not intended to be a whitewash. You will see some mistakes made; after all, our predecessors were human beings like us. There are defeats as well as victories, and you will see ships and aircraft and their crews lost. But despite the setbacks and the sacrifices, you will see a Navy that moves ever forward: avenging, learning, correcting, and growing stronger and smarter as tragedy is turned into triumph. This is a story that has no happy ending simply because it is far from ended. But a story emerges that has a happy *middle*, a story that is still being written as each day dawns.

If you are a Sailor reading this *heritage* book, never forget that you are one of the main characters of this ongoing story. Unlike the high school or college student who can merely *read* history, you are *writing* history every day that you serve in the U.S. Navy. The more you know about the Sailors who served before you, the better prepared you will be to do your job, and do it well. It is your turn to follow in the wakes of those who went before you, to lead the way for others who will follow you, and to make your contributions to the Navy's ongoing legacy of honor, courage, and commitment.

Don't forget to look in the mirror—you just might like what you see.

Acknowledgments

Authors who claim to have written a book all by themselves are either extraordinary or liars. This work is the product of a great many impressive and important people who generously took time out of their busy lives to help me create this book. Together, they served as a board of advisors who helped me locate information, provided creative advice, and vetted my chapters as I wrote them. I am tempted to describe what each one did to contribute, but this book would be many pages longer if I did. Suffice it to say that each played a vital role, and all have my everlasting gratitude.

Lieutenant Commander Richard R. Burgess, USN (Ret.)—Managing editor of the U.S. Navy League's *Sea Power* magazine.

Commander Anthony Cowden, USNR—Mobilized following the attacks of 11 September 2001 and served for two years as liaison officer to the Joint Staff and battle watch captain in the Navy Operations Center in the Pentagon.

Dr. Michael Crawford—Head of the Early History branch of the Naval Historical Center in Washington, D.C.

Captain Todd Creekman, USN (Ret.)—Executive director of the Naval Historical Foundation in Washington, D.C.

Deborah W. Cutler—Author, editor, critic, creative consultant, and loving wife.

Lieutenant Commander Youssef H. Aboul-Enein, MSC, USN—Author and director for North Africa and Egypt, and special advisor on Islamic militant ideology, for the Office of the Secretary of Defense for International Security Affairs.

Vice Admiral Robert F. Dunn, USN (Ret.)—President of the Naval Historical Foundation in Washington, D.C.

Journalist First Class Mark Faram, USNR—Military correspondent for *Navy Times* newspaper.

Dr. Alan B. Flanders—Naval historian at the Navy's Center of Naval Leadership in Norfolk, Virginia.

Colonel Charles Gentile, AUS (Ret.)—A former Army counterintelligence officer and staff assistant and tutor at the Schuler School of Fine Arts in Baltimore, Maryland.

Senior Chief Hospital Corpsman Mark T. Hacala, USNR—Director, Education Institute Foundation at the U.S. Navy Memorial in Washington, D.C.

Master Chief Petty Officer of the Navy John Hagan, USN (Ret.)—Master chief petty officer of the Navy (1992-98) and coauthor of the *Chief Petty Officer's Guide*; currently the human systems integration lead for the Navy's destroyer concept (DDX) program.

Dr. John B. Hattendorf—Ernest J. King Professor of Maritime History and chairman of the Maritime History Department at the U.S. Naval War College in Newport, Rhode Island.

Command Master Chief Delta Hinson, USN—Command master chief USS *Wasp* and former member of the U.S. Naval Institute's editorial board.

Vice Admiral Al Konetzni, USN (Ret.)—Chairman of the U.S. Naval Institute's board of control.

J. F. (Jack) Leahy—Executive director of the Naval Writers' Group and author of *Honor, Courage, Commitment: Navy Boot Camp; Ask the Chief: Backbone of the Navy*; and coauthor of the *Chief Petty Officer's Guide*.

Dr. Edward J. Marolda—Senior historian at the Naval Historical Center in Washington, D.C.

Rear Admiral Larry Marsh, USN (Ret.)—Vice president of the Olmstead Foundation in Alexandria, Virginia.

Force Master Chief Michael McCalip, USN—Force master chief at the Naval Education and Training Command.

Chief of Naval Operations Directed Command Master Chief Sean McGurk, USN—Executive assistant to the master chief petty officer of the Navy in Washington, D.C.

Chief Journalist Lisa Mikoliczyk, USN—Special assistant to the master chief petty officer of the Navy in Washington, D.C.

Vice Admiral Jerry Miller, USN (Ret.)—Author who has served the Navy as commander of fourteen sea commands, including special task forces and the U.S. Second and Sixth Fleets.

Chief of Naval Operations Directed Command Master Chief Bernard Quibilan, USN—Command master chief at the U.S. Naval Academy.

John C. Reilly Jr.—Ambassador J. William Middendorf Naval History Research Chair at the Naval Historical Foundation in Washington, D.C.

Rear Admiral Ann E. Rondeau, USN—Commander, Naval Service Training Command.

Captain David Alan Rosenberg, USN—Chairman of the secretary of the Navy's subcommittee on naval history and former head of the Navy's Task Force History project.

Vice Admiral James Stavridis, USN—Senior military assistant to the secretary of defense.

Master Chief Petty Officer of the Navy Terry Scott, USN—Master chief petty officer of the Navy, 2002 to present.

Commander Paul Stillwell, USNR (Ret.)—Director of the history division at the U.S. Naval Institute.

Captain Peter M. Swartz, USN (Ret.)—Author and commentator on naval affairs at the Center for Strategic Studies at the CNA Corporation (formerly Center for Naval Analysis).

Dr. Craig L. Symonds—Professor and former chairman of the U.S. Naval Academy's history department.

Chief Hospital Corpsman Anna Wood, USN—Special assistant to commander of Naval Service Training Command.

A few final words of acknowledgment are in order. This book would not have been possible without the trust and encouragement of Ron Chambers, former Naval Institute Press Director. Nor would it have been possible without the tireless efforts of an extraordinary team that expended a great deal of midnight oil to produce it in less than half the time it normally takes. In the long-standing tradition of the Naval Institute, each has served the Navy well, and I am deeply indebted to them all: Susan Artigiani, Patti Bower, Jim Bricker, Donna Doyle, Karen Eskew, Mark Gatlin, Tom Harnish, Linda O'Doughda, Fred Rainbow, Dewitt Roseborough, Sara Sprinkle, Faith Stewart, Mary Svikhart, Jennifer Till, Eddie Vance, Tom Wilkerson, and Jon Youngdahl.

About the Publishers

U.S. Naval Institute

The U.S. Naval Institute is a private, nonprofit, membership society for sea service professionals and others who share an interest in naval and maritime affairs. Established in 1873 at the U.S. Naval Academy in Annapolis, Maryland, where its offices remain today, the Institute has members worldwide. Membership includes the influential monthly magazine *Proceedings* and discounts on books, photos, and subscriptions to the Institute's bimonthly magazine *Naval History*, as well as reduced admission fees to Institute-sponsored seminars. The Naval Institute Press publishes about seventy new books a year, ranging from navigation guides and ship references to biographies and fiction. Nearly nine hundred titles are currently available online and at bookstores. For further information, please visit our Web site, www.usni.org.

Naval History & Heritage Command

The Naval History & Heritage Command (NHHC), located in the Washington Navy Yard not far from the U.S. Capitol, holds the keys to the history and heritage of the U.S. Navy from its creation in 1775 to the present. With good reason, NHHC has been called "the Navy's Smithsonian Institution." The Navy Department Library, Navy Art, and United States Navy Museum branches maintain thousands of books, artifacts, photographs, and paintings, and the Operational Archive holds the Navy's most important records from 1945 to the present. In support of the operating forces and their global mission, NHHC's civilian staff historians, curators, and artists deploy with uniformed members of Naval Reserve Combat Documentation Detachment 206 to capture the vital history of the U.S. Navy in the twenty-first century. For further information, please visit the Naval History & Heritage Command Web site at www.history.navy.mil.

U.S. Navy Memorial Foundation

The U.S. Navy Memorial Foundation is a not-for-profit organization founded in 1977 by naval, civic, and national leaders to perpetuate and honor the best that the Navy represents—its heritage, values, and traditions. The Foundation honors the legacy of those who have served, are serving, and will serve our nation at sea—in the Navy, Marine Corps, Coast Guard, and Merchant Marine—by preserving their history and educating the public about their bravery, sacrifices, and triumphs in keeping our nation free. The Foundation also seeks to inspire the nation's youth to follow in the footsteps of these American heroes. Through its commemorative ceremonies, education programs, and visitor facilities, the U.S. Navy Memorial Foundation passes on the values and traits of honor, courage, and commitment that have been the hallmark of the sea services for more than two centuries. For further information, please visit the Navy Memorial Web site at www.lonesailor.org.

About the Author

Thomas J. Cutler is a retired lieutenant commander and former gunner's mate second class who served in patrol craft, cruisers, destroyers, and aircraft carriers. His varied assignments included an in-country Vietnam tour, small craft command, and nine years at the U.S. Naval Academy, where he served as executive assistant to the chairman of the Seamanship & Navigation Department and associate chairman of the History Department. While at the Academy, he was awarded the William P. Clements Award for Excellence in Education (military teacher of the year). He is the founder and former director of the Walbrook Maritime Academy in Baltimore. Currently he is a professor of Strategy and Policy with the Naval War College and senior acquisitions editor for the Naval Institute Press.

Winner of the Alfred Thayer Mahan Award for Naval Literature, his published works include *Brown Water, Black Berets: Coastal & Riverine Warfare in Vietnam* (Naval Institute Press, 1988) and *The Battle of Leyte Gulf* (HarperCollins, 1994). His books have been published in various forms, including paperback and audio, and have appeared as main and alternate selections of the History Book Club, Military Book Club, and Book of the Month Club. He is the author of the 22nd and 23rd (centennial) editions of *The Bluejacket's Manual*. His other works include revisions of Jack Sweetman's *The Illustrated History of the U.S. Naval Academy* and *Dutton's Nautical Navigation*.

Cutler has served as a panelist, commentator, and keynote speaker on military and writing topics at many events and for various organizations, including the Naval Historical Center, Smithsonian Institution, U.S. Navy Memorial Foundation, U.S. Naval Academy, MacArthur Memorial Foundation, Johns Hopkins University, U.S. Naval Institute, Armed Forces Communications and Electronics Association, Naval War College, Civitan, and many veterans organizations. His television appearances include the History Channel's *Biography* series, A&E's *Our Century*, Fox News Channel's *The O'Reilly Factor,* and CBS's *48 Hours.*

Acronyms

ACP	Allied Communications Publication
ACTOV	Accelerated Turnover to the Vietnamese
CB	construction battalion
CIC	combat information center
CNO	Chief of Naval Operations
COD	carrier onboard delivery (aircraft)
CSS	Confederate States Ship
CV	escort aircraft carrier
CVE	escort aircraft
FDNY	Fire Department of New York
HMS	His (Her) Majesty's Ship
IBM	International Business Machines
LST	tank landing ship
NASA	National Aeronautics and Space Administration
NATO	North Atlantic Treaty Organization
NVA	North Vietnamese Army
NYPD	New York Police Department
PBR	patrol boat, river
PCF	patrol craft, fast (also "Swift boat")
PLAT	pilot landing aid television
POW	prisoner of war
PT	patrol torpedo
RSSZ	Rung Sat Special Zone
SAG	surface action group
SeaBee	construction battalion
SEAL	Sea, Air, Land (Navy commando)
SEALORDS	Southeast Asia Land, Ocean, River, Delta Strategy
SUV	sport utility vehicle
SWC	Surface Warfare Coordinator
TACAN	tactical air navigation (system)
TBM	torpedo bomber
UN	United Nations
USN	U.S. Navy

USNR	U.S. Naval Reserve
USS	United States Ship
USSR	Union of Soviet Socialist Republics
VA	U.S. Navy air attack squadron
VNN	Vietnamese Navy
WILCO	"will comply"
WPB	Coast Guard patrol boat

A Sailor's History
of the U.S. Navy

Part I

Core Values

All Sailors, from seaman to admiral, are guided in their everyday life in the U.S. Navy by three bedrock principles known as core values.

Honor

Those Sailors who have contributed the most to the great heritage of our Navy are those who have conducted themselves in the highest ethical manner: placing honesty and truthfulness above convenience, taking personal responsibility for their actions, and never compromising the high ideals of the great nation they serve.

Courage

The most obvious requirement for an effective fighting force is physical courage in the face of great danger. Less obvious is the need for moral courage. Yet both are absolutely necessary, and both are found in abundance in the annals of American naval heritage.

Commitment

The record of achievements by the Sailors of the U.S. Navy reflects a deep sense of commitment to the nation, to the service, and to fellow shipmates.

The chapters that follow will clearly show that *honor, courage,* and *commitment* are not merely words, but *actions.*

Honor

The United States Navy defends the nation's honor. The individual Sailor plays a crucial role in that vital mission by maintaining a personal sense of honor at all times. Sometimes this task can be challenging—for both the nation and the Sailor.

A Sailor's Honor

Like many other young people, nineteen-year-old Douglas Brent Hegdahl had joined the Navy to see the world. He grew up in Clark, South Dakota, and his travels had been limited to parts of the American Midwest. So, he was eager to expand his horizons, and he soon got his wish. In early 1967, just a few months after he had raised his right hand and promised to "bear true faith and allegiance," Seaman Apprentice Hegdahl found himself on the other side of the world as a member of the gunnery crew in USS *Canberra*, a guided missile cruiser serving as part of the Seventh Fleet in Southeast Asia.

The Vietnam War was in full swing by this time, and the U.S. Navy was carrying the war to the enemy in a number of ways. In the south, Sailors wearing black berets took to the rivers and littorals to fight Vietcong guerrillas "up close and personal." SEALs were involved in covert operations, and SeaBees built bases from the Cua Viet River in the north to the Mekong Delta in the south. Naval aviators shared the skies with U.S. Air Force pilots to pound targets in Communist North Vietnam. And cruisers, destroyers, and frigates of the surface Navy served on the gun line of Vietnam, striking enemy positions both north and south of that line. *Canberra* was one of those cruisers who had been called upon to bombard Communist targets with her six 8-inch, ten 5-inch, and eight 3-inch guns.

Although firing shells at enemy targets was exciting business, Hegdahl felt disappointed because his duties kept him down in the ammunition-handling spaces during the bombardments, where he could see nothing of the topside action. Some of his buddies told him that a night shelling was a spectacular event, kind of a Fourth of July celebration, except that it was more than symbolic—this was the real thing! Determined to get a look at this unique sight, Hegdahl decided to sneak a peek, even though he had

USS *Canberra* firing during a night mission against enemy targets in North Vietnam. Just one of the U.S. Navy's many roles in the Vietnam War. *U.S. Naval Institute Photo Archive*

been warned not to go topside during live firing. It was a decision that would change his life forever.

At about 0400 on the morning of 6 April, Hegdahl slipped out of his rack, quickly ate a cheese sandwich he had earlier stashed beneath his mattress, put on his uniform, and slipped out of the darkened berthing compartment. As he made his way through the passageways, lit only by the red lanterns designed to preserve night vision, he could feel the jarring jolts as *Canberra*'s guns fired in anger. His heart was pounding with excitement at the prospect of actually witnessing the great flashes of flame leaping from the muzzles of the guns that friends had described to him. He felt his way through a darkened light locker on the port side and undogged the door. A rush of humid air washed over his perspiring face as he stepped into the tropical night. The South China Sea was black like coal, and he could see nothing as he felt his way along the open deck.

Suddenly, a battery of 5-inch guns opened fire just above him and, in a flash, Seaman Apprentice Douglas Hegdahl learned the hard way why he had been forbidden to come out on deck when these weapons were at their deadly business. He found himself in the South China Sea, blown overboard by the concussion of the firing guns. Frantically, he began waving and yelling, but the darkness and the roar of the guns conspired against him; he watched helplessly as his ship steamed rapidly away.

Fortunately, he was a strong swimmer and had little trouble staying afloat. But as he slowly tread water there in the warm tropical sea, he suddenly remembered with horror the snakes he had seen making their way past the ship on bright sunny days. He had heard stories of their deadly poisons and now wished more than ever that he had stayed in his rack where he belonged.

As dawn broke, he was relieved that he could see no snakes, but he was discouraged that he could see nothing else but sea and sky. It was the loneliest feeling of his life. A few hours passed and then, to his relief, he caught sight of an object that at first he thought was a buoy. As he swam toward it, losing sight of it and then regaining it as he bobbed up and down in the swells, he realized it was a fishing boat. Within a short time, the Vietnamese fishermen saw him and hauled him on board. Hegdahl's hopes were soaring now as the six men treated him kindly, giving him a dry burlap sack to wear and offering him some clams to eat. Because of their apparent kindness, his hopes rose that they were friendly South Vietnamese rather than Communist enemies from the North.

Later in the day, however, when they passed by another fishing boat, the men yanked him to his feet and displayed him to the men in the other boat. The second group of men shook their fists and shouted things at him he could not understand, but he did not mistake their general meaning. It seemed certain that these were not South Vietnamese allies. His worst fears were confirmed when the fishing boat put in to shore. There, angry villagers attacked and might well have killed him had not local militiamen kept them at bay.

Hegdahl's nightmare was just beginning. It was one of imprisonment, interrogations, isolation, beatings, loneliness, fear, and horrible living conditions that would last for more than two years. He was moved to several different locations, eventually ending up in Hanoi, where he would share the ordeal with Navy and Air Force aviators who had been shot down over North Vietnam.

Early on, when the young seaman apprentice tried to convince his captors that he was not an aviator like the others, telling them that he had come from a ship, they accused him of being a commando, a "spy from the sea," and threatened to execute him. When his interrogators brought out paper and pens, demanding that he write a confession of his "crimes," he looked at the pens as though they were some complicated piece of machinery and told his tormentors that he couldn't read or write, saying, "I'm a poor peasant." The North Vietnamese believed him and then assigned a man to teach him. This did not go well. Hegdahl continued the ruse by proving to be a very poor student.

Continuing to act as though he was uneducated and slow-witted, Hegdahl was very convincing. The North Vietnamese began calling him something that translated to "the incredibly stupid one"; they soon gave him mundane camp duties that seemed fitting to his "limited" capabilities.

Hegdahl's captors moved him about quite a bit, but he eventually found himself sharing a cell with Lieutenant Commander Richard Stratton, a man who had caused his captors no small amount of trouble and who had been horribly tortured in return. In naval history there have not been many lieutenant commanders and seaman apprentices who have shared quarters, but these two men made the best of their unique situation and developed a strong friendship, based upon mutual respect and no small amount of humor. Stratton later described their first moments together.

It was a hot summer day when I first met Doug. I was in solitary confinement again. The Communists did not care for me, which was OK because I didn't like them either. My cell door opened and here was this big moose standing in his skivvie shorts [prison uniform of the day]: "My name is Seaman Douglas Brent Hegdahl, Sir. What's yours?" It is awful hard to look dignified when you are standing in your underwear, knock kneed, ding toed, pot bellied, unwashed and unshaven for 100 days. I automatically recited: "Dick Stratton, Lieutenant Commander, USS *Ticonderoga.*" Immediately I saw that I probably made a mistake as his eyes rolled back in his head and you could see what he was thinking: "Cripes, another officer!" But all he said was, "What do I call you, Sir?" I answered, "Beak." [Stratton had acquired the nickname years before and is known by it to this day.] Hegdahl pondered that briefly, then asked, "'Beak, Sir' or 'Sir Beak'?" I replied, "Just 'Beak' will do fine thank you, Doug."

The Communists took a siesta for two hours every afternoon, which was a good deal for us as we were free from torture and harassment. I was lying on the floor on my bed board and Doug was skipping, yes, skipping around the room. I asked: "Doug, what are you doing?" He paused for a moment, looked me in the eye and cryptically said: "Skipping, Sir" and continued to skip. A stupid question; a stupid answer. After a moment, I again queried: "What'ya doin' that for?" This stopped him for a moment. He paused and cocked his head thoughtfully, smiled and replied: "You got anything better to do, Sir?" I didn't. He continued skipping. I guess he did learn one thing from boot camp. You can say anything you want to an officer as long as you smile and say "sir."

During these siesta periods, the guards would often let Hegdahl out of his cell to sweep out the cell-block courtyard. Beak was at first relieved, "since it kept him from skipping and I could get some rest." But one day, curiosity got the better of him, and Stratton decided to peer out through a peephole they had bored through the door. What he saw was "one for the books."

He'd go sweeping and humming until the guard was lulled to sleep. Then Doug would back up to a truck, spin the gas cap off the stand-pipe, stoop down and put a small amount (Small, because it's goin' to be a long war, sir.) of dirt in the gas tank and replace the cap. I watched him over a period of time do this to five trucks. . . . There

Seaman Apprentice Doug Hegdahl sweeping out the cell-block courtyard as a prisoner of war in North Vietnam. This intrepid Sailor used such opportunities to sabotage enemy trucks. *U.S. Naval Institute Photo Archive*

were five trucks working in the prison; I saw Doug work on five trucks; I saw five trucks towed disabled out of the prison camp. Doug Hegdahl, a high school graduate from the mess decks fell off a ship and has five enemy trucks to his credit. I am a World Famous Golden Dragon [VA 192] with two college degrees, 2000 jet hours, 300 carrier landings and 22 combat missions. How many enemy trucks do I have to my credit? Zero. Zip. Nada. Who's the better man? Douglas Brent Hegdahl, one of two men I know of who destroyed enemy military equipment while a prisoner of war.

Despite their horrid circumstances and virtual helplessness, the POWs found ways to resist their enemies. It was essential that they not give in to despair, and one of the ways to keep it at bay was to fight back in whatever ways they could. Outright physical resistance was difficult under the circumstances—the Communists rarely hesitated to unleash extreme brutality when dealing with their helpless captives—but there were subtler ways to resist.

Although forbidden to communicate with one another, the Americans used a quadratic alphabet code that was simple to learn and could be used by tapping on the walls of their cells or even as a series of coughs. With practice, many became very proficient at using it. The letters of the alphabet were arranged in a five-by-five grid (excluding *K* as unnecessary, to keep it symmetrical).

A	B	C	D	E
F	G	H	I	J
L	M	N	O	P
Q	R	S	T	U
V	W	X	Y	Z

The first series of taps represented the number in a row (across) and the second indicated the number in the column (down). So five taps followed by four taps would be the letter *U*; three taps then four would be *S*; three taps followed by three would be *N*; and so on. With patience—and courage—a great deal could be transmitted this way.

Another means of fighting off despair was for the POWs to maintain their sense of honor. Their tormentors could take away the Americans' sense of dignity by providing just a tin can for a toilet. They could challenge their sanity by allowing them nothing to read except Communist propaganda. They could sap their strength by keeping them confined in leg irons that prevented them from exercising. They could torture them in ways that made death a tempting alternative. But as long as these men could maintain their sense of personal honor, the enemy could not defeat them. They accomplished this in a number of ways, not the least of which was their commitment not to accept an early release. At times, to serve their propaganda purposes, the North Vietnamese would offer to let one or more of the POWs go home to America. Accepting the opportunity to leave this hell, to be reunited with their families, was incredibly tempting. But through their tap code and other means of communicating, they vowed to each other that not one would go home until *all* could go home.

Doug Hegdahl was no exception. As any sane person would, he desperately wanted to go home, yet his sense of personal honor made that an impossibility. At a very young age, fate had placed him in the most challenging circumstance of his entire life. His fellow prisoners were older; they had college educations and a great deal more training, and they were being paid more than he was. But in spite of his youth, inexperience, and bizarre circumstances, Hegdahl's upbringing in South Dakota and the training he had received in the Navy made him wise enough to realize that while accepting an early release might be a welcome solution to his misery in the short term, it would mean a lifetime of regret. He had seen a few of the POWs accept early releases, and it was clear to him that they were wrong to do so. It was clear they had traded their honor for their freedom. Hegdahl resolved that if he were going to survive this ordeal, he wanted to live the rest of his life knowing he had behaved with honor.

But even this simple (if incredibly difficult) commitment was going to be challenged. As it happened, Dick Stratton and others had a different plan for Seaman Apprentice Hegdahl.

During one siesta period, Hegdahl asked Stratton if he knew the Gettysburg Address. Using a brick as a writing implement, the two men began to scrawl it out on the floor of the cell until they were convinced they had it right. Then Hegdahl, staring thoughtfully at their creation, asked, "Can you say it backward?" Not surprisingly, Stratton said, "No." Hegdahl began to do just that. Stratton followed along using their floor-inscribed version and, to his utter astonishment, found that Hegdahl was doing it without error. Stratton concluded that this was no ordinary memory. He was further convinced when Hegdahl revealed to him that an Air Force officer named Joe Crecca had taught him how to memorize the names, ranks, and services of all the pilots imprisoned in Vietnam, at that point more than 250. It was also clear that Hegdahl had memorized a great deal of information about his captors, the prisons he had been in, and what he had managed to see beyond the prison walls when his guards were napping.

Soon, tap-coded messages were flying about, and the senior POWs concluded that Seaman Hegdahl could do all of the POWs much good and their enemies more harm if he accepted an early release and carried his information home to the United States. The North Vietnamese had deliberately withheld the identities of the men they had in captivity as one part of their many attempts at undermining the will of the American people. Consequently, many Americans had no idea whether their loved ones were alive or dead. Finding out that your husband or son was a POW in North Vietnam was no pleasant revelation, but it was far better than living in uncertainty—and infinitely better than finding out he was dead.

And there was another factor. In those early days of the Vietnam War, the brutal treatment of the American POWs was not widely known or recognized. The North Vietnamese had convinced many sympathizers in the world that they were treating their captives humanely. Doug Hegdahl, of course, knew better.

If he could take his head full of information back to the United States, he could give renewed hope to many of those waiting in dreadful uncertainty, he could help to dispel the fiction of humane treatment, and he could also provide other knowledge to military authorities that might well prove useful. To the senior POWs, it was clear that Hegdahl should accept an early release.

But it was not so clear to the young seaman apprentice. Hegdahl had seen the way the other POWs had felt about those among them who had accepted an early release, and he shared their disappointment in those men. He had heard Stratton declare, "I'd have to be dragged feet first all the way from Hanoi to Hawaii screaming bloody murder all the way." From early in his captivity, Hegdahl, like the vast majority of his fellow POWs, had staked his personal honor on staying until the day they *all* would be released, no matter how long that might take. Some of the POWs had been there two years longer than he had. It just did not seem right for him to go.

Stratton worked on Hegdahl, trying to convince him that he was an exception, that he could go home and take his honor with him. Stratton told him: "You are the most junior. You have the names. You know firsthand the torture stories behind many of the propaganda pictures and news releases. You know the locations of many of the prisons."

In the end, it took a direct order before Hegdahl relented and accepted an early release, taking his head full of names and other accumulated intelligence back to the United States. Before going, he told Stratton he was worried that once he "spilled the beans" back in the safety of America, the Communists would take revenge on Stratton and the others. Stratton looked Hegdahl in the eye and said: "Don't worry about me. Blow the whistle on the bastards."

There was no question that the POWs had made the right decision in making an exception of Seaman Apprentice Hegdahl. The Communists soon learned that they had gravely misjudged "the incredibly stupid one." As predicted by Stratton and the others, Hegdahl's ability to recite the names of the other POWs proved invaluable, even if the people debriefing him were somewhat surprised to find that he *sang* the names to the tune of "Old MacDonald Had a Farm" (his unorthodox but effective way of remembering the information). The other information he brought back proved useful as well. He was able to pinpoint the exact location of the prison the POWs had dubbed "The Plantation," describing it as "located at the intersection of Le Van Binh and Le Van Linh, number 17," something he had learned one day while sweeping around the camp's front gate. He told all who would listen of the terrible conditions and torture. He eventually went to Paris, where North Vietnamese and American negotiators were meeting. When one of the North Vietnamese delegates said, "Our policy is very humane in the camps," Hegdahl responded, "I was there." That ended any further reference to "humane" treatment of the POWs.

One day back in Hanoi, Dick Stratton found himself facing another interrogation, but this one was to prove different from the many others he had endured over the years. His captors brought him into a room where a table had been laid with cookies, candy, sugared tea, and quality cigarettes. This was not unusual; the Communists would often tempt the POWs with such things or use them as a means of torment by letting the prisoners see such nice things but not allowing them to consume them. A North Vietnamese interrogator, dressed in a tailored suit and wing-tipped shoes instead of the drab military garb his interrogators normally wore, entered the room. It appeared that he might be some sort of government official—definitely higher up the North Vietnamese pecking order than the usual tormentors. With a very serious look on his face, the Communist asked, "Do you know Douglas Hegdahl?"

Stratton thought, "Uh-oh, here it comes." He answered, "You know I do."

Without changing expression, the interrogator said, "Hegdahl says that you were tortured."

Stratton laconically replied, "This is true."

"You lie," the Vietnamese said, his voice rising.

Stratton calmly rolled up the sleeves of his pajama-like striped prison uniform and pointed to the scars on his wrists and elbows. "Ask your people how these marks got on my body; they certainly are not birth defects!"

The interrogator examined the marks carefully and then sat back, staring at Stratton. At last he said a strange thing. "You are indeed the most unfortunate of the unfortunate." Stranger still, he then got up and left the room, leaving Stratton with the table full of food and cigarettes. It was not until some time later that Stratton was able to figure out what had happened. This encounter had occurred shortly after Doug Hegdahl had openly accused the Communists in Paris of having killed Stratton. "The incredibly stupid one" had figured that by doing so, the Communists would likely want to keep Stratton alive so that they could produce him at the end of the war to prove Hegdahl wrong.

Beak Stratton did survive. He eventually came home—along with the other POWs who had preserved their personal honor by remaining in captivity, some for more than eight years. Stratton remained in the Navy and retired as a captain after many years of service. Today, he maintains a Web site where he has posted the following words: "'The Incredibly Stupid One,' my personal hero, is the archetype of the innovative, resourceful, and courageous American Sailor. These Sailors are the products of the neighborhoods, churches, schools, and families working together to produce individuals blessed with a sense of humor and the gift of freedom, who can overcome any kind of odds. These Sailors are tremendously loyal and devoted to their units and their leaders in their own private and personal ways. As long as we have The Dougs of this world, our country will retain its freedoms."

Douglas Hegdahl went on to serve the Navy for many years as an inspirational and highly effective instructor at the James B. Stockdale Survival, Evasion, Resistance, and Escape School in Coronado, California, where he was able to prepare thousands of others for the challenges they might someday face if they fell into enemy hands. He never lost his wry sense of humor. One day, some thirty years after his imprisonment in Hanoi, Hegdahl confessed that he'd fooled Beak—he had *not* been able to recite the Gettysburg Address backward. He had been reading it over Stratton's shoulder as his gullible senior had his head down following along. That feat of memory may have been a ruse, but the one that counted was not.

The POWs have occasional reunions, where they gather to reinvigorate the bonds of friendship and mutual respect that were forged during their terrible ordeal. They do not invite those who took early releases without the consent of the others, but they *do always* invite Doug Hegdahl.

At a reunion in Yorba Linda, California, in 1998, Douglas Hegdahl paid a special tribute to his fellow POWs by singing a song. It was to the tune of "Old MacDonald Had a Farm," and the lyrics were, in alphabetical order, the names, ranks, and services of more than 250 American POWs who, like him, had come home with honor.

Guided missile cruiser USS *Wainwright*, also known as "The Lonely Bull," one of the Navy's participants in Operation Praying Mantis. *U.S. Naval Institute Photo Archive*

A Nation's Honor

Richard Molck and Robert Reynolds had come to Philadelphia on a sad mission. Both men had served in the Navy in the guided-missile cruiser *Wainwright* in the late 1980s. It had been a good time, when they had belonged to a special club where lifelong friendships were made and where boys became men. Today, 11 September 2001, they had come to bid farewell to their ship.

Wainwright's nickname had been "The Lonely Bull," and on this day she looked particularly lonely. Her days of service were over and she was slated to be committed to the deep as a target ship. Molck and Reynolds had come to the shipyard in Philadelphia to salvage a few artifacts from the doomed cruiser so that some part of her might live on. They had removed a number of items and had gone to get a truck to transport them. As they drove the truck back through the streets of the old shipyard, bumping their way over railroad tracks under a bright blue sky, bulletins began coming in over the radio, saying that an airplane had crashed into the World Trade Center's north tower. Not sure what was happening, but sensing that it was momentous and foreboding,

The Pentagon after being struck by a hijacked civilian airliner on 11 September 2001. All on board the aircraft and 125 people in the Pentagon were killed. *U.S. Navy (Cedric H. Rudisill)*

Molck felt a sense of comfort when they arrived at the pier and saw the American flag flying from *Wainwright*'s fantail, just as it had in those days when he had been a young fire controlman second class in her 4th Division.

Not knowing what else to do, and on a mission for which there might not be a second chance, the two men went back aboard their old ship. They climbed down into the after steering compartment to continue their salvaging. They had not been there long when they heard that a second plane had hit the other tower of the World Trade Center, and when they heard that the Pentagon had been hit as well, they knew the nation was, once again, at war.

As they continued to work, Molck heard approaching footsteps on the deck above; the sound reminded him of that April day in 1988 when he had heard the pounding of feet along the steel passageways as the Sailors in *Wainwright*'s crew rushed to their battle stations.

In the dimly lit missile plot room, Petty Officer Richard Molck listened intently as reports of the approaching Iranian fast attack craft *Joshan* continued to flow in. Four times, the Americans had warned the Iranians to turn back. But *Joshan* continued to close on *Wainwright* and the other ships of

SAG Charlie. *Joshan* was a 154-foot, 2,334-ton vessel whose name translated to "boiling oil." No stranger to combat, she was a veteran of earlier battles in the Iran-Iraq War, having once used her deadly Harpoon missiles to destroy two *Osa* patrol craft during an assault on the Iraqi ports of Al Faw and Umm Qasr.

When the Iranian vessel was within thirteen miles, Captain J. F. Chandler, *Wainwright*'s commanding officer and commander of SAG Charlie, took the ship's bridge-to-bridge radio in hand and said: "This is United States warship *Wainwright*. I order you to stop your engines and abandon ship. I intend to sink you."

Recounting this engagement in *Great American Naval Battles*, Michael Palmer wrote that "the scene was reminiscent of an earlier action" by a U.S. naval commander when, "in February 1800 Captain Thomas Truxtun, commanding the frigate *Constellation*, intercepted the French frigate *la Vengeance* [and using] a speaking trumpet, demanded that the French frigate 'surrender to the United States of America.'" The more heavily armed *la Vengeance* ignored the demand and was then soundly defeated in battle by *Constellation*. Like the Frenchman in 1800, the Iranian in 1988 also ignored the American demand. Just who was to be soundly defeated on this day remained to be seen.

Peering into the glowing cathode-ray tube of his radar repeater in *Wainwright*'s CIC, Operations Specialist Third Class Steven Twitchel stared at the glowing pip that represented the approaching Iranian vessel. With every sweep of radar the contact grew brighter. Suddenly, his keenly trained eyes detected video separation, and he knew what that meant. His natural impulse was to stare in shocked dismay at what he was seeing, but discipline and training took precedence, and he immediately reported a missile inbound. *Joshan* had fired a Harpoon at *Wainwright*.

Chief Gunner's Mate Douglas Brewer had been serving in "The Lonely Bull" since October 1986 and was *Wainwright*'s leading weapons chief. His actual battle station was gun repair, but his duties during general quarters required him to move about to the various weapons stations. When *Joshan* attacked, Chief Brewer was out on deck, just aft of the forward 25-mm chain gun that had been added to *Wainwright*'s armament to protect against small-craft attack. From his vantage point he could see some of the chaff launchers and was glad to see them firing soon after he heard the report of a missile inbound. With luck, these decoys might lure the missile away from *Wainwright* so they might all live to see another day.

On the bridge, Chief Warrant Officer Jon Fischman knew that chaff had to be employed carefully because if it were haphazardly placed, it could cause the missile to acquire one of the other ships in the SAG. As *Wainwright*'s officer of the deck, Fischman also knew that Captain Chandler's other options were limited. The Vulcan Phalanx close-in weapon system had locked on to the missile, but with the Harpoon coming "down the throat" as it was, the ship would probably be seriously damaged if the Phalanx caused it to detonate by engaging it. There was little they could do but hope that the missile missed.

Up in CIC, Operations Specialist Second Class Tom Ross, who had been serving in *Wainwright* since 1985, heard the captain tell all to brace themselves and felt his heart thumping in his chest. He remembered that an earlier Iranian propaganda broadcast had warned that the Americans would "never leave the Persian Gulf alive."

Out on deck, Doug Brewer actually saw the Harpoon as it roared in toward his ship. He fervently hoped the Harpoon's acquisition radar would prefer the fluttering chaff "tinfoil" to the ship beneath his feet.

From the starboard bridge wing, Jon Fischman watched as the missile grew larger at a very rapid rate. At less than one hundred feet, he could see the lettering on its side, and he realized that he would not be seeing those letters if the missile were coming straight at him.

Inside CIC, Tom Ross felt the bulkheads rattle as the Harpoon roared down the ship's starboard side, close aboard. It was a moment he was not likely ever to forget.

Brewer was most relieved when he saw the missile plunge into the sea astern of the ship, hitting just fifty to seventy-five yards from *Wainwright*. As Palmer later wrote, "In a literal sense, *Wainwright* had 'dodged a bullet.'"

With the roar of the missile still echoing in CIC, rapid but disciplined orders and reports filled the air: "Whiskey, this is Alfa Whiskey. Red and free!"

"Fire SWC!"

"Birds affirm."

"Birds away on hostile track 1077."

Again, the bulkheads rattled as several surface-to-surface missiles left *Wainwright*'s rails in retaliation. The other ships in SAG Charlie—frigates *Simpson* and *Bagley*—opened fire as well.

Ross heard the air tracker's radio crackle with a report from a helicopter that the first missile had reached *Joshan* and "blew the top right off." The Americans were shooting better that day than were the Iranians. Several more missiles found their marks and *Joshan* was, in Ross's words, "turned into metal composite and sank."

Wainwright's trial by fire was not yet over, however. A number of Iranian aircraft had sortied from bases on the southern Iranian coast, and one of them was headed straight for the American cruiser. Like *Joshan*, this aircraft ignored all warnings. Again, missiles ran out on *Wainwright*'s rails, and again she opened fire. One of the missiles damaged the Iranian fighter, which quickly turned heel and ran back to the safety of its base in Bandar Abbas. This was the first time in history that an American warship had simultaneously engaged both surface and air targets with missiles. The action continued on into the day, with other SAGs and U.S. aircraft engaging designated targets, repelling Iranian attacks, and retaliating with devastating effect. When the sun finally set on the Persian Gulf, half of Iran's operational navy had been destroyed.

When the battle had subsided and *Wainwright* was steaming out of the area, Chief Warrant Officer Fischman decided that, under the circumstances, it would be all right to break one of the rules; he announced that the smoking lamp was lighted on the bridge. He and the other smokers immediately began to light up, and he noted that several of the nonsmokers were joining in too. Just as eight cigarette lighters fired up, Captain Chandler emerged from CIC and, looking at his officer of the deck, asked what was going on. Fischman replied, "Well, Captain, since you've been filling my pilothouse with smoke from the missile rails, I figured the smoking lamp was lit." Chandler smiled at Fischman and countered: "First of all, this is not *your* pilothouse, it's mine. I just let you play out here for a few hours. And second, the lamp goes out unless someone can run me out a cigar." One quickly appeared from somewhere in CIC.

From his ringside seat in CIC, Tom Ross had seen his ship and his shipmates in action, and he later summed up the action well when he said it was "the best feeling I ever had in my life . . . and the job that everyone in combat did that day was an awesome testament of just how bad ass our ship was under that kind of pressure. I would go to war any day with those guys anytime!" He also added proudly, "If you mess with the Bull, you'll get the horns."

Memories of that day had momentarily distracted Richard Molck from the unfolding drama at the World Trade Center and the Pentagon. But the footsteps he had heard earlier turned out to be those of a Sailor coming to tell him that he and Reynolds would have to leave the ship. In light of the terrorist attacks, the shipyard was being closed down for security reasons and all "civilians" would have to depart the area.

Before they departed, Molck took one more look around. Standing there in the dark cavern of the after steering compartment, inside the steel skin of the once potent warship, he suddenly felt reassured. He sensed that, despite the devastating news of passenger airliners serving as the guided missiles of a fanatical enemy against the American homeland, the nation would survive these attacks just as *Wainwright* had survived those attacks in 1988, when he and his shipmates had gone to war with the Iranian navy in the confines of the Persian Gulf. Then and now, the nation's honor had been challenged and, now as well as then, it would be the enemies of the United States who ultimately would pay the price. Bull's horns or eagle's talons, it didn't matter: Americans don't run from a fight.

Praying Mantis

The sinking of the *Joshan* had been just one part of a larger sea battle that took place on that day in April 1988—the first U.S. Navy surface battle since World War II—at a time when U.S. forces rarely were permitted to engage in combat operations. It had come about for a number of reasons, not the least of which was the matter of honor.

In recent times, combat in the Middle East has become an all too frequent occurrence for American Sailors. But during the many years of the Cold War, the United States was legitimately concerned about the terrible destruction that would come about if the use of force led to a nuclear war with the Soviet Union. Because both superpowers had vested interests in many parts of the world, including the Middle East, American statesmen and military commanders had been very reluctant to risk combat operations in any of those hot spots for fear they might have disastrous consequences. Many U.S. Sailors spent an entire career making arduous deployments under the constant threat of all-out war, yet never hearing a shot fired in anger.

But in 1988, economic considerations centering largely on oil and a growing realization that the United States could no longer afford to remain politically disengaged in the Middle East brought about a new level of involvement there. When, during the Iran-Iraq War, the Iranians began attacking oil tankers and other vessels in the Persian Gulf as a means of putting economic pressure on their enemies, the United States made the bold decision to place many of these vessels under U.S. protection.

The Iranians responded by sowing mines in the Persian Gulf, and on 14 April 1988 USS *Samuel B. Roberts* struck one of those mines and nearly sank. The explosion ripped a seven-hundred-square-foot hole in the frigate, injured ten of her crew, and nearly broke her in two. Only an extraordinary damage control effort by the crew saved her.

It could be argued that responding militarily to this attack on a U.S. Navy ship would accomplish little in either a political or a strategic sense. It also could be argued (and was) that responding by force of arms would be risky in light of the world situation. But there was no question that the nation's honor had been injured, and not to respond ran other risks, not the least of which was a virtual invitation for future attacks on U.S. warships and installations. Within a very short time, President Ronald Reagan ordered the U.S. Middle East commander to take appropriate retaliatory action.

Just four days after *Roberts* had been hit, three SAGs, consisting of three ships each and supported by a carrier battle group in the nearby Arabian Sea, headed into battle in an operation code-named Praying Mantis. Two of the SAGs, designated Bravo and Charlie, first destroyed two Iranian offshore oil platforms in the Persian Gulf that the Iranians had been using as outposts in support of their attacks on merchant ships. When the Iranian navy counterattacked, the *Joshan* was not the only vessel dispatched to the bottom. As part of SAG Delta, the frigate *Jack Williams* directed a group of A-6 Intruders from the carrier battle group onto a group of attacking vessels, including five high-speed, Swedish-built Boghammars. Loaded with Rockeye cluster bombs, the attack aircraft sank one of the Boghammars, causing the others to retreat into port.

As the day wore on, two Iranian frigates—*Sahand* and *Sabalan*—joined the battle. After *Sahand* fired on U.S. aircraft, they and the destroyer USS *Joseph Strauss* retaliated with a barrage that included three Harpoons, four

The Iranian frigate *Sahand* burns in the Persian Gulf after an attack by U.S. Navy aircraft in retaliation for the mining attack on USS *Samuel B. Roberts*. *Naval Historical Center*

Skipper infrared homing rockets, and several laser-guided bombs. A number of the weapons struck home, and *Sahand* was left a flaming wreck that later sank. *Sabalan* too had fired on U.S. aircraft and paid the price by receiving a 500-pound laser-guided bomb that penetrated her superstructure amidships and left her dead in the water.

In one day of sea combat, American ships and aircraft had soundly thrashed the Iranian navy, and U.S. honor had been upheld by force of arms in a time when *cold* war was the watchword of the day. Nations rarely go to war for the sake of honor alone. Yet a nation's credibility is closely tied to its honor, so there comes a time when the use of force becomes a necessity if that nation is to maintain its stature on the world stage. Even the threat of a widened war takes second place to the need to defend the nation's honor.

Brave Yankee Boys

Operation Praying Mantis was not the first time that the U.S. Navy had been called upon to defend national honor. And it was not the first time such defense had been undertaken in the face of significant risk.

One of the earliest challenges to the honor of the United States of America came in 1797, barely ten years after the signing of the U.S. Constitution in Philadelphia. Although France had come to the aid of the Americans during the American Revolution, relations between the two nations soured in the years following. When the United States signed a treaty with England—France's longtime enemy—the French began to seize American ships on the high seas. The new nation's Navy was very weak, and the idea of taking on the powerful French navy seemed to be a very bad idea. So President John Adams sent a delegation on a peace mission to France. The French foreign minister refused to meet with the members of the delegation, and, even worse, some go-betweens suggested that the Americans must first pay a bribe before the minister would see them. In dispatches back to the United States, the three primary go-betweens were not mentioned by name but were instead referred to as simply X, Y, and Z.

When word spread in the United States about the insulting treatment the American delegation received, many were outraged and demanded an appropriate response to this serious insult to our national honor. Much of the American anger was summed up by the legendary slogan, "Millions for defense, but not one cent for tribute." With no army to speak of, and because much of the trouble had begun with French seizure of U.S. ships, Congress ordered the Navy to take action, authorizing it to "subdue, seize, and take any armed French vessel." This was a tall order for a tiny fleet facing the second largest in the world. But the Americans had taken on the most powerful army and

 frigate *Constellation*, key player in the so-called Quasi-War with France. *U.S.*
Naval Institute Photo Archive

navy in the world just a few years before and had won their independence, so
they did not shrink from this challenge, despite formidable odds. Because
Congress did not go so far as to formally declare war on France, what followed has become known as the "Quasi-War with France."

On 9 February 1799, USS *Constellation* was cruising in Caribbean
waters when a lookout reported an unidentified ship just over the horizon.
Captain Thomas Truxtun ordered his ship to come about, then went below
to record in his log: "At noon saw a sail standing to westward, gave chase.
I take her for a ship of war."

The pursuit continued for about an hour, with *Constellation* gaining on
the other vessel. As they drew closer, it became apparent that the other ship
was a heavily armed frigate. A lesser captain with a lesser crew might have
decided to look for an easier conquest to carry out Congress's edict to "subdue, seize, and take any armed French vessel" in this "Quasi-War," but
Truxtun was not lacking in courage, and he knew that *Constellation*'s crew
was well trained and ready for a fight.

When the two ships were close enough to exchange signals, Truxtun
attempted to learn her identity. The other ship ran up an American flag but

would not reply to any of Truxtun's coded signals. It was looking fairly certain that this was a Frenchman. In fact, the men of *Constellation* would later learn that she was *l'Insurgente,* a French frigate that had earlier taken part in the capture of USS *Retaliation.* This was truly shaping up as a matter of honor.

A naval ballad of the day titled "Brave Yankee Boys" recorded this incident in a number of verses, the first of which began

'Twas on the 9th of February at Monserat we lay,
And there we spied the *L'Insurgente* at the break of day.
We raised the orange and blue,
To see if they our signal knew,
The Constellation and the crew
Of our brave Yankee boys.

Truxtun again recorded in his log that he "had no doubts respecting the chase being a French frigate." On his orders, a young Marine drummer began to beat to quarters and all hands took up their stations and prepared the ship for battle. A young seaman named Neal Harvey was assigned to a gun crew in Third Lieutenant Andrew Sterett's division, one of several divisions that manned the cast-iron cannons that fired 24-pound balls and made up a major part of *Constellation*'s firepower. Not wanting to displease Lieutenant Sterett, Harvey raced to his station at the first rattle of the drum, pausing just long enough to let several Sailors cross his path as they took to the ratlines and climbed up to their stations among the ship's sails. By the time Harvey arrived at his station, other members of the gun crew had already opened the gun port and were releasing the 24-pounder from the lashings that held it securely in place. This was no time for carelessness. The gun weighed close to three tons; should the crew lose control of it on the rolling ship, disaster would quickly follow. Still today, we refer to someone who is dangerously out of control as a "loose cannon."

Once the gun was unlashed, Harvey and the others maneuvered it away from the gun port into its recoil position, removed the tompion from the gun's muzzle, and quickly loaded the weapon. Then, hauling on the tackles at each side, they rolled the massive gun forward until its muzzle protruded from the open port.

Elsewhere in the ship, Sailors were busy putting out the galley fires, removing furniture from the captain's cabin and striking it below, opening scuttles to the magazine and shot locker, laying out the surgeon's dreaded instruments, and sanding down the decks for better traction. Young boys called *powder monkeys* ran back and forth from the gun decks to the powder magazines, the two best quartermasters manned the helm, carpenters made ready their stocks of plugs and oakum in case shot holes in the hull had to be repaired, and Marines armed with muskets positioned themselves in the rigging and at the rails.

Two hours into the chase, a serious squall arose, and within minutes the two ships had a common enemy in the gale-force winds. *Constellation* fared better, having let go her sheets and braces in time to avoid serious damage, but the French frigate lost her mainmast to a violent gust.

As the squall subsided, *Constellation* continued to close, and within another hour she was ranging up on the French ship's lee quarter. All this time, Neal Harvey and the others waited at their guns for the battle to begin. It was nerve-wracking business, being unable to go anywhere, with little to think about except the coming battle. Some of the men tried several times to make conversation on idle topics, but soon silence would settle in again and someone would peer out the gun port to see how much they had gained on the other ship.

Then all hands were called to quarters while we pursued the chase,
With well primed guns, our tompions out, and well spliced the main
    brace.
Then soon to France we did draw nigh,
Compelled to fight, they were, or fly,
These words were passed: "Conquer or Die,"
My brave Yankee boys.

When they were close enough to see the faces of their counterparts peering out the other ship's gun ports, the men at last heard the long-awaited order, and a great roar echoed across the sea as the 24-pounders fired at the French frigate less than one hundred yards away. The heavy balls crashed through the enemy's side and careened across her deck, inflicting great damage to men and material.

Almost immediately, the enemy answered *Constellation*'s broadside with one of her own, and suddenly wood splinters were flying about like snowflakes in a winter flurry. There was a tearing sound and then a loud crash as a boom fell to the deck, trailing a tangle of lines. Shouted orders mingled with angry curses. In the midst of all of this noise and crashing violence, Harvey and his fellow Sailors continued to service their gun to keep it firing.

Confirming Newton's law of action and reaction, the propelling explosions deep in the cannon's cast-iron bore caused the three-ton monster to leap backward in recoil, barely stopped by the hawserlike breeching slung across its rear. With the wind in their faces, a great cloud of choking smoke blew back on the crew, momentarily blinding them. Harvey was aware of a strange, metallic taste in his mouth as he breathed in the foul gunpowder vapors.

Moving as fast as they possibly could, the gun crew prepared the cannon for another shot. With a moistened sponge on the end of a pike, one man swabbed out the inside of the gun, removing residue and dousing any sparks that might be lingering there. The loader then placed the flannel cartridge bag full of gunpowder into the muzzle, and another man shoved it to the far end of the bore with a long rammer. A wad of scrap fibers followed; then came the 24-pound ball. Another wad was rammed in to prevent the ball from rolling back out should the ship's motion in the seaway tip the muzzle downward. Through the touch hole in the top of the barrel near the breech, the gun captain pricked the cartridge with a long needle-like spike, and loose gunpowder was then poured into the touchhole from a funnel-shaped horn. With its truck wheels squeaking loudly under the ponderous weight, the cannon was hauled out so its muzzle again pointed through the gun port at the enemy across the narrow stretch of water. Within seconds, Lieutenant

A gun crew at work. *Naval Historical Center*

Sterett barked the order to fire, and once again there was a great thunderclap as a tongue of flame emerged from the cannon's mouth.

For more than an hour, Harvey and the others of Lieutenant Sterett's division repeated the process. As they labored, the confused sea frequently doused them with wind-driven spray, causing clouds of steam to rise from the cannon's heated barrel. The noise was deafening, the odors of burning powder and running perspiration filled the air, and musket balls and deadly wooden splinters—some of them several feet long—flew about, threatening to tear off a limb or snuff out a young life in an instant. As Harvey and his mates rolled their gun forward to fill the opening, the young Sailor caught occasional glimpses of the enemy ship and saw the terrifying sight of her cannons winking bright flashes at them.

And then it was over. With the French ship's rigging a shambles, her crew decimated and in disorder, her rails shattered, and her hull pierced in many places, l'Insurgente's captain struck his flag in surrender.

> Loud our cannons thundered, with peals tremendous roar,
> And death upon our bullets' wings that drenched their decks in gore.
> The blood did from their scuppers run,
> Their chief exclaimed, "We are undone,"
> Their flag they struck, the battle was won,
> By brave Yankee boys.

When the French captain was brought on board *Constellation* in the aftermath, Captain Truxtun asked him, "Your name, sir, and that of your ship."

"I am Capitaine de Fregate-Citizen Michel-Pierre Barreaut, commanding the French national frigate *l'Insurgente* of forty guns," came the reply.

Truxtun then said, "You, sir, are my prisoner," and, in the custom of the day, relieved the Frenchman of his sword.

Barreaut later told Truxtun that "your taking me with a ship of the French nation is a declaration of war." Truxtun responded by reminding the Frenchman of early transgressions by the French that had led the United States to take such action. "If a capture of a national vessel is a declaration of war," Truxtun said, "your taking the *Retaliation* commanded by Lieutenant Bainbridge, which belonged to the United States and regularly placed in our Navy, was certainly a declaration of war on the part of France against the United States." Barreaut did not respond.

French casualties were high. Lieutenant John Rodgers was the first to board the defeated ship, and in a letter home he described what he saw: "Although I would not have you think me bloody minded, yet I must confess the most gratifying sight my eyes ever beheld was seventy French pirates (you know I have just cause to call them such) wallowing in their gore, twenty-nine of whom were killed and forty-one wounded."

In contrast, just one American died in the battle, but it was a tragic loss. Ironically, while defending the honor of his nation, poor Neal Harvey failed to uphold his own. In the heat of battle, he ran from his post. Upon noticing his absence, Lieutenant Sterett ran him down and then ran him through with his sword. The incident later caused a great deal of debate, and Sterett inspired his supporters and appalled his detractors when he wrote to his brother, "You must not think this strange, for we would put a man to death for even looking pale in *this* ship."

Such passion—however extreme—was no doubt a contributing factor to the one-sided outcome of the battle. "*This* ship," as Sterett had referred to *Constellation,* had won an amazing victory. A fledgling navy had stood up to a considerably more powerful one and prevailed. It was a risky venture for the Americans, considering the world situation and the possible reactions of a much more powerful French nation, which by that time was well on its way to conquering most of continental Europe. But it had been dictated as a matter of national honor. To do otherwise would have jeopardized the new nation's position in the world. Sometimes respect is earned through diplomacy and restraint, but other times it must be demanded by force of arms.

President Adams told his cabinet that *Constellation*'s victory would ensure that American ministers would not again be treated so dishonorably when they came to negotiate. The secretary of war added, "The only negotiation compatible with our honor or safety is that begun by Truxtun in the capture of *L'Insurgente.*"

Even in London, where respect for the tiny U.S. Navy was not abundant, the merchants and underwriters of Lloyd's, the world's foremost maritime insurance company, sent Truxtun a beautiful silver urn in recognition of *Constellation*'s achievement.

When word spread throughout the United States, there was a great outpouring of appreciation and congratulations. All over the country, parades, cheering crowds, special dinners, and gun salutes honored *Constellation*'s victory. Toasts were heard everywhere, calling the ship the "vanguard of America's naval glory" and, referring to the infuriating XYZ Affair, naming Truxtun "our popular envoy to the French, who was accredited at the first interview."

And there were songs. In Baltimore there was "Huzza for the Constellation"; in Philadelphia, "Constellation: A Wreath for American Tars"; and in Boston, "Truxtun's Victory." And in taverns up and down the coast, there was "Brave Yankee Boys."

Now here's a health to Truxtun who did not fear the sight
And all those Yankee sailors who for their country fight,
John Adams in full bumpers toast,
George Washington, Columbia's boast,
And now to the girls that we love the most,
My brave Yankee boys.

Two Honors

So, in the end, Sailors of all ranks in the U.S. Navy must defend two kinds of honor. First, there is the nation's honor, which must be upheld through various means if this great nation is to remain free and effective on the world stage. Second, there is the personal honor of each individual Sailor, which must be maintained if Sailors are going to remain true to themselves and their shipmates—and to continue to like what they see in the mirror for the rest of their lives.

Courage

2

There are many kinds and degrees of courage. It takes courage for a young man or woman to enlist in the armed forces of their nation; for a Sailor to climb down a Jacob's ladder to a boat that is pitching violently in a stormy sea; for a petty officer to tell his chief that he made a mistake; for a coxswain to make her first landing; for a corpsman to stop a Marine's arterial bleeding while enemy rounds are cracking all about; for a fireman to take the test for third class petty officer; for a gunner's mate to man a weapon as a replacement for her shipmate who was just killed a moment before; for a brand-new ensign to lead for the first time; for an airman to report a case of sexual harassment; for an electronics technician to climb the mast to fix a wiring problem in the TACAN antenna; for a nozzle man to lead a hose team into a compartment full of flames and smoke; for an officer to put his career on the line over a matter of conscience; for a master chief to put in his papers for retirement after thirty years of service. These are all acts of courage that occur every day in the United States Navy.

The rewards for these acts of courage vary. On rare occasions they result in the awarding of a medal such as the Bronze Star or Navy Cross. Sometimes they result in the achievement of a qualification or a promotion. Often, the only reward is in knowing, "I did the right thing."

It is not by accident or random choice that courage is one of the three standards the Navy has chosen to live by. Honor and commitment must be teamed with courage—both moral and physical—if the Navy is going to carry out its many missions and overcome the myriad challenges that arise every day.

While there have been and always will be moments when courage fails, the long history of the Navy is an impressive record of Sailors having the courage to do what is right, what is needed, what makes the difference between success and failure, what ultimately decides victory over defeat.

No Exit Ramp

PBRs 105 and 99 of River Section 531 were closing rapidly on two sampans loaded down with uniformed troops in the middle of the My Tho

River. The PBRs were running at full throttle, their American flags stretched taut, great white rooster tails following close behind.

In October 1966 it was not unusual for American Sailors to be seen on the waterways of Vietnam. The U.S. Navy had expanded its traditional large-fleet, "blue-water" role to take the fight to the enemy in the "brown-water" world of the Mekong Delta and RSSZ. Using modified fiberglass recreational boats powered by jet pumps, many Sailors voluntarily left their jobs as yeomen, signalmen, and the like to "get up close and personal" with the Communists, who were using the waterways to smuggle war-making contraband and to disrupt the vital flow of rice from the paddies to the marketplace along South Vietnam's vital rivers. Small yet well-armed PBRs patrolled the jungle-lined waterways to keep them open, often boarding and inspecting junks and sampans to make sure they were legitimate commercial traffic.

On this particular day, there was no doubt that these two sampans were not commercial. Heavily armed men wearing North Vietnamese military uniforms were clearly visible in the craft. The two sampans split up; one

A PBR under way in the Mekong Delta. These dark green craft were a mere thirty-one feet long and were manned by a crew of four. They had no propellers; they were driven, instead, by a water-jet system that allowed them to operate in extremely shallow water. Because their fiberglass hulls provided no protection against enemy fire, speed and armament were their main defenses. *U.S. Naval Institute Photo Archive*

headed for the north shore, the other toward the south. The soldiers in the sampans fired at the approaching patrol boats and were almost instantaneously answered by the staccato bark of the forward twin fifties of each PBR. The two American craft veered off after the southbound sampan. When they got close enough, they slowed down to stabilize the careening fire of their gunners, and in less than a minute they had destroyed the fleeing enemy craft. Boatswain's Mate First Class James Elliott Williams throttled up and banked the 105 in a tight turn that caused the skidding PBR to burrow nose-down into the river before dashing out across the water in hot pursuit of the other sampan. Williams was boat captain for the 105 and patrol officer in charge of both PBRs.

Before the Americans could get to it, the second sampan reached the north bank of the river and disappeared into a channel too small for the PBRs. Williams knew that part of the Mekong Delta like the back of his hand, so he radioed the 99 and said in his South Carolinian drawl: "Stay with me. I know where he has to come out. We'll get 'im." The two boats raced, prows high, to head off the sampan. A short way down the riverbank they turned into a canal. Some months before, Williams had removed all of the armor from his boat, except that which surrounded the engines, in order to get more speed and to permit the 105 to carry more ammunition. She was a fast boat flying through the canal at about thirty-five knots. The trees lining the banks were a peripheral green blur to the Sailors on the dashing craft.

As they raced around a bend in the canal, Seaman Rubin Binder, the 105's forward gunner, suddenly shouted something colorful. Before them were forty or fifty boats scattered over the canal, each carrying fifteen to twenty troops. The sampans were so full of men, they barely had two inches of freeboard remaining. It would be difficult to assess who was more startled—the crews of the PBRs upon suddenly finding the waterway full of an enemy "fleet," or the soldiers of the 261st and 262nd NVA regiments upon seeing two patrol craft careening around the bend and hurtling down on them.

Binder's shoulders shook violently as he opened up with his fifties. The NVA soldiers stood up in the sampans to return fire with their rifles. Williams had merely a split second to think: there was little room to turn around, there were no alternative routes to either side, and they were damned near among the enemy craft already. As he later said in an interview: "Ya'll got to understand. There weren't no exit ramp." He pressed on.

The banks erupted in heavy fire. The unmistakable *thoonk* of mortar rounds could be heard in the midst of the chattering of automatic weapons and the cracking of rifles. Williams swerved left a little, then right, as much as the narrow canal would permit, trying to give his after gunner's grenade launcher a clear shot. The enemy mortar rounds were not up to the PBRs' speed and missed both boats; the small-arms fire was equally unsuccessful. In another few seconds, the 105 had reached the first of the enemy sampans. Although they were already at full power, Williams leaned on the throttles and ran right over the first boat—then another, and another. The enemy was reduced to chaos as soldiers spilled into the canal from the stricken sampans and still others were rolled into the water by the PBRs' wakes. Soldiers along both banks fired at the boats as they streaked by, not realizing in the confusion that they were hitting their own men on the opposite banks.

The waterway narrowed even more, but still the PBRs roared on. Two 57-mm recoilless rifle rounds lashed out from the right-hand bank, hitting the 105 in the bow on the starboard side, but passing completely through, emerging from the port side and exploding among the NVA troops on the opposite bank. Throughout, Binder and his fellow crew members—Castlebury, Alderson, and Spatt—were firing for all they were worth. Brass shell casings rained onto the fiberglass decks as hundreds of rounds spewed out in every direction. The 99 was likewise spraying metal at a phenomenal rate as she followed close behind. The North Vietnamese were suffering staggering losses.

The two PBRs emerged from the gauntlet practically unscathed. The boats were pockmarked and holed, but miraculously no men were injured, all weapons were still working, and the engines were intact. Williams called on the radio for assistance from Navy Seawolf helicopters. Among the myriad troop-carrying sampans behind him, he had spotted several good-sized junks he suspected were carrying ammunition and supplies. Those and the troops remaining would make good hunting for the helicopter gunships.

Clear of the havoc, Williams slowed the patrol, intending to move on down the canal a safe distance and wait for the Seawolves before taking on that armada again. The PBRs cruised on for about 150 yards. The men on the boats were just beginning to relax when, after a right turn, they found themselves confronted by yet another imposing concentration of junks, sampans, and troops, even larger than the first. Prudence might have dictated that the PBRs should back off and wait for the Seawolves, but Williams never hesitated. He jammed on full power and headed in for an encore.

With the roar of the engines resonating off the banks of the canal, guns hammering relentlessly, and wakes boiling up behind them, the PBRs charged into battle. As in their previous encounter, they caught the NVA unprepared. The canal erupted in shooting, shouting, and explosions. Bullets slapped the water on both sides of the 105, and fragments of fiberglass flew in every direction. Death was poised everywhere. But the Americans roared on through, their weapons chewing up sampans and felling enemy soldiers. PBRs 105 and 99 emerged from the battle area, once again essentially intact, leaving a swath of destruction in their wake. But the battle had not yet ended. The radio came alive, announcing the arrival of the Seawolves. The pilots had made a pass over the two enemy staging areas that Williams's PBRs had passed through, and the lead pilot told Williams that the NVA was still there and that there were plenty of them left.

Williams replied, "I want y'all to go in there and hold a field day on them guys."

"Wilco," agreed the helicopter commander, adding, "What are *your* intentions?"

Williams hollered, "Well, I damn sure ain't goin' to stay here! I'm goin' back through." And once again the 105 and 99 tore through the North Vietnamese regiments, this time with Seawolf support.

The helicopters swooped over the area again and again, 7.62-mm ammunition cascading from their M-60s. Rockets leaped from their side-mounted pods into the troop-infested jungle. Williams took full advantage of the PBRs' extraordinary maneuverability as he ran his craft among the enemy like a skier on an Olympic slalom. He had guessed right about the junks: the secondary explosions that erupted from the four that the PBRs and the helicopters nailed sent debris rocketing one thousand feet into the air. Williams pressed the attack relentlessly, undeterred by the maze of bullets and rockets and mortar rounds. As darkness came, the battle raged on, and Williams ordered the PBRs' searchlights turned on. When the water was finally devoid of targets, Williams drove in close to the shore seeking the enemy.

The whole battle had lasted more than three hours. The final assessment revealed that the NVA had lost hundreds of men. Sixty-five enemy vessels had been destroyed, and many prisoners were taken. Williams discovered a small piece of shrapnel in his side after the battle was over. Binder had taken a bullet through the wrist, which passed cleanly through the flesh and had not broken any bones. These were the only American casualties.

On 13 May 1968, in ceremonies held at the Pentagon, President Lyndon Johnson was having difficulty fastening the snaps at the back of the cravat of the Medal of Honor as he attempted to place it around the neck of James Elliott Williams. The struggling president said into Williams's ear, "Damn, Williams, you've got a big neck." It's a wonder that Williams did not have a big head as well, for that Medal of Honor was placed in good company: along with his previously earned Navy Cross, two Silver Stars, the Navy and Marine Corps Medal, three Bronze Stars, the Navy Commendation Medal, the Vietnamese Cross of Gallantry (with Palm and Gold Star), and three Purple Hearts.

Operation Seadragon

Long before the carrier-centered fleets and amphibious task forces marched across the Pacific during World War II, U.S. submarines took the war to the Japanese by operating well behind enemy lines, even in the home waters of Japan. The courageous crews of these tiny, incredibly cramped warships took on the Japanese navy when they could and relentlessly attacked logistical shipping, slowly but surely depriving the enemy of fuel, food, and other necessities of war. It was a campaign that required a special kind of Sailor who was able to endure hardships for long periods of time, to face the dangers of the sea and the violence of the enemy on a regular basis, and to be ever adaptable and resourceful. Indeed, early in the war, the submarine *Seadragon* barely escaped from her base in the Philippines when the Japanese invaded, yet she returned time and again to the island of Corregidor, leaving her torpedoes behind to make room for food and other supplies desperately needed by the Allied forces trapped there.

USS *Seadragon.* One of the many American submarines that lurked behind enemy lines many hundreds of miles from their home bases during World War II. *U.S. Naval Institute Photo Archive*

On 11 September 1942, she was patrolling well behind enemy lines in the southwest Pacific when Seaman First Class Darrell Dean Rector fell to the deck unconscious. Submarines did not often have the luxury of a doctor on board, so the matter fell to twenty-three-year-old Pharmacist's Mate Wheeler Lipes to diagnose the problem. Under the arduous conditions presented by life in a submarine, a collapsing Sailor was not all that unusual; men often succumbed to the gradually worsening atmosphere in a submerged sub or were brought down by simple exhaustion in the demanding environment.

But there was something about Rector's appearance that concerned Lipes. He kept the young Sailor under observation for a time and noted a rising temperature, increasing rigidity of the abdominal muscles, and a tendency for the patient to flex his right leg up toward his abdomen for relief from the increasing discomfort he felt. Lipes went to see the skipper, Lieutenant Commander William Ferrall, and told him that he was certain Rector had appendicitis and that it was a severe case, requiring surgery sooner rather than later.

The captain asked, "What can we do for him?"

The pharmacist's mate answered, "Without a surgeon, nothing."

Ferrall looked at Lipes for a long moment, then asked, "Can you do it?"

Forerunners to those miracle workers we call hospital corpsmen today, Navy pharmacist's mates in World War II were very capable people. They routinely saw to a wide variety of medical needs and treated many different kinds of ailments aboard naval vessels. But major surgery was not among their practical factors for advancement. Lipes was understandably reluctant to take on such a responsibility.

Ferrall pressed, "I fire torpedoes every day and miss."

Lipes responded, "But *I* only get one shot."

Yet Rector was certainly going to die unless something drastic could be done. *Seadragon* was hundreds of miles from the nearest friendly doctor. Lipes seemed the only hope. He told his captain he would do it.

Rector was told of the situation and the plan. Frightened as he was, the suffering Rector said, "Whatever Lipes wants to do is okay with me."

The skipper ordered *Seadragon* to submerge to a quiet depth, and Lipes selected a team of assistants from among the crew. Surgical implements were as scarce as surgeons on the submarine, so Lipes had to improvise. Shipmates rigged a searchlight over the wardroom table, bent spoons to serve as muscle retractors, and converted a tea strainer into an ether mask. They sterilized the instruments by boiling them in torpedo alcohol and water. While these preparations were going on, Lipes carefully studied the medical books in sick bay.

When all was ready, they carried the patient into the wardroom and stretched him out on the table where the officers ate their meals. With his shipmates at the controls of the submarine holding the vessel as steady as they possibly could, Darrell Rector went under the knife held by Wheeler Lipes. After a clean incision, with one of the assistants holding back the layers of muscle with the bent spoons, Lipes went in.

To his consternation, he could not find the appendix at first. "Oh, my God!" he thought. "Is this guy reversed?" He knew that a very small percentage of people had their appendix on the opposite side. But after some careful probing beneath the cecum—the so-called blind gut—he discovered the elusive organ. Lipes later described the procedure: "I turned the cecum over. The appendix, which was five inches long, was adhered, buried at the distal tip, and looked gangrenous two-thirds of the way. What luck, I thought. My first one couldn't be easy. I detached the appendix, tied it off in two places, and then removed it after which I cauterized the stump with phenol. I then neutralized the phenol with torpedo alcohol. There was no penicillin in those days."

Lipes then sewed up the incision with catgut and applied an antiseptic powder he had made by grinding up sulfa tablets, and *Seadragon* went back to war, her complement intact.

A later official report, written by the Submarine Squadron Two medical officer, summed up that doctor's assessment of the operation: "It is by no means desirable to encourage major surgical procedures on naval personnel by other than qualified surgeons, yet in this particular instance, it appears that deliberation and cautious restraint preceded the operation; the operation was performed under difficult circumstances and with pioneering fortitude and resourcefulness; and the result was entirely satisfactory."

Like most professionals, submariners have a language all their own. During the war, it was common practice for submariners to refer to a radioman as a "brass pounder" (because he spent much of his time operating a brass Morse-code key), a sonar man as a "ping jockey" (because of the sound emitted by an active sonar), and a pharmacist's mate as a "quack." After 11 September 1942, the crew of *Seadragon* referred to Wheeler Lipes only as "Doctor."

Saving Taffy 3

As darkness gave way to morning light on 25 October 1944, the wind barely whispered across the calm surface of the Philippine Sea. Intermittent rain squalls occasionally disturbed the otherwise tranquil scene but provided the six small escort aircraft carriers (CVEs), three destroyers, and four destroyer escorts of Taffy 3 with "fresh-water wash-downs" that rinsed some of the glistening salt from their weather decks. This northernmost of three Seventh Fleet escort carrier task groups (with designated radio call signs "Taffy 1," "Taffy 2," and "Taffy 3") had been steaming all night east of the island of Samar, waiting for daybreak so that flight operations could be resumed in support of the amphibious landing on Leyte Island.

Officially, these diminutive floating airfields were "escort carriers," but they had many unofficial names as well. To the men in the fleet the CVEs were frequently referred to as "baby flattops," "Kaiser coffins" (because many were built by Henry Kaiser's shipyards), "tomato cans," "jeep carriers" (because they often were used to transport vehicles and aircraft to forward bases), and "wind wagons." Some Sailors had informed their awed civilian friends that the CVE stood for "combustible, vulnerable, and expendable." They were what the Sailors called "thin-skinned," meaning they had no double hulls, no armor, no torpedo blisters for defense. They were also very slow. During the war, Captain Walter Karig aptly described their speed capabilities when he wrote, "In a calm sea and with a following breeze these little ships might make eighteen knots provided the engineering officer had been leading a good life."

Rear Admiral Clifton A. F. "Ziggy" Sprague was the commander of Taffy 3 and had his flag in USS *Fanshaw Bay,* one of the so-called baby flattops. At daybreak, Sprague watched from her bridge as planes took off from the short flight deck, some loaded with depth charges in case any Japanese submarines appeared in the area, and others carrying antipersonnel bombs and strafing ammunition for use against targets on Leyte Island.

At 0637, one of the men who had been monitoring the interfighter director net from the *Fanshaw Bay*'s CIC began to hear voices speaking in what sounded like Japanese. He turned to the man next to him and said, "What do you make of that?" The second man listened for a moment and then replied, "Somebody's playing a joke." The first man shrugged and said: "Yeah, maybe. Or it could be long-range jamming." Taffy 3 continued the morning's routine.

Sprague looked out the bridge windows at the sea, now quite bright in the morning light. Ahead of *Fanshaw Bay* were the other CVEs under his command: *Kalinin Bay, White Plains, Saint Lo, Kitkun Bay,* and *Gambier Bay,* all launching aircraft as the group headed northeast into the light morning wind. Screening the carriers were the destroyers *Johnston, Hoel,* and *Heerman,* and the destroyer escorts *Samuel B. Roberts, Dennis, Raymond,* and *John C. Butler.*

At about 0745, an excited voice called from CIC, reporting that one of the pilots had spotted an enemy surface force of four battleships, seven

USS *Fanshaw Bay* (CVE 70), one of the many "baby flattops" that played many important roles in World War II. Sailors often told their awed civilian friends that "CVE" stood for "combustible, vulnerable, expendable." *U.S. Naval Institute Photo Archive*

cruisers, and eleven destroyers just twenty miles northwest of the task group and closing at thirty knots. Sprague leaned over the "squawk box" and pressed the lever. "Air plot, tell that pilot to check his identification." Sprague's voice reflected the irritation he felt. The last thing he needed was for some overzealous aviator to get everybody excited by a misidentification of an American task group.

A moment later, air plot called the bridge. "The pilot insists that these ships are Japanese. He says they have pagoda masts!" This was a sure sign that these were enemy ships. Japanese warships had distinctive, unusually formed masts that were indeed reminiscent of pagodas.

Sprague looked northwest and could see puffs of antiaircraft fire above the horizon. There was no denying it: a major Japanese fleet had come to contest the landings at Leyte. "Come to course zero-niner-zero," Sprague barked. "Flank speed. Launch all aircraft." Taffy 3 turned due east in response, and puffs of black smoke from the CVE stacks signaled their increase in speed.

Away to the northwest, the pilot who had spotted the Japanese fleet dove in on the nearest enemy cruiser and released his weapons. They were depth charges meant for submarine targets, but they were all he had.

A few minutes later, the Japanese ships had closed to within eighteen miles of Taffy 3, and several geysers appeared within two thousand yards of the fleeing carriers. The next salvo fell even closer. It seemed simply a matter of time before these deadly projectiles would find their mark. Closer still, the rounds walked in, and Admiral Sprague wondered what he could possibly do to save his task group.

Aboard the destroyer *Johnston,* Commander Ernest E. Evans ordered general quarters. Evans was a short, barrel-chested man with a booming voice whom nearly everyone described as a born leader. At the commissioning ceremony for USS *Johnston* on 27 October 1943, Evans told the crew and assembled guests that when war had broken out in the Pacific, he had been serving in an old World War I–vintage destroyer, USS *Alden,* in the Java Sea near the Dutch East Indies. He explained that after the Japanese navy had sunk the heavy cruisers *Houston* and *Marblehead* and the situation had become hopeless for the remnants of the U.S. Asiatic Fleet, *Alden* had been forced to beat a hasty retreat out of the Java Sea. Indicating the bunting-draped *Johnston* and recalling the words of John Paul Jones, Evans said, "Now that I have a modern, fighting ship, I intend to go in harm's way." Then, speaking with a conviction that many of the crew sensed was sincere and irrevocable, Evans declared, "I will never again retreat from an enemy force."

Almost a year to the day from that moment, Evans was about to get the chance to prove just how sincere he had been when making that promise. With Japanese ships closing on Taffy 3 and USS *Johnston* directly in their path, his moment had come.

Just below the bridge on the port side, Bill Mercer, who routinely worked in the ship's laundry, sat at his battle station as trainer for one of the twin 40-mm gun mounts. From that position he could hear the captain giving orders up on the bridge. Having seen the masts of Japanese ships poking above the horizon off *Johnston*'s port quarter when he first arrived at his station, Mercer was most gratified to hear the captain order, "All engines ahead flank." Heading away from the enemy as fast as possible seemed like an excellent idea to the eighteen-year-old Mercer. His happiness was short-lived, however. Before long, he heard the captain's booming voice order, "Left full rudder," and Mercer watched with dismay and mounting concern as *Johnston*'s bow swung rapidly around *toward* the Japanese ships. He quickly began strapping on his life jacket. Evans was clearly taking his ship "in harm's way."

"Taffy 3" escorts laying a smoke screen during the Battle of Samar. *U.S. Naval Institute Photo Archive*

Captain Evans started zigzagging between the Japanese ships and the fleeing carriers. Intent upon obscuring the CVEs from Japanese view, he ordered the engineers to make black funnel smoke while the ship's smoke generator detail began producing cottony white clouds that seemed to cling to the sea like a heavy fog. At the captain's order, the crews manning the 5-inch guns commenced firing on the nearest Japanese cruiser. Soon Mercer could see hits registering on the enemy cruiser's superstructure, which prompted the Japanese to retaliate. Giant splashes rose from the ocean's surface close to *Johnston*. Evans "chased the splashes" by steering the ship toward the last shot to fall, a tactic based on the theory that the shooting ship will correct a missed shot, making the site of the last shot a relatively safe place to be.

Quartermaster-striker Robert M. Billie watched the geysers leaping out of the sea from his lookout station on the port side of the flying bridge and felt the ship heeling over from one side to the other as she veered rapidly about in pursuit of the last enemy shell bursts. It was the only time he could remember wanting to dig a foxhole.

As most of the carriers disappeared from view behind the smoke curtain laid down by *Johnston* and the other escorts, more of the Japanese ships turned their guns on *Johnston* in frustration. Billie listened in awe as battleship rounds passed overhead, sounding like fast-moving freight trains as they roared by. It seemed to him that the destroyer's chances of survival were poor at best and rapidly diminishing.

The splashes began closing in on the destroyer from all sides, and Evans too must have been thinking of the ship's demise, for he turned to Officer of the Deck Lieutenant Ed Digardi and said, "We can't go down with our fish aboard." True to his commissioning day promise, Evans ordered, "Stand by for a torpedo attack." He then told Digardi to head right for the formation of cruisers still bearing down from the northwest. As the ship came about, guns still firing at a furious rate, Digardi could clearly see the massive cruisers ahead, their dull gray forms highlighted by the flashes of gunfire. Beyond them he could make out the ominous forms of an echelon of battleships. This was sheer madness! One tiny destroyer charging an armada of such formidable firepower.

Once the ship had fired her torpedoes, Digardi steered *Johnston* into her own smoke screen to gain some respite from the cascading Japanese gunfire. Moments later, the sound of distant underwater explosions indicated that some of the torpedoes had found their mark. As *Johnston* emerged from the smoke screen, those crew members who could look were treated to the welcome sight of flames burning brightly on the fantail of the nearest Japanese cruiser.

Any elation the crew felt at that moment was quickly extinguished, however, as *Johnston*'s phenomenal luck ran out. Three 14-inch shells slammed into the destroyer's after engine and fire rooms, followed by a 6-inch salvo that struck *Johnston*'s port bridge wing and penetrated her 40-mm magazine. The ship immediately lost steering control and all power to her after gun mounts.

On the flying bridge, a piece of shrapnel struck the mouthpiece of Robert Billie's sound-powered phone set, shattering the instrument and filling the young Sailor's mouth with blood and broken teeth. A subsequent explosion lifted Billie into the air and slammed him down on the steel deck, knocking him unconscious. Upon reviving a few seconds later, he saw his shoes lying next to his head, still neatly tied.

A few minutes after the rounds had hit, Bill Mercer heard someone above him call, "Stand by below." Mercer watched as a pair of khaki-clad legs dangled into view. Someone on the bridge was lowering one of the officers to the main deck. As the khaki shirt appeared, Mercer could see that it was covered with blood. Then the lowering paused for a moment, and Mercer saw, to his dismay and horror, that the officer's body had no head.

The decapitated officer was not the only victim on the bridge. Lieutenant Digardi had rushed out of the pilothouse to the port bridge wing right after the shells had crashed into the ship. There he found terrible carnage. Besides the headless officer, Digardi discovered that the torpedo officer had lost a leg and a signalman had been blown to bits. The captain was still alive but bleeding from shrapnel wounds to his neck, chest, and hand.

On the flying bridge one deck up, Robert Billie discovered that he was bleeding from every limb and that he could only move his left arm. In a state of shock, he again lost consciousness.

As Mercer looked about the mangled ship, trying to forget the image of the headless body that had dangled in front of him, he saw that Mount 52, one of the forward 5-inch gun mounts, was still firing at a furious rate, but the deck around the mount was filling up with expended brass shell casings that threatened to inhibit the mount's rotation. Mercer and another 40-mm gunner, J. B. Strickland, ran forward and began jettisoning the brass casings as fast as they could. When they had cleared most of the brass from the deck, Mercer and Strickland returned to their guns. Almost immediately after their departure from the Mount 52 area, the gun took a direct hit.

On the bridge, the ship's doctor tried to minister to the captain's wounds. But Evans, whose shirt and helmet had been blown off his body, refused treatment, saying: "Don't bother me now. Help some of those guys who are hurt." Ignoring the wounds to his neck and chest, Evans then wrapped his bleeding hand in a handkerchief and returned to the business of fighting his ship.

By this time, steering had to be accomplished by emergency cables and the destroyer was under way on only one engine, reducing her to half speed and half power. She had no gyrocompass, her search radar antenna dangled uselessly from the mast, and—although power had been restored to two of the three after gun mounts—Mount 54 was reduced to firing manually in local control.

From his vantage point in the gun director, Lieutenant Robert C. Hagen, the ship's gunnery officer, could see three other escort ships—destroyers *Hoel* and *Heerman* and destroyer escort *Samuel B. Roberts*—racing by at full speed to take on the giant Japanese force. It seemed apparent to Hagen that *Johnston* was out of the fight. With her speed reduced to barely seventeen knots, she had no hope of keeping up with the other escorts. But Evans had other ideas. In his booming voice he ordered his ship to fall in astern of the other escorts to provide gunfire support. As he prepared to direct *Johnston*'s gunfire, Hagen said to himself, "Oh, dear Lord, I'm in for a swim."

As the four American escorts charged boldly at their formidable Japanese adversaries, the two sides were firing at one another at a furious rate. Tiny 5-inch shells bounced off the thick hides of the Japanese ships, while heavy-caliber rounds roared through the air and peppered the water all around the Taffy 3 escorts, some of them slamming into the already wounded *Johnston.* Generating smoke and still armed with torpedoes, the three escorts charged in to deliver these more potent weapons, while the limping *Johnston* valiantly struggled to keep up, firing her remaining guns with amazing persistence.

Mercer had been driven from his battle station by a raging fire that engulfed his gun mount. He and seven or eight other men were huddled under a gun tub as the relentless pounding of Japanese shells continued. Suddenly, without really knowing why, Mercer headed forward, leaving the other men still huddled beneath the gun tub. When he was a few yards away, he heard and felt a tremendous explosion behind him. When the smoke cleared sufficiently, he saw that a Japanese round had landed directly beneath the gun tub, killing all of the men who had just seconds before been his companions. Turning away from the awful sight, he again started forward. But another round detonated close aboard, this one forward of Mercer's location. He immediately felt a searing heat on his face as he saw cascades of water pouring over *Johnston*'s gray superstructure.

The tenacious courage displayed by the American escorts was not wasted. The cruiser *Kumano* was out of the battle, licking the wounds inflicted by *Johnston*'s earlier torpedo attack. The cruiser *Suzuya* also withdrew from the battle so she could transfer the commander of Heavy Cruiser Division Seven and his staff from the crippled *Kumano.* And this latest torpedo run by the other escorts had scored several hits and forced the world's largest battleship, *Yamato,* to turn away and temporarily head north, taking with her the longest-range guns in the force and losing about seven miles in her pursuit of the carriers.

Meanwhile, *Hoel* had been scampering about for quite some time, engaging Japanese ships without sustaining any major damage to herself. But her nine lives eventually expired when she found herself surrounded by a battleship and several heavy cruisers who began to chew at her mercilessly. Firing more than five hundred rounds in defiance, *Hoel* eventually succumbed to the more than forty hits she received over a period of about twenty minutes. Listing heavily to port with one magazine on fire and her engines completely knocked out, her captain ordered abandon ship at approximately 0830.

Roberts had hit one of the Japanese ships with several torpedoes and had been dealing with this vengeful cruiser ever since. Both she and *Johnston* had managed to get so close to this Japanese ship that the latter had been unable to lower her guns far enough to get a proper bead on her tiny adversaries. *Roberts*'s gun crews had been firing so long and so continuously that they had given up worrying about what type of ammunition to use. The men in the ammunition handling rooms beneath her two 5-inch gun mounts had been grabbing whatever was closest at hand and feeding it to the blazing guns above. As a result, the Japanese cruiser was being hit with all sorts of strange rounds, including some designed as illumination projectiles and even some dummy practice rounds loaded merely with sand.

After several minutes of this relentless firing, one of the lookouts yelled, "Captain, 14-inch splashes coming up astern!" From the pattern he saw astern, Lieutenant Commander Robert Copeland knew that the next rounds would hit his ship if he didn't do something fast. He immediately ordered, "All engines back full," and the little destroyer escort began to tremble violently as alert engineers down below answered the astern bell. The ship shuddered to a halt so quickly that her fantail was nearly engulfed by her own wake wave. A second later, a 14-inch round roared overhead and struck the sea just ahead of the ship.

But *Roberts*'s luck had run out. In avoiding the approaching battleship rounds, she had made herself vulnerable to the cruiser who had been her particular nemesis for the better part of two hours. Three 8-inch armor-piercing shells struck her on the port side forward. Because her hull contained no armor, the Japanese shells did not detonate but instead passed completely through the ship, entering the port side and exiting the starboard, leaving neat, round holes at each location.

While preferable to the terrible destruction that would have occurred upon internal detonation, these holes in the hull were not without serious consequences. Two of the shells exited below the waterline, which caused flooding in both the forward ammunition handling room and the compartment containing the ship's master gyro. The latter was the more serious because it shorted out all electrical power to the radios, radars, and gun mounts. It also took the lives of two electricians who were trapped in the small compartment and drowned. But the third round, which cut right through the ship's main steam line in the forward fire room, did the most serious damage. High-pressure steam roared into the fire room instead of the turbines where it was meant to be, instantly killing three of the five men on station there. The other two men were badly scalded—one of them doomed to a more lingering and extremely painful death, the other, an eighteen-year-old named Jackson McKaskill, destined to survive as a hero.

Although already burned by the ferocious steam, McKaskill made his way through the intense heat and confusing darkness to shut off the air and fuel supplies to the offending boiler. He then removed the sound-powered phones from one of his dead shipmates and reported the damage and casualties. By the time he had completed these level-headed actions, all the flesh had been seared from the bottoms of both of his feet.

With half her engine power gone, *Roberts* had lost much of the agility that had kept her alive for so long. Almost simultaneously, four rounds smashed into the wounded destroyer escort. Another round sapped still more of her power and her speed was further reduced. Then round after round crashed into the hapless ship, piercing her flimsy hull, ripping into her inner compartments, smashing her vital equipment, and tearing apart her human components.

Captain Copeland was trying to assess his damage when out of the swirling bands of smoke came the spectral image of USS *Johnston*. By now, her bridge was a total shambles, smoke and flames adorned her almost everywhere, her mast was bent double, and her large radar antenna dangled loosely, banging against her superstructure with every roll of the ship. One of her gun mounts had been completely obliterated, and there was just a hole where one of the torpedo mounts had once resided. But to Copeland's utter amazement, *Johnston* was still under way, still firing at the enemy.

As the mangled destroyer passed close by, Copeland could see her skipper standing on the fantail, calmly calling conning orders down through the hatch leading to the after steering compartment. The only way she could be steered was by nearly exhausted Sailors laboring in the after steering compartment to operate the heavy rudder by hand. Evans was stripped to the waist and covered with blood. As *Johnston* steamed by, Evans looked up at Copeland and casually waved.

As *Johnston* disappeared into the veils of smoke as hauntingly as she had appeared, Copeland began receiving his damage assessments. Both 5-inch gun mounts were finished. The after mount had gone out in a particularly tragic and awe-inspiring manner. During most of the long engagement the after mount had lost power, and the Sailors had manually crewed the gun. This required not only that pointing and training had to be laboriously done by hand, but also that the 28-pound powder cases and 54-pound projectiles had to be lifted up from below decks to be loaded. Despite this handicap, the gun crew had kept the gun firing at an incredible rate.

With the relentless firing, however, the gun had become quite hot. When the crew was down to their last seven rounds, they suddenly lost the compressed air supply to the gun. Used to clear the barrel of dangerously hot gases between rounds, this air was essential to the safe firing of the weapon. To fire such a hot gun without the ejecting air was a hazardous undertaking, but shunning the danger, the men continued to fire the weapon. As they were loading the final powder charge, it "cooked off" before they could close the breech, blowing the mount apart and killing or fatally wounding all but one of the ten-man crew.

When a member of the repair party entered what was left of the shattered mount, he found the gun captain, Gunner's Mate Third Class Paul Henry Carr, torn open from neck to crotch with most of his internal organs exposed to view. Carr, still alive, was holding the last projectile, begging for someone to load it in the gun and fire it. He died a short while later lying next to the gun he had served so well.

With so much damage, no weapons left with which to fight, enemy shells still raining in, and his ship sinking beneath him, there seemed no alternative for Copeland but to order, "Abandon ship." Copeland gave the onerous order and men began helping their wounded shipmates over the side.

As *Roberts* slowly gave up the ghost, it was clear that *Johnston,* too, was mortally wounded. Like hungry wolves, a pack of Japanese cruisers and destroyers had closed in on the gallant destroyer and were pounding her into submission. She had fought long and hard, several times interposing herself between the attackers and the helpless CVEs still fleeing for their lives. She had endured the intense barrage much longer than anyone ever could have imagined. But her time had run out, and Captain Evans at last gave the order for her crew to leave her.

By this time Robert Billie had regained consciousness. Barely able to move and unable to talk, he lay helpless as several men passed by him, apparently assuming him dead. With only his left arm still functioning, he pulled himself slowly across the deck. Each pull was agonizing, and his many shrapnel wounds oozed blood with each exertion, leaving a red smear behind to mark his path. At last he reached the rail, but he was too weak to pull himself over. Struggling at the rail, he suddenly got help from an unexpected source. A close salvo hit lifted him over the side and threw him into the sea.

Bill Mercer had left the ship in a more conventional manner, jumping off the port side amidships and swimming quickly away, where he joined up with a friend who, supported by his kapok life jacket, was neatly combing his hair. When the Sailor finished the task, he tossed the comb into the water, saying, "I don't guess I'll ever need that again."

As *Johnston'*s survivors floundered about in their new environment, watching their ship slowly being swallowed by the sea, they were horrified to see a Japanese destroyer bearing down on them. Fearing they were about to be strafed, many slipped out of their life jackets and dove beneath the water for protection. Others feared being depth charged and tried to float on their backs, believing they would sustain less injury this way. Still others watched in fatalistic terror as the Japanese vessel loomed very large above them. But the Japanese ship neither strafed nor depth-charged these men. Instead, some of the crew tossed cans of food to their enemies now floating helplessly in the water. And then many of *Johnston*'s survivors witnessed something they would never forget. There on the bridge wing of the Japanese destroyer, an officer stood watching as *Johnston,* his mortal enemy of just moments before, slipped beneath the waves. As the noble ship went down, this Japanese officer lifted a hand to the visor of his cap and stood motionless for a moment . . . *saluting.*

The crews of the Taffy 3 escorts saved the day. Just one of the CVEs failed to escape—USS *Gambier Bay* succumbed to the Japanese gunfire and was lost. The Japanese commander of the powerful surface force eventually broke off his attack and retired from the scene, allowing all three Taffy groups to survive and leaving the vulnerable amphibious area unmolested.

Bill Mercer, Robert Billie, Ed Digardi, Robert Hagen, Robert Copeland, and Jackson McKaskill all survived this incredible battle. Captain Ernest Evans and several hundred more men did not.

The actions of the Sailors in those hopelessly outclassed destroyers are among the most courageous acts in the whole of the U.S. Navy's history. Together, as crews, they accomplished the seemingly impossible. As individuals, they leave us images that most of us can barely imagine, much less firmly comprehend: Paul Henry Carr with his body mortally wounded, holding up the last projectile to be fired; laundryman Bill Mercer running onto the exposed forecastle to clear away empty shell casings; Jackson McKaskill enduring terrible burns to secure steam valves; Ernest Evans refusing treatment for his wounds as time and again he took his ship into harm's way; the hundreds of Sailors who carried out a thousand duties while their ships were being torn apart around them. This is courage of the highest order and is fitting to the high ideals of a great nation.

Salvage

When they rolled Chief Boatswain's Mate Carl Brashear into the emergency room at Torrejon Air Force Base in Spain, he had no discernible pulse and barely the faintest of heartbeats. He had lost massive amounts of blood despite the two tourniquets that had been applied to his leg, and when the bandages that had been applied at the scene of the accident were removed, his foot fell off.

Eighteen pints of blood later, Brashear began to come back from the threshold of death. For most people, surviving would have been enough. But Carl Brashear had just begun to fight.

Hours before, Chief Brashear had been the picture of health. A Navy diver, he was among the most physically fit people in the world. It was March 1966, and Brashear and his shipmates were diving off the coast of Spain, trying to locate a nuclear bomb that had been lost at sea when two U.S. Air Force planes suffered a midair collision. It was a mission of vital importance, and Brashear and the other divers had been diving around the clock for two months, investigating every possible sonar contact that might prove to be the lost weapon.

When they at last located the bomb, a salvage operation began, and Brashear was in the thick of it. After the weapon was brought to the surface from 2,600 feet of water, Brashear was supervising the final operation of getting it aboard when a line parted. Every experienced Sailor knows that a parting line can be as lethal as a bullet, and Chief Brashear grabbed a nearby Sailor to yank him out of the deadly path of the whipping line. At that same moment, a pipe to which another line had been secured tore loose and flew across the deck, striking Brashear in the leg.

First aid was immediately administered, but it was clear that Brashear was in very bad shape. He was bleeding profusely, and his muscle-bound leg would not accept tourniquets well. The small salvage vessel was not equipped to handle an accident of this severity, so the mangled boatswain's mate was evacuated to the hospital in Torrejon.

Despite the best efforts of the hospital personnel, infection and then gangrene set in. Brashear was flown to a hospital in the United States, but things did not improve much, and doctors decided that amputation was the prudent answer.

Chief Brashear lost his leg. To all around him, and to the Bureau of Naval Personnel, it was apparent that this Sailor's career was over; he would have to retire on disability.

But Carl Brashear had other ideas. He was no stranger to challenges—as an African-American in a nation still adjusting to full integration and equal rights, he had overcome numerous obstacles to achieve what he had. He made up his mind not only to stay in the Navy but also to continue serving as a deep-sea diver.

He began reading about other people who continued to do amazing things after losing limbs. He studied how prostheses worked. As he recovered his strength, it soon became obvious to the hospital personnel that they had no ordinary case on their hands. Before his doctors thought it prudent, Brashear was working out to stay in shape. One session was so rigorous, in fact, he broke off the temporary cast that had been rigged to shrink the stump of his leg. He refused to use crutches and worked around the hospital, doing chores to help out and prove that he was capable. A few people began to wonder if maybe, just maybe, this crazy man was going to achieve the comeback he kept promising. But convincing hospital personnel and convincing a Navy medical board were two different things, and Chief Brashear knew it.

Through his persistence, he managed to get himself transferred to Portsmouth Naval Hospital so he could be nearer to the diving school there in Virginia. At the first opportunity, he went to the school and told the officer in charge, Chief Warrant Officer Clair Axtell, that he wanted to dive. He also wanted to get some photographs taken to prove that he could do it. Axtell knew that if anything went wrong, it would be the end of his own career. But there was no getting around the look of determination in Brashear's eyes, and Axtell decided that, if this man had the courage to fight these tremendous odds, he would have the courage to risk his career.

Soon the one-legged man was diving in a deep-sea rig. Then in a shallow-water rig. Then in scuba gear. All the while, he had an underwater photographer snapping pictures as proof, which he then sent to the Bureau of Medicine along with the paperwork for his medical board.

Carl Brashear eventually convinced the Navy to give him the chance to prove himself. A captain and a commander were assigned to dive with and observe him in underwater action during a number of arduous tests, and every morning they watched as he ran around the building and then led the other divers in calisthenics.

The day finally came that decided Brashear's future. He appeared before a medical board tasked with deciding what to do with this man who had fewer limbs than the average, but who had mountains more courage and determination. The captain heading the board began with this observation: "Most of the people in your position want to get a medical disability, to get out of the Navy, and do the least they can and draw as much pay as they can. But then you're asking for full duty!" He then asked, "Suppose you were diving and tore your leg off?"

Chief Brashear smiled and said, "Well, Captain, it wouldn't bleed."

The Navy relented in the face of Brashear's courageous determination. He was sent to the Navy Diver School for a yearlong trial under the tutelage and watchful eye of Chief Warrant Officer Raymond Duell. Cutting Brashear no slack, Duell had the amputee diver go down every single day that year. At the end of the trial, Duell wrote a powerfully convincing letter recommending that Brashear be restored to full diving status and duty. By now the answer was obvious. For the first time in history the Navy had a one-legged diver.

Brashear not only made history as the Navy's only master diver missing a leg, but he also became Master Diver of the Navy in 1975, the only black man to date to hold that position.

In 2000, Twentieth Century Fox made an inspiring movie about Carl Brashear called *Men of Honor.* Cuba Gooding Jr. played Brashear and Robert De Niro played a composite character named Billy Sunday, who represented the men like Axtell and Duell who had helped Brashear achieve his goal. Gooding told reporters what it was like to wear a 220-pound diving rig and simulate the action of a Navy diver during the filming of the movie: "At the end of the day I would sit on my steps in the trailer. I couldn't even walk into my trailer; that's how fatigued I was. I would rest my elbows on my knees and my whole body would start to shake, so I would have to sit up. It was a very strenuous movie." Describing the man he was portraying, Gooding said Brashear is a man who "took everything seriously but not personally."

Retired Sailor Carl Brashear and actor Cuba Gooding Jr. together at a preview of the movie *Men of Honor.* Gooding played Brashear in the 2000 film based on the master chief's inspirational commitment to service. *U.S. Navy (Dolores L. Parlato)*

Years after Master Chief Carl Brashear's retirement from the Navy, he told his story to the Naval Institute's historian, Paul Stillwell. When asked about that trial year, Brashear confided that because he was a chief, he led the diving school students in calisthenics each morning and "sometimes I would come back from a run, and my artificial leg would have a puddle of blood from my stump." Fearing that a trip to sick bay might cause him to fail the trial, he would just "go somewhere and hide and soak my leg in a bucket of salt water—an old remedy." Matter-of-factly he added, "Then I'd get up the next morning and run."

Courage comes in many forms.

A Final Word on Courage

The form of courage we most often think of and frequently celebrate is *physical* courage, as exhibited by the Sailors of Taffy 3 and Medal of Honor recipient James Elliott Williams. It is in our nature to admire such deeds. And well we should. Less often, however, do we recognize *moral* courage, the kind that does not risk one's body but does risk other aspects of one's life.

People sometimes face decisions that will affect their lives in some significant way. It may be as relatively small a thing as giving up a much-wanted leave period to help a shipmate in need, or it may be as significant as risking a promotion or even an entire career.

I have personally witnessed acts of physical courage that I will never forget, but I have also seen many more acts of moral courage during my years in the Navy. For example, there was the young petty officer who came to Vietnam late in the war, newly married and consequently terribly homesick. By chance, he happened to be in the personnel office in Saigon when a personnel drawdown was implemented; the officer in charge offered him the chance to go home after just a few days in-country. I could see in his eyes that he desperately wanted to say yes. But after a moment's hesitation, he answered: "No, there are others who have been here much longer. Let one of them go."

There was the chief on a cruiser who was being pressured by his department head to find ways to spend leftover budget money at the end of the fiscal year "so they don't take it away from us next year." The chief, who was eligible for promotion to senior chief that year, told the officer he could not spend the taxpayers' money that way.

There was the captain of an aircraft carrier who was facing an operational readiness evaluation that would determine the ship's deployability and thus affect the captain's chances of being selected for admiral the next year. The night before the big evaluation was to begin, his battle stations officer of the deck—who had been training in that slot for months—received a telegram that his wife's father had passed away. That captain must have been tempted to keep the man on board for obvious reasons, but instead he insisted that the man be flown off at first light so that he could be with his grieving wife in her time of need.

These are acts of moral courage, not risking life or limb but sacrificing or risking personal needs and wants. They occur far more often than do the death-defying feats we celebrate, and they sometimes have serious consequences, yet they are rarely recognized. Unlike acts of physical courage, which often occur spontaneously, acts of moral courage are often reached after careful deliberation, when rationalization is a ready ally.

Although we will probably never find a way to give full recognition to these acts, it is vitally important that we recognize they do happen and they are just as important as the inspiring acts of physical courage we rightfully admire.

When young Americans append the letters USN or USNR to their names, they accept the responsibility of defending a nation; of following in the footsteps of Boatswain's Mate Williams, Commander Evans, and Master Chief Brashear; of finding within themselves the physical and moral courage that are among the necessary tools of a Sailor. This is no small challenge to be sure, but history has proved that we need not worry. As each new day dawns, we can rest assured that the nation is in good hands, that courage—along with honor and commitment—is alive and well, and that the U.S. Navy will continue to do its job in the tradition set by ordinary people who have left us an extraordinary legacy.

Commitment 3

While a sense of honor is a prerequisite to military service, and it takes courage to face the dangers of the sea and the violence of the enemy, it takes a special kind of commitment to be a Sailor in the United States Navy.

Among the many things that have always made Sailors different from other people is the way they live and work. There is some truth in the popular image of Sailors visiting beautiful and exotic places and enjoying the comforts of hot meals and a warm bed while their Soldier counterparts are eating cold rations and sleeping on the ground. There is another side of life in the Navy, however, that is often challenging, sometimes difficult to bear, and yet a source of great pride.

Even in times of peace, the life of a Sailor can be arduous. While the vast majority of people live and work in places that do not move, Sailors since the earliest days of seafaring eat, sleep, and do their work—whether it is maintaining weapons, typing reports, or launching aircraft—on decks that move at the whim of wind and sea. They share their quarters with highly explosive substances, dangerous inflammables, and toxic chemicals. Theirs is a world where they perform daily duties on the crest of a storm-driven wave, in the dark and foreboding depths of the ocean, or in the turbulence of a cloud-covered sky. Despite their bond with the sea, many Sailors find themselves in the frigid arctic, a steaming jungle, or a blazing desert.

Many professions have their challenges and difficulties, but it has always taken a unique sort of individual to stand up to the rigors of life in the Navy, whether in surface ships, submarines, aircraft, or the many other branches of the sea service. This is one of the reasons why Sailors can justifiably be proud of the uniform they wear and stand just a little taller when wearing it. They share the knowledge that they come from a long line of tough individuals who, as part of a crew, endured hardships and faced dangers while accomplishing vitally important things for the safety and well-being of their fellow citizens and their nation.

Even though much has changed, much has remained the same in the more than two hundred years that the U.S. Navy has guarded the nation and projected its power to distant places. Although today's Sailors draw higher pay, have more comforts, and are treated more justly than were their predecessors, they still must contend with many of the same challenges that faced those "Tars" and "Bluejackets" who first took to the sea in the earliest days of the American Revolution. They face many of the same perils and hardships and must still deal with the sadness of leaving loved ones behind as they carry out their duties the world over.

Today's Sailor copes with a very different way of life from the one he or she left behind, one that is rich with tradition of the past yet steaming full speed ahead on the cutting edge of modern technology. Today's Sailor often functions under uncomfortable, taxing conditions, carrying on the necessary tradition of sacrifice that has been one of the hallmarks of the U.S. Navy since its earliest days. It is a tradition shored up by honor, by courage, and not least by commitment, for no one could possibly be a Sailor in the finest sense of the word without being deeply committed to this great nation and its defense.

Earliest Days

At the very beginning, the men who chose to go to sea as part of the newly formed American Navy (first called the Continental Navy) were committed to the idea of revolution, to casting off the ties that held them to England in hopes of creating a new nation based upon the rights of man and the principles of life, liberty, and the pursuit of happiness.

When John Kilby joined the Navy in July 1779, he joined a tiny force that not only was facing battle with the most powerful navy on earth, but also was one that had to compete for sailors with several other "navies." All but two of the colonies (New Jersey and Delaware) had formed navies of their own, and—far worse for the fledgling Continental Navy—there were countless privateers roaming the seas. It was a common practice of the day for warring nations to encourage private shipowners to capture enemy merchant shipping. If successful, they would share in the profits gained from the sale of the goods carried in the captured vessel.

While this practice was beneficial to the war effort because of the damage it did to the enemy's economy (more than two thousand American privateers took to the sea, seizing British merchant ships and their cargoes and causing insurance rates to skyrocket), it made recruiting for the Continental Navy much more difficult. It took an extra measure of commitment for a young, able-bodied seaman to choose that tiny Navy—whose mission included facing the warships of the professional and powerful Royal Navy—for a mere eight dollars a month, when privateers were likely to make more money while facing less danger. The naval Sailor was far more likely than the privateer to be killed, wounded, or captured.

Recruiting

The Continental Congress offered grants of land to men who would fight as Soldiers in the Army, but no such offer was ever made to those who chose the Navy. So it is no wonder that recruiting for the Navy was challenging in those days. An example of the methods used survives in the record of one of those who, despite his apparent cynicism, signed on.

> All means were resorted to which ingenuity could devise to induce men to enlist. A recruiting officer, bearing a flag, and attended by a band of martial music, paraded the streets to excite a thirst for glory and a spirit of military ambition. The recruiting officer possessed the qualifications to make the service appear alluring, especially to the young. . . . When he espied any large boys . . . he would attract their attention by singing in a comical manner:
>
> > All you that have bad masters,
> > And cannot get your due,
> > Come, come, my brave boys,
> > And join our ship's crew!

Recruiting posters were plastered on walls along the waterfront of American seaports, offering whatever incentives recruiters could devise. One such poster created in March 1777 used patriotism as its primary incentive, beginning with the heading "Great Encouragement for Seamen":

> ALL GENTLEMEN SEAMEN and able-bodied LANDSMEN who have a Mind to distinguish themselves in the GLORIOUS CAUSE of their Country

Yet this same poster did not rely upon love of country alone. The ship seeking the recruits was described in these glowing terms:

> The Ship RANGER, in the Opinion of every Person who has seen her is looked upon to be one of the best Cruizers in America.—She will always be able to Fight her Guns under a most excellent Cover; and no Vessel yet built was ever calculated for sailing faster, and making good Weather.

As recruiters have always done, this one painted a slightly "enhanced" description of what the volunteer could look forward to.

ANY GENTLEMEN VOLUNTEERS who have a Mind to take an agreeable Voyage in this pleasant Season of the Year may, by entering on board the above Ship RANGER, meet with every Civility they can possibly expect.

Those who actually signed on might describe this "agreeable voyage" in different terms. Under routine sailing conditions, Sailors like John Kilby could expect to be on watch fully half of their time under way—because the ship was divided into merely two watch sections—and the remaining time was allocated to additional work assigned (which was often considerable) and to the necessary functions of sleeping and eating.

Danger as Routine

The work aboard a sailing ship in those times could be quite dangerous. While the odds were thirteen to one that Kilby would be killed in battle, they were a frightening three to one that he might die in an accident. Indeed, by his own account, Kilby described an incident that occurred shortly after reporting aboard his ship: "The first thing that happened was, as we were beating down to the island of Groix, a man fell off the main topsail yard onto the quarterdeck. As he fell, he struck the cock of [the Captain's] hat, but did no injury [to the Captain]. He was killed and buried on the island of Groix."

The Kedge Anchor, a book published some years after the Revolution "as a ready means of introducing Young Sailors to the theory of that art by which they must expect to advance in their profession"—a forerunner to today's *Bluejacket's Manual,* which first appeared in 1902—understated the situation when it advised "men perched aloft in a perilous situation will adopt that method which will eventually cost the least time and trouble." Among the Sailors themselves, it was commonly understood that the rule was "One hand for the ship, one hand for yourself."

Sails have long since disappeared from the Navy, yet danger has not. Sailors must still climb masts, and although these masts are more user-friendly in many ways, invisible gremlins in the form of volts and amps now lurk there, waiting to do harm to the careless Sailor. There are far fewer lines in the modern warship, yet it takes only one to give way under strain to leave a swath of death and injury in its path. Modern weapon systems are in many ways safer than those cumbersome cannons, yet their

G R E A T

ENCOURAGEMENT

F O R

SEAMEN.

A LL GENTLEMEN SEAMEN and able-bodied LANDSMEN who have a Mind to diftinguifh themfelves in the GLORIOUS CAUSE of their COUNTRY, and make their Fortunes, an Opportunity now offers on board the Ship RANGER, of Twenty Guns, (for FRANCE) now laying in PORTSMOUTH, in the State of NEW-HAMPSHIRE, commanded by JOHN PAUL JONES Efq; let them repair to the Ship's Rendezvous in PORTSMOUTH, or at the Sign of Commodore MANLEY, in SALEM, where they will be kindly entertained, and receive the greateft Encouragement.---The Ship RANGER, in the Opinion of every Perfon who has feen her is looked upon to be one of the beft Cruizers in AMERICA.---She will be always able to Fight her Guns under a moft excellent Cover ; and no Veffel yet built was ever calculated for failing fafter, and making good Weather.

Any GENTLEMEN VOLUNTEERS who have a Mind to take an agreable Voyage in this pleafant Seafon of the Year, may, by entering on board the above Ship RANGER, meet with every Civility they can poffibly expect, and for a further Encouragement depend on the firft Opportunity being embraced to reward each one agreable to his Merit.

All reafonable Travelling Expences will be allowed, and the Advance-Money be paid on their Appearance on Board.

IN C O N G R E S S, MARCH 29, 1777.

RESOLVED,

T HAT the MARINE COMMITTEE be authorifed to advance to every able Seaman, that enters into the CONTINENTAL SERVICE, any Sum not exceeding FORTY DOLLARS, and to every ordinary Seaman or Landfman, any Sum not exceeding TWENTY DOLLARS, to be deducted from their future Prize-Money.

By Order of CONGRESS,

JOHN-HANCOCK, PRESIDENT.

DANVERS: Printed by E. RUSSELL, at the Houfe late the Bell-Tavern.

A Revolutionary War poster used to recruit Sailors for service in the new Continental Navy. *Naval Historical Center* explosive power is far more devastating when something goes wrong. Fire, flooding, and falling overboard are the ever-present dangers common to eighteenth- and twenty-first-century Sailors alike. Fuels, electricity, heavy machinery, heights, depths, extremes of temperature, erratic motion, the dark of night, and nature's unpredictable moods are all potentially deadly shipmates to today's Sailor. It takes vigilance and prudence to survive these hazards and serious commitment to meet them head-on in today's Navy.

Elusive Sleep

Sleeping was itself a challenge in Kilby's day. Although there were some on board—known as "idlers" (cooks, sailmakers, clerks, for instance)—who stood no watches and therefore could sleep the night through, Kilby and the vast majority of his fellow Sailors could sleep for merely four hours at a time (the two-section watches were "four on, four off"). To make matters worse, they were permitted to sleep only during the hours of darkness, so one night they would get barely four hours of sleep and the next night they might get seven and a half, but with a four-hour watch dead in the middle. Further, a sudden squall or some other emergency could necessitate a call for "all hands" at any time of day, and virtually all the crew (even the idlers) would have to go to their assigned stations to reef topsails or carry out whatever major evolution was needed.

The wristwatch was a long way off, so most on board relied upon the sounding of the ship's bell to know when it was time to go on or off watch. The bell was rung each half hour of the watch—beginning with one bell on the first half hour, two on the second, and so on—so that by the time a Sailor heard seven bells, he knew he had but half an hour before it was time to relieve the watch.

The Sailor's bed of the day was a hammock, a wonderful place to catch a nap in one's backyard, but not the place to try to sleep night after night. When a Sailor could at last crawl into his hammock, other obstacles to coveted slumber often intervened. The motion of the ship could be quite violent and counter to the swing of the hammock. There was no source of heat or air conditioning, and ventilation was poor at best. Herman Melville, who went to sea in the frigate *United States,* a much larger ship than the earlier one Kilby signed onto, colorfully described sleeping (or trying to) in a sailing man-of-war in his narrative *White-Jacket.*

> Your hammock is your [prison] and canvas jug; into which, or out of which, it is very hard to get; and where sleep is but a mockery and a name.

Eighteen inches a man is all they allow you; eighteen inches in width; in *that* you must swing. Dreadful! They give you more swing than that at the gallows.

During warm nights in the Tropics, your hammock is as a stew-pan; where you stew and stew, till you can almost hear yourself hiss. . . .

One extremely warm night, during a calm, when it was so hot that only a skeleton could keep cool (from the free current of air through its bones) . . . I lowered myself gently to the deck. Let me see now, thought I, whether my ingenuity cannot devise some method whereby I can have room to breathe and sleep at the same time. I have it. I will lower my hammock underneath all these others; and then—upon that separate and independent level, at least, I shall have the whole berth deck to myself. Accordingly, I lowered away my pallet to the desired point . . . about three inches from the deck—and crawled into it again. But alas! this arrangement had made such a sweeping semicircle of my hammock, that while my head and feet were at par, the small of my back was settling down indefinitely. I felt as if some gigantic archer had hold of me for a bow.

But there was another plan left. I triced up my hammock with all my strength, so as to bring it wholly *above* the tiers of pallets around me . . . but alas! it was much worse than before. My luckless hammock was stiff and straight as a board; and there I was—laid out in it, with my nose against the ceiling, like a dead man's against the lid of his coffin.

When not in use, the hammocks were rolled up and stored in netting triced to the overhead. An early instruction to officers provided guidance for the supervision of this daily ritual: "Nothing adds more to the smart and favorable appearance of a vessel of war than a neat stowage of hammocks. . . . In the stowage of the hammocks, the officer should stand on the opposite side of the deck, a position which will enable him to preserve a symmetrical line, and guide and direct the stower in his progress fore and aft the netting; they are also enjoined to be careful that the hammocks of the men be properly lashed up. Defaulters in this particular should be reported to the First Lieutenant. Seven turns at equal distance is the required number of turns with a hammock-lashing."

Sustenance

Food, another necessity of life, was a constant concern for Sailors of the early Navy. Of the forty-four articles making up the *Rules for the Regula-*

tion of the Navy of the United Colonies of North-America (the first "Navy Regulations," written largely by founding father and future president John Adams), six pertained to the acquisition, stowage, inspection, and issuing of food. Article 17, for example, directs: "All ships furnished with fishing tackle, being in such places where fish is to be had, the Captain is to employ some of the company in fishing." Article 22 requires: "The Captain is frequently to order the proper officer to inspect into the condition of the provisions, and if the bread proves damp to have it aired upon the quarter-deck or poop, and also to examine the flesh cask; and if any of the pickle be leaked out, to have new made and put in and the cask made tight and secure."

The meals of the day were breakfast at 0800, dinner at noon, and supper at 1600. No other meals were served ("mid-rats" did not come along until much later), so a Sailor had nothing to eat from 1600 till 0800 (a full sixteen hours) unless he managed to stuff a biscuit in his shirt during supper.

The reefer would not be invented for a long time, so keeping food from spoiling was a challenge that severely limited what could be taken to sea for long periods. Meats were dried and preserved with a heavy coating of salt. When it was time to eat some of the beef, for example, it was removed from the barrel where it (hopefully) had been kept from the marauding rats, the salt chipped off as much as possible, and then immersed in water for a time to help cut the remaining salt and make the meat something close to chewable.

Food in general was called "tack" in the Sailor's jargon. "Hardtack" was an ever-present, if not terribly appetizing, form of sustenance that is roughly similar to today's dog biscuit (but harder). Made of flour, salt, and water—leavening was conspicuously absent—it could keep a man alive but not happy. As the cruise went on, the battle with small insects would gradually go the way of the weevil, and it became the habit of Sailors everywhere to tap their hardtack on the deck (or table if they were among the few who rated one) for a time before eating so that most of the unwanted vermin would fall out. Charles Nordhoff, who wrote from first-hand experience about life in the sailing Navy, recalled, "I have seen a biscuit literally crawl off the mess cloth."

Sailors ate in messes consisting of eight to ten men. Typically, one representative of each mess would bring the food to his shipmates, who would gather together between two of the cannon and seat themselves on a tarp spread out on the deck. Melville described this process vividly.

> The common seamen are divided into messes, put down on the purser's books as *Mess No. 1, Mess No. 2, Mess No. 3,* etc. The members of each mess combine their rations of provisions, and breakfast,

dine, and sup together in allotted intervals between the guns on the main deck. In undeviating rotation, the members of each mess (excepting the petty officers) take their turn in performing the functions of cook and steward. . . . It is the mess-cook's business to have an eye to the general interests of his mess; to see that, when the combined allowances of beef, bread, etc. are served out by one of the master's mates, the mess over which he presides receives its full share. Upon the berth-deck he has a chest, in which to keep his pots, pans, spoons, and small stores of sugar, molasses, tea, and flour.

But though entitled a cook, strictly speaking, the mess-cook is no cook at all; for the cooking for the crew is all done by a high and mighty functionary, officially called the "ship's cook," assisted by several deputies. . . .

From this it will be seen that, as far as cooking is concerned, a *"cook of the mess"* has very little to do. . . . Still, in some things, his office involves many annoyances. Twice a week, butter and cheese are served out—so much to each man—and the mess-cook has the sole charge of these delicacies. The great difficulty consists in so catering for the mess, concerning these luxuries, as to satisfy all. Some guzzlers are for devouring the butter at one meal, and finishing off the cheese the same day; others contend for saving it up till *Banyan Day,* when there is nothing but beef and bread; and others again, are for taking a very small bit of butter and cheese, by way of dessert, to each and every meal through the week. All this gives rise to endless disputes, debates, and altercations.

Discipline

Discipline in the old sailing Navy could be harsh. John Kilby described what he saw in his first moments aboard his new ship.

The first sight that was presented to our view was thirteen men stripped and tied upon the larboard [port] side of the quarterdeck. The boatswain's mate commenced at the first nearest the gangway and gave him one dozen lashes with a cat-o'nine-tails. Thus he went on until he came to the coxswain, Robertson by name. (These men were the crew of the captain's barge and Robertson was coxswain.) When the boatswain's mate came to Robertson, the first lieutenant said: "As he is a bit of an officer, give him two dozen." It was done.

Now it is necessary to let you know what they had been guilty of. They had carried the Captain on shore, and as soon as he was out of sight, they all left the barge and got drunk. When [the Captain] came down in order to go on board, not a man was to be found. [The Captain] had to and did hire a fishing boat to carry him on board.

Far more graphic versions of the practice of flogging have been recorded, but it takes little imagination to know that it was a barbaric form of discipline, and although it was a standard practice in all the navies of the day, it would be abolished in the U.S. Navy ten years before the American Civil War.

Lesser punishments were available and often administered without the prerequisite of a captain's mast or other judicial proceeding. Even a Sailor guilty of no wrongdoing could expect to be encouraged to carry out his duties expeditiously by a petty officer not opposed to a swift kick or a blow from a knotted rope.

The regulations drawn up by John Adams included such things as: "If any shall be heard to swear, curse or blaspheme the name of God, the Captain is strictly enjoined to punish them for every offence, by causing them to wear a wooden collar or some other shameful badge of distinction, for so long a time as he shall judge proper."

Those same regulations limited a captain to ordering a maximum of twelve lashes for any offense (far less than the limits imposed in the Royal Navy), but there were few restrictions on a captain's authority, and many could be quite creative in how they enforced discipline or solved personnel problems within their ships. For example, noting that seasickness was a serious problem among his crew, Captain Charles Biddle responded: "Knowing that exercise is an excellent remedy for sea sickness, and wishing to make the young men on board learn to go aloft whenever the weather was fair, I had the hand pump taken up to the head of the main top-mast and there lashed, and every one of them that wanted a drink of water was obliged to go up, bring the pump down, and after they had taken a drink carry it up again. For the first five or six days many of them would come up on deck, look wistfully at the pump, but rather than go aloft would go down again. However, they were soon reconciled to it and I believe it was a great service to them."

A Special Kind of Commitment

Despite all the deprivations and harsh conditions, Sailors went to sea, committed to carrying out their duties, to fighting for those things they believed in, and even to giving their lives when and if the time came.

By the law of averages, most Sailors serve in times of peace. Even when war comes, many never see actual combat. This requires a special kind of commitment, for there is a disappointment, however perverse, in not being permitted to do what you train for. The Navy exists to defend the nation, and, while there are many kinds of operations that do not require the actual exchange of fire, in the end, a Sailor's training, a Sailor's routine, is ultimately aimed at supporting or participating in victory over the nation's enemies. There can be great frustration in spending great quantities of time preparing for the moment of truth, simply to find that the moment never comes for you personally. There can be a sense of disappointment when others are called upon to do battle and your task is support. While it is obvious that who will play which role is largely a matter of chance, and it is equally obvious that both roles are vital to victory, it requires a strong sense of commitment to be ready for either.

For those few who indeed must face hostile fire, yet another kind of commitment is mandated. Courage conquers fear, but commitment counters confusion, fatigue, horror, and setback when the chaos of war changes your world forever. John Kilby was one of those Sailors who would be called upon in that moment of truth for that unique form of commitment, and it was his fate to serve with one of the most famous naval captains of all time during one of the greatest naval battles in history.

Kilby's challenge began early in the Revolution when he served for a time as a privateer but had the misfortune of being captured by the British. Some of that spirit and sardonic humor that are often characteristic of Americans in grave circumstances show through in his brief description of what happened: "We were put on board the old *Princess Amelia* of ninety guns, then a guard-ship, where we lay two months. Then we were carried up to Hazel Hospital for trial and condemnation (a mock trial to be sure). After calling over all our names, the Judge rises up and pronounced sentence in these words, to wit: 'You are all condemned for piracy on His Majesty's high seas.' (Here permit me to say I wish to know who gave him the high seas.)"

Kilby would suffer as a prisoner of war for several years before being released as part of a prisoner exchange in 1779. Finding himself in the French city of Nantes along with a number of the other former prisoners, Kilby learned that an American warship was in the port city of l'Orient getting ready for sea. It was the *Bonhomme Richard* of forty guns, named in honor of Benjamin Franklin, who had long written a periodical known in Philadelphia as *Poor Richard's Almanac* and translated into French as *Les Maximes du Bonhomme Richard*. They learned that the ship was commanded by John Paul Jones, a man whose reputation had already been established by the capture of many British ships and by the daring raid on Whitehaven on the west coast of England itself. Jones was hailed as a naval hero in America and condemned as a pirate in England. Kilby and his mates found this very appealing. "Thirty-three of us determined to get with Captain John Paul Jones," Kilby later explained. "One reason why we came to this determination was, you know revenge is sometimes quite pleasant to men, and we then believed the said Jones would not disappoint us in our great wish and desire."

John Kilby made the 108-mile trip to l'Orient and signed on with Jones as an "ordinary seaman." He must have been somewhat disappointed when he first laid eyes on his new ship. She was a converted merchantman whose keel had passed over many miles of seawater. Her crew included Sailors from nine different nations, of whom merely about a third were American and many had far less experience than Kilby. Her armament was an odd mixture of cannons, some of which did not appear reliable.

To Sea

The old ship and her mongrel crew put to sea in August 1779 in company with several French ships and the American frigate *Alliance,* commanded by French captain Pierre Landais. Within a month, the small squadron had sailed around Ireland and Scotland, capturing, sinking, and destroying a number of British ships.

Jones soon promoted Kilby to "able seaman" and then to petty officer as a gunner's mate. At one point during the cruise, the captain took aboard a British pilot as he ventured into a Scottish river. Jones had deliberately disguised *Bonhomme Richard*'s identity so that the pilot was unaware that he had boarded an American ship. With obvious pride (and a little taste of that revenge he sought), Kilby described the encounter: "Jones asked the pilot what was the news on the coast. 'Why,' said he, 'very great and bad news! That rebel Paul Jones is expected to land every day.' Jones asked him then what they thought of the rebel Jones, saying he wished he could come across him. 'What!' said he, 'he is the greatest rebel and pirate that ever was and ought to be hanged.' Jones then asked him if he knew whom he was talking to, and observed, 'I am Paul Jones.' The poor pilot dropped on his knees and begged for his life. Jones said 'Get up! I won't hurt a hair of your head, but you are my prisoner.'"

Her hold loaded with prisoners, *Richard* and the other ships in the little squadron arrived off Flamborough Head on the east coast of England in the late afternoon of 23 September 1779. Lookouts sang out, reporting first one, then another mast sprouting up from the flat line of the horizon. Though the light was beginning to fade, it was clear that they had encountered a convoy of some sort: rich pickings on the one hand, serious danger on the other. Convoys did not usually travel without escorts, even this close to the English shore. Before long, any hopes that this might be an exception were extinguished.

HMS *Serapis*

Looming up over the horizon were the three tall masts of a British frigate. It was HMS *Serapis,* rated at forty-four guns, and she was accompanied by the sloop of war *Countess of Scarborough* of twenty guns. The two warships came on quickly, moving into position to protect the merchant convoy. Although the other ships in Jones's squadron began behaving erratically (the sole exception being *Pallas,* who moved in to fight the British sloop), Jones immediately maneuvered to engage *Serapis.*

From his station as quarter-gunner at one of *Richard*'s 18-pounder cannons on the lower deck, Kilby peered out through the gun port at the British frigate across the water, who grew larger every minute as the two ships closed upon one another. *Serapis*'s sails glowed faintly red in the gathering darkness as they caught the last vestiges of light from the sun now vanished over the horizon. Kilby recorded no emotion except perhaps a hint of pride as he recounted what he saw: "In order to protect that valuable convoy, as it was his duty, he (the enemy) hove to, hauled up his canvas and prepared for action. Side lanterns, of course, were up throughout the enemy's ship and every man at quarters was plain to be seen. We were then but a very small distance from them and you may be sure that our ship was as well prepared for action as it was in the power of man to have a ship."

Kilby's assessment of his ship's readiness was no doubt accurate, but the American Sailors were not going to have an easy time of it. In his monumental biography of John Paul Jones, Admiral Samuel Eliot Morison described the two ships about to do battle.

> HMS *Serapis* . . . , commanded by Captain Richard Pearson RN, was a new copper-bottomed frigate [which substantially increased her speed]. Rated at 44 guns, actually she had 50; a main battery of 20 eighteen-pounders on a lower gun deck (compared with *Richard*'s six of that caliber); 20 nine-pounders on an upper covered deck (compared with *Richard*'s 28 twelve-pounders), and 10 six-pounders on the quarterdeck (where *Richard* had 6 nine-pounders). . . . There is no doubt that *Serapis* was a newer, faster, and more nimble frigate than *Richard*; and in fire power, owing to her far greater number of eighteen-pounders, she was definitely superior.

Unremitting Fury

Despite these circumstances, Jones never flinched; Kilby and his mates were likewise committed to following their intrepid captain into battle. The moon was rising and the weather clear as the two ships moved across the now blackened waters, ever closer for the impending fight. The creaking of the rigging and an occasional luff in one of the sails were the only sounds to be heard until a voice drifted across the water from *Serapis,* demanding, "Tell me what ship that is directly or I will sink you." Kilby recalled his captain's response: "Jones then answered: 'Sink and be damned!' Both ships were within fifty yards of each other and at the words 'sink and be damned,' I fully believe no man living could tell which ship fired first, but so it was that each ship fired a broadside."

Jones himself later wrote in his official report that "the battle thus begun was continued with unremitting fury." And furious it was. Round shot and grapeshot poured into both vessels, smashing into masts and bulkheads, splintering wood into deadly shards, crushing bones, and tearing flesh. Suddenly, two of *Richard*'s 18-pounders exploded, killing most of their crews, blowing a gaping hole in the deck above, and reducing the ship's weight of fire to a mere 195 pounds compared to *Serapis*'s 300. The smell of burning flesh spread about the deck as flames erupted from the explosions.

Bonhomme Richard and *Serapis* fighting one of the most famous sea battles in history. John Kilby and the other American Sailors were inspired to fight with "unremitting fury" when they saw the American colors flying at the top of the after mast. *U.S. Naval Institute Photo Archive*

Undaunted by the setback, Kilby and the others continued to serve the remaining weapons, firing at a rapid rate. Kilby noted how Jones's leadership strengthened the crew's commitment to fight on despite all the chaos and carnage around them: "At this time, Jones ordered the helm to be put hard up and to run the enemy on board. It was done. In doing this, her jib-boom ran between our mizzen-shrouds and mizzen mast. Her jib-boom carried away our ensign staff and colors. At this, they gave three cheers. We answered them with one cheer. Jones at the same time cried out: 'Look at my mizzen-peak!' at which place was run up the glory of America, I mean the most handsome suit of colors that I ever saw. They were about thirty-six feet in the fly."

The inspiring sight of the large national ensign flying from the after mast was further strengthened when Jones personally seized *Serapis*'s jib stay, which had fallen across *Richard*'s quarterdeck, and "belayed it to our mizzen cleats," lashing the two ships together in a deadly embrace. Kilby heard Jones say, "Now we'll hold her fast by this until one or the other sinks." When the British commander ordered his men to board *Richard,* Jones, standing at the gangway with a long pike in his hands, shouted: "Come on. I am ready to receive you." Kilby and some of the others joined Jones, and together, in fierce hand-to-hand fighting, they repulsed the British sailors and marines trying to come across.

The fighting continued for some time, with both ships firing into one another at point-blank range. Men fired muskets down from the rigging above, fire raged in both ships, and water rose fast in *Bonhomme Richard.* The ship's carpenter, who functioned in those days much as the damage control assistant does today, reported to Captain Jones within Kilby's hearing that "the ship then had six feet six inches of water in the hold and that she was sinking fast."

Alliance at last made an appearance, but instead of coming to the aid of her American ally, she inexplicably fired on *Richard,* killing a number of men and adding further damage to the already decimated ship.

As noted earlier in this chapter, it takes a special person to be a Sailor, to remain committed to one's personal sense of honor, one's shipmates, one's ship, one's Navy, even one's nation in the face of such adversity. But John Kilby, Richard Dale, William Hamilton, John Paul Jones, and scores of other Sailors of this newly formed U.S. Navy never faltered despite the raging fires, exploding ordnance, rising water, flying shrapnel, flowing blood, and screams of agony. They fought on and on, loading and firing time and again, swinging pikes and cutlasses with all their strength, shoring up damaged bulkheads, slipping in the blood that ran across the decks, manning the pumps in a losing battle with the sea, fighting back fires, choking on great clouds of smoke, ignoring the crushing fatigue that strained their laboring muscles, and suppressing the terrible fear that clutched at their hearts.

In the midst of all this, though Kilby did not witness it, First Lieutenant Dale later told of a moment that would define the new Navy forever. Noting early on that the odds were in his favor and that *Richard* was taking a terrible beating, the British captain called across to Jones, asking if he wished to surrender. Jones's defiant reply echoes across the ages and serves as a battle cry of commitment that has made the United States Navy the greatest in the history of the world. Surrounded by terrible devastation and chaos, John Paul Jones defiantly replied, "I have not yet *begun* to fight!"

And he was right. The battle raged on, both sides fighting fiercely. But the advantage in firepower that *Serapis* had enjoyed had been diminished when the two ships became grappled together. And the top men and Marines in *Richard* were delivering a withering fire down upon *Serapis*'s exposed decks, slowly but surely diminishing the size of the opposing crew and wearing away both their ability and their resolve to fight.

To add to *Serapis*'s misery, Hamilton climbed into the rigging with a basket of hand grenades and a live match. Shinnying out along one of *Richard*'s yardarms that stretched over *Serapis,* he reached a point directly above an open hatch on the enemy ship. With musket balls flying about him, Hamilton coolly lit the fuze on one of the grenades and with great precision dropped it through the gaping maw of the hatchway. The grenade exploded among some powder bags that were scattered about. The magnified detonation killed at least twenty men and seriously injured many others.

Jones had been concentrating fire on the enemy's mainmast to make sure she could not escape should the two ships become disentangled. When that great spar began to topple, the British captain at last lost his will to fight and personally tore down his national ensign as a signal of surrender. It was 2230, and the great struggle was over.

A Most Glorious Sight

Once the formalities of surrender were concluded, other matters became paramount. Though victorious in her struggle with a superior British frigate, poor *Bonhomme Richard* was fighting for her life. John Kilby described the aftermath:

> Our ship was on fire within three feet of her magazine. The fire on board both ships was at last conquered, though by much harder work than the fighting during the action. By the time all this was accomplished, daylight began to make its appearance. . . . We then cleared

the ships' decks of the dead and at the rising of the sun, we hove overboard one hundred dead bodies. One hundred more were wounded, between thirty-five and forty of whom died the next day before four o'clock. During this time, we also rigged up jury masts on board the *Sea-Raper* [Kilby's name for *Serapis*]. At four o'clock in the afternoon, our good ship *Bonhomme Richard,* which had so short a time before carried us through all the dangers of the night, sank. . . . O heavens! It was enough to bring tears from the heart of the most unthinking man! She went down head foremost with all sails set—studding sails, top-gallant sails, royals, sky-scrapers, and every sail that could be put on a ship—jack, pennant and that beautiful ensign that she so gallantly wore while in action and when we conquered. A most glorious sight!! Alas! She is gone! Never more to be seen!

Jones, too, later described the last moments of *Richard* in his journal: "As she plunged down by the head at the last, her taffrail rose momentarily in the air; so the very last vestige mortal eyes ever saw of the *Bonhomme Richard* was the defiant waving of her unconquered and unstricken flag."

Commitment

As we have seen, Sailors must develop within themselves several kinds of commitment. They must remain committed to their shipmates and to their nation when their living conditions are practically unbearable, or when demands are made upon them that most other citizens will never face. They must remain committed even knowing that the odds dictate they are preparing for a test that may never come. And they must be committed to giving their all when and if the day comes that they must meet the kinds of challenges that John Kilby faced and conquered.

As the hapless *Richard* went to rest on the ocean floor, Kilby and the other Sailors who watched her go had no idea that their commitment to fight on, even when defeat seemed inevitable, was just the *beginning* of a tradition—a *standard*—that would guide those who followed through times of violent war and arduous peace, taking the new Navy to heights unimaginable to those iron men fighting in wooden ships. As these Sailors said farewell to their gallant little ship, it probably did not occur to any of them—not even to Jones himself—that their Navy had just begun to fight!

Part II

Traditions

In the more than two hundred years that Sailors of the U.S. Navy have been defending their nation, they have created certain consistencies in the way they do things, and these consistencies have become traditions. Sometimes these traditions manifest themselves in language used, in inspirational sayings, in special customs and ceremonies, or simply in the unique way things are done. Sometimes traditions are merely quaint or colorful, and sometimes they seem to serve no purpose. But some traditions are born of core values and have the power to inspire noble deeds, to overcome hardship and fear, to set standards that ensure greatness. The chapters that follow are about the traditions that make the Navy stronger, that give Sailors an extra measure of confidence, and that help them to achieve victory at sea.

What's in a Name? **4**

It has long been a tradition in the U.S. Navy that when a ship is lost in battle or dies of old age, her name is sometimes given to a newly built ship to carry on the legacy.

Retribution

The USS *Enterprise* moved effortlessly across the black surface of the Arabian Sea, displacing nearly one hundred thousand tons of seawater as she cut a trough through the dark waters. Her great bulk disturbed millions of the tiny bioluminescent sea creatures, causing them to glow and leave an eerie green swath of light to mark her passage. A more sophisticated enemy with satellites or reconnaissance aircraft might have used that glowing wake to locate and attack the ship, but her enemy was neither the Soviet Union nor the Empire of Japan. This latest enemy had no great fleet to oppose her, nor a powerful air force to challenge her mastery of the skies. Yet, an insidious new threat had emerged from the back alleys of the Middle East and the foreboding mountains of Central Asia to strike at the very heart of American power. With hijacked airliners and a fanaticism born of misguided religious fervor, long-festering envy, and irrational hatred, terrorists had destroyed the World Trade Center towers and seriously damaged the Pentagon, killing thousands of Americans and other innocent bystanders. Now, less than a month later, USS *Enterprise* was poised to strike back.

On the great flat deck of this largest of combatants was the smallest of airfields. In the faint illumination of subdued flight-deck lighting, hundreds of Sailors—whose average age was a mere nineteen and a half years—went about their duties as though it were any other day of routine flight operations. Yellow-shirted petty officers waved their light wands to direct tractor-drivers in blue shirts as they repositioned F-14 Tomcats and F-18 Hornets, while brown-shirted plane captains perched in the cockpits rode the aircraft brakes. Purple-shirted Sailors wrestled with snakelike fuel hoses, while others in green prepared the steam-hissing catapults. Beneath the wings and fuselages of the attack aircraft, aviation ordnancemen in red

The nuclear-powered aircraft carrier USS *Enterprise* was among the first Navy ships to strike at terrorists in Afghanistan after the attacks on the World Trade Center and the Pentagon on 11 September 2001. *U.S. Naval Institute Photo Archive*

shirts hoisted the bombs and missiles into the waiting latches on the undersides of the airplanes.

As one of the 500-pound bombs rolled off an ordnance elevator, a young airman pulled a piece of chalk from his pocket and, with a wide smile on his soot-smeared face, scrawled across the side of the weapon, "Hijack this!" A red-shirted chief petty officer squatting beneath a nearby aircraft, his weathered features contorted into a scowl, carefully wrote the letters "NYPD" on one side of a Mark 83 bomb and "FDNY" on the other, in tribute to the courage of other uniformed men and women who had raced into the stricken World Trade Center towers, heedless of the great danger that would soon take their lives. "It's payback time," he said, slapping the side of the olive-colored bomb.

The date was 7 October 2001, and Operation Enduring Freedom was about to begin. Several weeks before, "Big E"—as *Enterprise* Sailors called their ship—had just completed a six-month deployment and, on 9 September, had headed for home. With her crew happily anticipating the joyous homecoming, she had barely begun the long trek across the Atlantic

Aviation ordnancemen hoisting precision-guided munitions to the wing pylon of an aircraft that will soon launch and take the war to the enemy. *U.S. Navy (Philip A. McDaniel)*

Ocean when news of the 9/11 terrorist attacks stunned the world. In what will long be remembered as the famous "*Enterprise* U-turn," the ship's captain, without waiting for orders from higher authority, turned the carrier around and headed back for the troubled part of the world that had spawned the terrorist attacks.

The feelings of many of *Enterprise*'s Sailors at the time were summed up well by a young third class gunner's mate from Brooklyn when he told a reporter: "I was ready to go home, but I felt I needed to go back and get whoever was responsible for this. From my building I can see all of Manhattan. When I go home and see the big empty space [where the World Trade Center towers used to be], it will really hit me."

Now, in conjunction with other U.S. and allied ships, *Enterprise* was about to launch air strikes into Afghanistan, a dark corner of the world with a tragic history recently made worse by an oppressive regime known as the Taliban. These Islamic extremists ruled with an iron fist, severely punishing nonbelievers, denying basic rights to women, and keeping the general populace in a state of fear, ignorance, and deplorable poverty. Not only had this oppressive regime done much to hurt the image of Islam, they also had provided sanctuary to some of the world's nastiest terrorists. The Taliban had permitted al Qaeda and other radical groups to set up terrorist training camps in the desolate areas of the region, and they had provided a haven for the likes of Osama bin Laden, acknowledged perpetrator of the 9/11 attacks and alleged mastermind behind the terrorist attacks on American embassies and the destroyer *Cole*. In the aftermath of the 9/11 tragedy, the obvious first target in the newly declared War on Terrorism was Afghanistan.

As the hour approached for the air strikes to commence, more off-duty Sailors than usual joined the reporters who lined the railing of the observation area known as "Vulture's Row." Some of these Sailors had come out merely to get some air before reporting to watch stations somewhere below decks, where night and day were indistinguishable and the only air that flowed came from man-made ventilators. Others had come to Vulture's Row because they sensed that history was being made, and they wanted to witness it with their own eyes. But most were there because it somehow felt like the right thing to do, as though their collective presence might breathe an extra measure of vitality into the coming launch, might somehow help lift those lethal machines into the air, and might speed them on their way to seek vengeance for a terrible wrong. More than one reporter noted that the faces of these Sailors were set with grim determination as they watched the aircraft taxi up to the catapults amidst the deafening whine of powerful jet engines and the pungent odor of JP5 fuel thick in the night air.

There was no wild cheering as the first aircraft rocketed down the catapult track and roared into the black sky. There were no high fives as, one after another, Hornets and Tomcats took to the air and headed for the enemy's territory far to the north. Instead, there was an almost palpable sense of relief as the observers felt the dissipation of the feeling of helplessness that had gripped them since they first stared, horrified, at television screens, watching airliners full of innocent people forced to crash into buildings full of more innocent people. Unlike the vast majority of Americans who could do little more than seethe or grieve, the men and women of USS *Enterprise* were striking back. And as many would attest, it felt very good indeed.

Had this been a training exercise in friendlier waters, the strike aircraft from *Enterprise* would have to have flown from the Gulf of Mexico to the Great Lakes region to travel a distance equivalent to that being flown this night. Refueled twice by combinations of Navy S-3 Vikings and Air Force tankers on the way to their targets, the Big E's aircraft reached Afghanistan while the rugged mountains and barren deserts were still enshrouded in darkness. The American fliers rained down bombs, missiles, and rockets on terrorist training camps, airfields, weapons storage areas, and Taliban troop concentrations. Although subjected to antiaircraft fire in various forms, not a single aircraft was lost in the raids, not a drop of American blood was shed. But as the aircraft turned southward for the long return trip, they left behind an assortment of smoldering remains, signaling the coming demise of the Taliban and the beginning of the end for al Qaeda.

Six hours after their launch, Big E's brood returned safely to the nest. Again, there were no overt celebrations—simply a strong sense of accomplishment and a realization that this was just the beginning. Indeed, as the crews from this first sortie headed for a belated breakfast and much-needed rest, other sorties were shuttling to and from enemy targets, keeping the pressure on.

Over the next several weeks, *Enterprise*'s Sailors displayed the courage needed to carry out their commitment to defend their nation with honor as they ran sortie after sortie into Afghanistan. Along with other ships in the task force, they hammered away at the enemy, keeping him on the run, breaking down his infrastructure, making him pay for his terrible deeds, teaching him that an angered America is a formidable foe indeed. Big E's attack aircraft flew the length and breadth of Afghanistan, from Kabul to Kandahar to Jalalabad to Herat to Mazar-e-Sharif. They struck at the Taliban's military academy, artillery garrisons, radar installations, and surface-to-air missile sites. They rained fire and destruction down on mountaintops and guided precision weapons into cave entrances. They attacked terrorists attempting to flee by SUV and by camel. They maintained safe zones where C-17 aircraft could deliver food, clothing, and medical supplies to long-suffering Afghanis. By the time *Enterprise* was released to go home, her mission planners were having difficulty finding meaningful targets.

On 13 October, six days after the initial strike, Big E's crew paused briefly to celebrate the U.S. Navy's birthday. As they shared ice cream and cake especially prepared for the occasion, the ship's captain told the crew: "Two hundred and twenty-six years ago we were fighting the British for our freedom. Today it's the same thing. We're fighting for freedom from terrorism."

When the captain spoke of the struggle for freedom 226 years earlier, he might also have told the Big E's crew that the *Enterprise* had been there too. Obviously, she was not the nuclear-powered giant that had struck at Afghanistan. She was the first of *eight* American naval ships to carry that name. She was involved in the first American naval attack in history and would subsequently play a role in one of the most strategically important battles of the American Revolution.

First Blood

When the American colonies revolted against royal authority in 1775, Great Britain had a tremendous advantage over its rebellious subjects because the Royal Navy was the most powerful in the world. This was particularly significant because travel along the eastern seaboard of America, from New England to the South, was easier by sea than by land. Relatively few bridges spanned the many rivers that flowed through the colonies, making it much easier for troops to be moved from place to place by ship than by road.

The Americans, by contrast, had *no* navy at all. George Washington, Commander in Chief of the American Army, and John Adams, one of the more influential members of the Continental Congress, were among those who recognized the importance of having a navy, but it would be some time before the Americans could put together even a small naval capability. In May 1775, however, not even a month after the first shots of the Revolution had been fired at Lexington and Concord, a series of events began that would bring about two significant naval engagements that would have far-reaching effects.

Both the American colonists and their British adversaries recognized the importance of the string of waterways in the wilderness north of New York City that led down from Canada into the very heart of the rebellious American colonies. From the St. Lawrence River in Canada, a natural invasion route followed the Richelieu River, Lake Champlain, Lake George, and the Hudson River. If the British could control this water highway, they could effectively cut off the New England colonies from the rest, making their ultimate subjugation a much simpler matter.

Recognizing this strategic vulnerability, an American force led by Colonel Ethan Allen and Colonel Benedict Arnold captured Fort Ticonderoga at the southern end of Lake Champlain. Arnold, who would later become infamous for betraying the American cause, was, in the early days of the Revolution, one of the ablest of American commanders. The capture of the British fort was significant because it not only blocked a British invasion from the north but also provided much-needed cannon and gunpowder that would be used in the siege of Boston.

Learning that the British had a ten-gun sloop of war named *George* at a place called St. Johns at the northern end of the lake, Arnold feared that this vessel—the largest on the lake—could bring down enough Redcoats to recapture Ticonderoga. Therefore, he decided that the best way to prevent this would be to capture the British sloop.

Although a colonel in the newly formed Continental Army, Benedict Arnold had spent much of his earlier life at sea and was a capable mariner. He devised a plan and sent some of his men farther south to Skenesboro to bring back a small schooner named *Katherine*. Arnold later wrote that upon the little schooner's arrival, "We immediately fixed her with four carriage guns and six swivel guns." The Americans then cut gun ports in her sides and practiced running the carriage guns out with block and tackle rigs until they were proficient. They renamed the small warship *Liberty* and, along with two thirty-three-foot boats armed with swivel guns along their gunwales and one larger gun in the bow, the Americans got under way and headed north.

It took several days of variable winds for the small naval force to travel the length of Lake Champlain. When they dropped anchor near Point au Fer at the Canadian frontier, the wind vanished and the surface of the lake shone like a polished mirror. A scout took a canoe and headed down the Richelieu River to infiltrate the British lines and reconnoiter St. Johns. By nightfall, he was back and reported that the sloop *George* was indeed there, moored at the wharf. He also brought news that Arnold had been correct to worry about a British counterattack—hundreds of Redcoat reinforcements were on their way to St. Johns from Montreal with plans to sail south in the sloop and retake Fort Ticonderoga. There was little time to act.

Deciding that they could not afford to wait for a favorable wind, Arnold decided to use the small boats to row downriver for the attack. Leaving fifteen men behind to guard the becalmed *Liberty,* the other thirty-five climbed into the two small boats and rowed all night, arriving before dawn at a point half a mile upriver from St. Johns. Pulling into a small creek, the men waited while another scout went ahead to see if the British had detected their coming or if the reinforcements had arrived from Montreal, either of which would have doomed the mission. The men sat quietly in their boats, resting their aching muscles and fighting off the effects of fatigue, with swarms of gnats and mosquitoes adding to their misery. The sun had risen by the time the scout returned with the happy news that the Redcoats seemed unaware of their presence and that the reinforcements had not yet arrived.

The Americans lost no time in mounting the attack. The small naval force headed downstream and landed about one hundred yards from the British barracks. The surprise attack was a complete success; without firing a shot, the Americans overwhelmed the troops in the barracks. They moved on to *George* and swarmed over the sides of the British ship. The unsuspecting crew was rudely awakened by the sound of musket butts pounding on doors and hatch covers, and they quickly surrendered.

Interrogating the prisoners, the Americans learned that the reinforcements were expected at any time. For two hours they loaded guns, powder, blankets, food, rum, and two brass cannon into the captured sloop; sank five boats they had to leave behind; and then got under way with four small British gunboats added to their force. The wind had picked up, and soon the captured sloop and her six escorts emerged from the Richelieu and rejoined *Liberty* on Lake Champlain.

The audacious American capture of the British sloop prevented the planned British counterattack. It would be more than a year before the British would attempt to come south over the waterways guarded by Fort Ticonderoga.

As the small armada of eight vessels headed south along Lake Champlain, Arnold removed the name *George* from the sloop's stern and replaced it with a new, more appropriate name: *Enterprise.*

Valcour Island

In the aftermath of the capture of *George*—now *Enterprise*—the Americans were emboldened to strike into Canada, capturing and holding Montreal for a time and unsuccessfully attacking Quebec on New Year's Eve 1775. After their defeat at Quebec, they were forced to abandon their position in Montreal in the face of a growing British force and fell back to Lake Champlain, where they began to prepare for a British thrust south. What followed would be remembered as the Battle of Valcour Island, one of the most significant battles of the American Revolution.

Intent upon taking control of the Richelieu-Champlain-George-Hudson waterways to separate New England from the rest of the colonies—in effect "cutting off the head of the rebellion," as one British commander described it—Major General Sir Guy Carleton moved his Redcoats down from Canada along the Richelieu River. Arriving at St. Johns near the northern end of Lake Champlain, the British commander received word that the Americans not only had *Liberty* and *Enterprise* down at the south end of the lake but also were building more vessels at Skenesboro. Determined that he must have control of the lake before moving his troops farther south, the cautious Carleton decided to put together his own "fleet" before proceeding.

Gradually, the British assembled a strange but effective mixture of vessels, some of which were built from scratch, while others were disassembled, moved in pieces to St. Johns, and then reassembled. It would be the first inland fleet for the Royal Navy.

Embarked in *Enterprise,* Arnold had arrived at Skenesboro in July and begun organizing the American shipbuilding effort. Dividing those men with at least some useful skills into crews of twenty-five, he tasked each group with building a ship. He sent five hundred more men into the forest to cut down trees and drag them out using oxen, and another hundred worked in shifts to keep the sawmills running.

While the British had experienced sailors, carpenters, and blacksmiths at

St. Johns, the Americans at Skenesboro had far less expertise to draw upon as they set about building their fleet. Most of these men had signed on to be soldiers, not sailors; but the circumstances were such that only a naval force could stop or at least slow the British advance that now threatened an early end to the Revolution.

In remembering great moments in history, such as key battles like the one that was about to occur, most of us remember—as well we should—the courage of those who face the terrors of combat and somehow prevail. But we should also remember that countless others give of themselves in other ways—less glamorous, but no less vital. Such was the case in the days preceding the Battle of Valcour Island. Not only would many brave men eventually face a formidable enemy, many others would also labor through the summer of 1776, building vessels from scratch and preparing for the critical battle that was to come.

Sweltering in the summer heat, and losing many of their number to the ravages of smallpox, the Americans set about the task, their determination offsetting their lack of equipment, materials, and skills. The many miles of rope needed to rig vessels of the time and the oakum needed to waterproof the hulls were in very short supply and had to be brought great distances. Because the British had long maintained restrictions on the American iron industry, nails were also hard to come by. The story of how the supplies, manpower, and technical expertise were all assembled is beyond the scope of this telling, but it was a gargantuan task; its accomplishment, under the able leadership of Benedict Arnold, makes his later defection all the more tragic.

By the time the leaves on the trees had changed to various shades of gold and red, the American fleet consisted of sixteen ships. The smallest vessels were the so-called gondolas, built low to the water to make them difficult targets and armed with one 12-pound gun in the bow, a pair of 9-pounders amidships, and several swivel guns. The latter were rigged like large shotguns to fire grapeshot, effective at destroying enemy rigging as well as serving as a lethal antipersonnel weapon. These eight gondolas were named *Spitfire, Philadelphia, Boston, Providence, New Haven, Connecticut, New York,* and *New Jersey.* Four galleys, powered by oars and armed with an array of cannon ranging from 6-pounders up to 18-pounders, were christened *Congress, Lee, Trumbull,* and *Washington.* The largest vessels were the schooners *Royal Savage, Revenge,* and *Liberty* and the sloop *Enterprise,* each carrying various combinations of cannon ranging from 2- to 6-pounders. All totaled, the little fleet could fire about 600 pounds of shot, which seemed quite potent until compared with the British total of 1,100 pounds.

The American fleet, as ready as it ever was going to be, got under way and headed north in the face of an early winter. Taking station part way up

The gondola *Philadelphia*. These craft were built low to the water to make them difficult targets to hit. This one, which sank after the Battle of Valcour Island in 1776, was raised from the bottom of Lake Champlain in 1935 and is now on display at the Smithsonian Institution's National Museum of American History in Washington, D.C. *U.S. Naval Institute Photo Archive*

the lake, the men were soon sleeping on the open decks, snow falling on their shivering bodies and gale winds frequently buffeting the little fleet. As September drew to a close, the storms worsened, and Arnold decided to move around to the relative shelter provided by the kidney-shaped Valcour Island on the western side of the lake. While there, sheltering from the wind, Arnold made his plans.

If the Americans confronted the British as they came south along the lake with the north wind at their backs, the Redcoats would have what was known as the *weather gage,* a decided advantage when trying to maneuver sailing vessels, particularly those rigged with square sails. By remaining hidden there in Valcour Bay, however, the Americans could wait until the British had passed by, thereby gaining the upwind advantage over their adversaries. If successful, the British would have to beat against the wind to get at the Americans. For camouflage, the Americans cut spruce trees and rigged them along the sides of their vessels, not only making them more difficult to see but also providing some protection against small arms fire. They anchored the vessels stem to stern in a gradual crescent formation across the waterway formed between the island and the western shore. Vessels coming into the bay would thus be forced to come one or two at a time through the narrow channel and would be subject to the full force of American firepower.

Coming from the north was an enemy force of nine thousand men in more than six hundred ships and boats, ranging from Indian canoes to the *Inflexible,* a square-rigged ship armed with a powerful battery of eighteen 12-pounder cannons. Among these many vessels were several well-armed sailing schooners, twenty-seven smaller gunboats carrying heavy brass field pieces in their bows, and twenty armed longboats. The Redcoats also created a very large raftlike vessel that was by far the most heavily armed in either fleet. Armed with six cannon that fired 24-pound balls, six 12-pounders, and two large siege howitzers, she was appropriately named *Thunderer.* To make her even more formidable, she had an onboard furnace to heat cannonballs until they were red hot, all the better to set wooden ships on fire.

The British fleet sailed past Valcour Island without spotting the Americans. Once the bulk of the force was well south—downwind—of the island, several American vessels came out of the bay to lure the British into the trap. *Royal Savage* and *Enterprise* ran ahead of three of the American galleys, racing toward the British force with their newly created battle flags held taut in the steady wind.

Once the Americans were sure they had been spotted, the decoys turned and headed back toward Valcour Bay. Several of the British ships gave chase, *Inflexible* in hot pursuit of *Royal Savage,* and the schooner *Carleton* chasing *Enterprise.* The British flagship *Maria* followed close behind.

Enterprise successfully led her pursuer into the bay. As the British schooner closed on the American ship, Arnold's crescent formation loomed ahead. The British barely had time to realize what they were seeing when the line of American vessels disappeared behind a great cloud of white smoke. A great rumble rolled across the water as geysers erupted from the water close aboard the British ship. The American trap had been sprung.

Royal Savage proved less elusive than *Enterprise*. *Inflexible* began firing heavy broadsides as she pursued the American schooner, her first salvo including cannonballs connected by a length of chain that tore into the target's rigging just as it was designed to do. A second salvo sent a heavy shot slamming into the hapless vessel's mainmast, and further broadsides began chewing her to bits. *Royal Savage* was no match for the much larger *Inflexible*; under the relentless barrage, she ran onto the shallow bar near the entrance to Valcour Bay, and her crew began abandoning ship.

British gunboats began pouring into the bay, and the firing from both sides intensified. The battle became, in the words of a German soldier fighting on the British side, "very fierce." The British flagship *Maria* neared the crescent line, and the American flagship *Congress* opened fire. A cannonball passed between Major General Sir Guy Carleton and his brother Thomas; the latter was seriously injured by the concussion of the near miss, and General Carleton appeared to be stunned as well. The captain of the *Maria,* apparently concerned for the safety of the British commander, ordered his ship to withdraw, taking the flagship out of the battle.

The schooner *Carleton,* having been lured into the American trap by *Enterprise,* had sailed headlong into the crossfire from the crescent line. From her angle of approach, she was unable to bring her twelve guns to bear. Murderous American fire raked the schooner, heavy shot holing her hull in several places, grapeshot spraying her decks. A cannonball grazed the head of *Carleton*'s captain, knocking him unconscious, while another shot tore off the first mate's arm. Relentlessly, the Americans continued to hammer away at the ship as she began to fill with water and list heavily to one side. She would no doubt have been lost had it not been for two longboats that braved the heavy fire to take her under tow and row her out of the range of the American guns.

As the battle wore on, the crews on the American vessels served their guns well, sustaining a high rate of fire that proved effective. Firing, clearing, loading, and firing again, time after time, was a laborious business made all the more difficult as the British gunboats began to get the range and score hits. Eyes burning from powder fumes peered out from blackened faces to see more and more British gunboats pressing the attack. Shells crashed into the wooden hulls, crushing men under their weight, casting showers of lethal splinters about. Wounded men could receive little attention, and many died lingering deaths as they lay unattended. The dead were quickly thrown over the side. And still these men—who just a short while before had been merchants, farmers, fishermen, teachers, and all manner of things but soldiers or sailors—fought on.

Liberty, Lee, and *Washington* were close enough to the western shore that they were exposed to small arms fire from British marines and their Indian allies who had landed there. Fortunately, the spruce screens added before the battle made this fire less effective than it might have been.

The big bruiser *Thunderer* eventually arrived on the scene, but she was too cumbersome to work into the narrow confines of the battle, so she remained at long range ineffectively lobbing shells in the general direction of the American line.

As the shadows lengthened signaling the approaching end of the short October day, *Inflexible* at last entered the main battle, suffering the gauntlet of American fire to move up into position where the huge vessel could bring her heavy firepower to bear. She began pounding away at the American vessels and gradually turned the tide. Hit after hit took its toll. *Washington* suffered the most, but all of the American vessels were in danger of succumbing to the overwhelming firepower of this most powerful ship. Had darkness not intervened, the battle might well have ended there, with the American vessels shattered into so much driftwood. With barely enough light for safe navigation, the British vessels retired from the bay, delaying just long enough to set fire to the grounded *Royal Savage.*

Gathered in a council of war illuminated by the flickering firelight of the burning *Royal Savage,* the Americans assessed their situation: sixty men dead, many others seriously wounded, three-quarters of their gunpowder expended, every vessel severely damaged, *Philadelphia* settling into the mud at the bottom of the bay even as they conferred. Yet surrender was not an option to these determined men.

A blanket of fog enhanced the darkness, and soon a plan took shape. Muffling their oars by tying pieces of clothing around them and hanging horn-shaped lanterns over their sterns that emitted no more than a tiny beam of light directly aft, the vessels got under way in single file, hugging the shore as closely as they dared. *Trumbull* led the way, followed by *Enterprise,* and then the remaining vessels. They could see Indian campfires along the shore and hear voices aboard General Carleton's flagship as they stole past the unsuspecting British fleet.

By the time dawn broke, the Americans were seven miles to the south. After much initial confusion, in which Carleton first sailed north after stranding a number of his men on Valcour Island, the British eventually gave chase. But the wind had by this time shifted to the south, making progress difficult. It took another full day for the British to catch up to the Americans. When they did, another battle ensued in which the Americans miraculously held their own for five hours. Only *Washington* surrendered under a merciless barrage from *Inflexible*. At one point, *Congress* was surrounded by seven British vessels chewing away at her. More than a third of her crew was dead, her ammunition was exhausted, and she had twelve holes below her waterline. Yet she and several other remaining vessels managed to escape into the shallows of Buttonmould Bay where the British could not reach them. Deliberately running their vessels aground, the Americans removed what they could, jettisoned their guns, and set the vessels on fire. They then disappeared into the wilderness, found their way to the bastion at Crown Point, burned it to prevent it from falling into British hands, and moved on to Fort Ticonderoga where they were reunited with *Enterprise* and four other vessels that had managed to escape the British.

What may have seemed a decisive British victory was not. Carleton arrived at the smoking remains of Crown Point as heavy snow began falling; convinced that further advance was not possible, he decided to retreat back to Canada for the winter. This bought the Americans another year, priceless time that permitted them to prepare for the next British attempt to strike from the north. The resulting American victory in the Battle of Saratoga the following summer was one of the most decisive of the entire Revolution; it prevented the British from severing the colonies, dealt them a terrible blow to their morale, and brought the French into the war as an American ally.

Famed naval historian Admiral Alfred Thayer Mahan would later write of the Battle of Valcour Island: "Save for Arnold's flotilla, the British would have settled the business. The little American Navy was wiped out, but never had any force, big or small, lived to better purpose."

As the British came south in the days just prior to Saratoga, *Enterprise* was there again, taking part in the evacuation of Fort Ticonderoga before she was overwhelmed by a fresh British fleet, forced aground on 7 July 1777, and burned by her crew to prevent her capture. Reminiscent of Viking funeral pyres of ancient times, it was an honorable death for a ship that had served honorably and well.

Three "Wars"

After the Battle of Valcour Island, the American Revolution would go on for seven more years before ending with the Treaty of Paris in September 1783. During that time, a second American naval vessel was named *Enterprise*—a twenty-five-ton schooner fitted out with eight guns. She served in the Continental Navy for a brief time, convoying transports, performing reconnaissance missions, and guarding against British foraging raids in the Chesapeake Bay. Most of the records of her service were lost, so little is known about her.

In the years following the Revolution, the euphoria of victory and independence had been accompanied by the challenges of building a new nation virtually from scratch. There was a sizable war debt to be paid off, a national economy to be built, and governmental structures to be put in place. Of necessity, the nation's leaders needed to prioritize their time and resources, and with no immediate threat on the horizon, both the Army and Navy were seriously neglected, the latter virtually disappearing for a time.

But the rest of the world did not wait patiently for the United States to get around to all it had to do. To begin with, much had changed since France had been an American ally during the Revolution. In the aftermath of a revolution of their own, the French were now fighting much of Europe, and the relationship between the two former allies had seriously deteriorated. French vessels began taking advantage of the naval weakness of the United States and were plundering American shipping. To make matters worse, the North African states of Morocco, Algiers, Tunis, and Tripoli had long taken advantage of their geographic location to demand tribute from vessels using Mediterranean waters. Without a navy, American shipping was particularly vulnerable. As if this were not enough, relations with Great Britain were gradually worsening as well.

It became clear that a navy was going to be needed, so the U.S. Congress at last began allocating money for that purpose. One of the ships authorized was the third *Enterprise*. Built in 1799 as an eighty-four-foot schooner similar in design to the famed Baltimore Clippers, which were known for their extraordinary speed, she was fitted out with twelve 6-pounder cannons. Her first challenge was to take on the French vessels that had been attacking U.S. commercial ships. These were not naval vessels but privateers—privately owned ships that had been authorized by the French government to capture helpless American shipping vessels. As part of a squadron led by the frigate *Constellation, Enterprise* captured eight of these privateers and liberated eleven previously taken American vessels.

In 1801, *Enterprise* sailed for the Mediterranean where the Barbary States of Morocco, Algiers, Tunis, and Tripoli continued to harass American commercial shipping.

Encountering a Barbary corsair of fourteen guns named *Tripoli, Enterprise* engaged her in a three-hour battle. Twice during the fierce engagement the Tripolitans struck their colors as a sign of surrender, but when the Americans sent a boat to board, the enemy reopened fire and hoisted their colors. After a third resumption of devastating fire, the Tripolitan captain tore down his colors and tossed them into the sea. Amazingly, the American Sailors had sustained no losses while their defeated enemy had fifty killed or wounded. The Americans jettisoned the Tripolitan guns and ordered the defeated corsair into the nearest port. Upon his return to Tripoli, the defeated captain—already wounded in the fierce battle—was ordered by the monarch to ride through the streets on the back of a jackass and was then beaten with a stick five hundred times on the soles of his feet. Needless to say, there were considerably fewer volunteers for service in the Tripolitan Navy after that.

Enterprise later captured the Tunisian ship *Paulina* and, with the frigate *Constitution,* the Tripolitan ketch *Mastico.* She also bombarded the North African coast on several occasions, sent landing parties inshore, and together with other ships of the American squadron attacked the capital city of Tripoli. In this latter engagement, *Enterprise* led a group of gunboats into the inner harbor, where her crew boarded and captured several enemy gunboats after fierce hand-to-hand combat.

In the early summer of 1805, the Tripolitan monarch signed a treaty that effectively ended the so-called Barbary War, and *Enterprise* was then laid up *in ordinary,* a term similar to the more modern "in mothballs," meaning that the vessel was put out of commission but preserved for possible future use. That future use was not far off. Relations with Great Britain continued to deteriorate, and in 1809 she was refitted and back at sea.

When war was declared in June 1812, the Navy quickly converted *Enterprise* into a more capable brig, armed with two long-range 9-pounders and fourteen shorter-range 18-pounders called *carronades,* so named because they were originally designed in Carron, Scotland. For the first year of hostilities she cruised along the East Coast of the United States, searching for English quarry. On 4 September 1813, near Pemaquid Point, Maine, an *Enterprise* lookout called down from his perch near the top of the mainmast, reporting that he had spotted another brig anchored in a small inlet. *Enterprise* cleared for action and hoisted battle ensigns to the tops of her two masts. The other brig, HMS *Boxer,* did likewise, and the two stood out to open water, loaded with various arrays of round shot and grapeshot.

For several hours the two ships lay becalmed, unable to get at one another. Then at about 1130 a breeze sprang up from the south. Fortunately for *Enterprise,* she lay to the south of *Boxer,* which gave the Americans the advantage of the weather gage, just as the earlier *Enterprise* had enjoyed for a time at Valcour Island.

With local residents watching from the nearby shore, *Boxer* evaded for a time, trying to work herself into a more favorable position. But *Enterprise* managed to keep her advantage, all the while closing on her British adversary. Finally, at just past 1500, what sounded to those on shore like a sudden clap of thunder rolling across the water signaled the beginning of the battle as *Enterprise* fired a broadside from her starboard side. *Boxer* responded immediately with all the guns along her opposite side, then known as the larboard.

This first exchange of fire was hardly decisive, yet it was very significant. A cannonball struck and killed Samuel Blyth, the British captain, leaving the ship's only other officer in command. A musket ball fired by one of the *Boxer*'s sharpshooters struck down the American captain, Lieutenant William Burrows. As he lay mortally wounded upon the deck, his head propped up by a rolled hammock, Burrows looked up at the ensign fluttering in the breeze, its peppermint stripes already rent by several shrapnel holes, and said to Lieutenant Edward McCall, who had assumed command, "Never strike that flag." Both vessels fought on, their seconds in command carrying on in a manner that each navy expected of them.

Seventeen-year-old William Barnes had grown up in the small town of Woolwich, Maine, and now worked with six other men serving one of *Enterprise*'s large carronades. Each time the 2,700-pound gun fired, young Barnes had to stand clear to make sure the heavy carriage did not run over his

The fourth USS *Enterprise* and HMS *Boxer* engaged in battle during the War of 1812. Seventeen-year-old William Barnes "wormed out the bore," inserted the "wadding," and manned the tackles while serving in one of the American ship's gun crews during the battle. *U.S. Naval Institute Photo Archive*

feet as it flung itself backward in recoil. A heavy rope, called a *breeching,* was fastened to the ship's side on either side of the gun and passed through a ring on the bulbous after end of the weapon, the *cascabel* in ordnance parlance; the breeching stopped the cannon's recoil just enough to allow Barnes to get at the muzzle of the weapon. It was his responsibility to run a corkscrewlike tool called a *worm* down inside the still-smoking barrel to dislodge the chunks of smoldering powder left behind by the firing of the weapon. If he failed to clear it sufficiently, the remaining residue could prevent the fresh powder cartridge or the ball from being properly loaded.

Half-blinded by the smoke and coughing from the fumes, Barnes had just a few seconds to do his work before another Sailor would swab out the inside of the bore with a sponge fixed to a long pike to cool the chamber and douse any burning embers that might prematurely ignite the new powder charge. Another crew member followed with a fresh cartridge, a flannel bag that earlier had been carefully and precisely filled with explosive black powder by the ship's gunner down in the copper-lined magazine well below the ship's waterline. A twelve-year-old boy, known as a powder monkey, shuttled between the guns and the magazine, bringing fresh cartridges up from the magazine to replace those expended. Next down the bore went the 18-pound iron ball.

Barnes again stepped to the muzzle to force a hunk of wadding down the cannon's throat that prevented the ball from rolling out as the ship heaved and rolled in the seaway. He then helped several others man the tackles that were used to reposition the gun in the gun port. As Barnes heaved on the line with all his strength—his arms feeling as though they were coming out of his shoulder sockets, and his lungs burning from the pungent smoke-filled air—the heavy gun rumbled forward into place. The gun captain quickly supervised the aiming of the weapon, which at this range—"a half-pistol shot distance" as later described by McCall in his official report—required little adjustment. When the gun went off, Barnes felt as though someone had clapped him on both ears simultaneously.

The two ships hammered at one another for the better part of an hour. Twice during the engagement, *Enterprise* managed to cross *Boxer*'s bow, a maneuver called *crossing the T* that is highly advantageous because it allows the crossing vessel to bring all the guns along her side to bear on her opponent's bow, where few if any guns can be positioned. After the second such crossing, *Boxer*'s main topmast came crashing to the deck, bringing the main yard down with it. Continuing her murderous fire, *Enterprise* punched holes in *Boxer*'s hull with well-placed round shot and shredded her sails with hailstorms of grapeshot. At about 1600, *Boxer*'s guns fell silent, and a voice called across the water, "We have surrendered." Using a voice trumpet, McCall asked why *Boxer* had not struck her colors. The answer came back that her captain had nailed her ensign to the mast before the battle and ordered, "Do not let these colors come down while I still have life in my body."

Three days later, young William Barnes made his way through the streets of Portland, Maine, as part of a large procession. He felt unsteady, as though the street were moving beneath his feet, an odd but common affliction among sailors who have spent long periods at sea upon decks constantly in motion. The whole town had turned out, and he couldn't help but smile when a tall man walking solemnly at his left flinched noticeably when a cannon went off out in the harbor. It was *Enterprise* firing a shot every minute in salute to the funeral procession. Full honors were being accorded the deceased.

The large entourage reached the Portland cemetery where everyone gathered around the gravesite as best they could. Barnes was fortunate to find a small hillock upon which to stand, giving him a good view. Over the heads of the town fathers and more senior members of *Enterprise*'s crew, he could see a casket over which was draped an American flag, its fifteen stars and fifteen stripes bright in the morning sun. Next to it was a second casket, its flag also red, white, and blue, but the colors arranged in the combined crosses of Saints George, Andrew, and Patrick. William Burrows, captain of the brig USS *Enterprise,* whose dying words were "Never strike that flag," and Samuel Blyth, captain of His Majesty's brig *Boxer,* who had told his crew, "Do not let these colors come down while I still have life in my body," were being laid to rest side by side, where they would remain for the ages.

Interims

Successful in major engagements against the French, Barbary States, and Britain, the third *Enterprise* came to be known as "Lucky Little *Enterprise*" and continued her service after the War of 1812, fighting pirates, smugglers, and slavers, mostly in Caribbean waters. Though her luck seemed to have run out in 1823, when she ran aground in the West Indies and broke up, she had one last bit of good fortune in her. Even in that dark moment of her demise, not one of her crew was lost.

The fourth ship to bear the name *Enterprise* was a schooner commissioned in December 1831, who spent much of her time patrolling South American waters and made an around-the-world voyage in 1835–36. She was sold out of the Navy in 1845, and there would not be another *Enterprise* in the U.S. Navy until 1877, when a ship described as "a steam-powered sloop of war, rigged as a bark" received the honored name. This fifth *Enterprise* also circumnavigated the Earth, serving in a naval hydrographic mission and bringing back a wealth of data that contributed much to our knowledge of the oceans. She ended her career as a training ship, first at the U.S. Naval Academy, then at a maritime school in Massachusetts. Sold in 1909, she was followed by the sixth *Enterprise,* a small motor patrol craft purchased by the Navy in 1916 to serve a homeland security role during World War I. She left the Navy in 1919.

For more than a century following the War of 1812, the name *Enterprise* seemed to have seen its greater days of glory. While the fourth, fifth, and sixth namesakes served honorably and well, they went the way of the great majority of naval vessels. In much the same way, many young Sailors sign on for great adventure, hoping for a moment of glory, but the laws of chance dictate that only a few will see their aspirations fulfilled; the rest must carry out the mundane and the routine, the vital yet unexciting tasks of patrolling, showing the flag, keeping watch, gathering information, serving as deterrent, waiting for the day of challenge that may never come. Yet

The fifth USS *Enterprise,* seen here in 1893. She was a steam-powered sloop of war who once sailed around the world. *U.S. Naval Institute Photo Archive*

their importance cannot be overstated; just as the policemen on patrol on an uneventful night are essential to the security and well-being of the neighborhood they are protecting, so the Navy—its ships and Sailors—must carry on during the quiet times in history. There may be no obvious glory, and the ongoing work may not seem as important as those crescendos of crisis that capture the imaginations of writers and moviemakers, but there could be no security, no glorious responses to those rare challenges, no continuation of American democracy, without the dedication of those who serve quietly and stand ready.

Such was the lot of the interim *Enterprise*s and the Sailors who manned them. But all of that would be turned around in ways Benedict Arnold and William Barnes could never have dreamed of when *Enterprise VII* sailed into the Pacific Ocean in the late 1930s.

The First Big E

Eighteen-year-old Alvin Kernan reported aboard *Enterprise* in November 1941. He later remembered his first encounter with her as he arrived in a boat dispatched from USS *Procyon,* the ship that had brought him from the West Coast of the United States to Pearl Harbor, Hawaii. "The *Enterprise* was tied up on the western side of Ford Island taking on fuel and bombs, and as the motor whaleboat came up under her counter on her seaward, port, side, she towered a hundred feet above us, grayish white, nearly nine hundred feet long, beautifully shaped despite her size. . . . It was a total and instant love affair with this great ship, never lost and never felt again in quite the same way for another."

Commissioned in May 1938, this seventh *Enterprise* was one of the U.S. Navy's earliest aircraft carriers, as evidenced by her hull number, CV-6. It was a time when battleships were still considered supreme among naval vessels, and carriers were seen as supportive rather than primary in naval warfare. That was about to change.

Kernan was assigned to an aircraft squadron embarked in *Enterprise*. As a seaman second class, his duties would be unexciting at first. But that too would change.

On his first day aboard, Kernan wandered about the ship, "staring with wonder at the complicated machinery, stowage spaces, elevators, and spare planes tied up in the overhead of the vast hangar deck. It was all so extraordinarily busy, the Sailors in spotless white shorts and T-shirts rushing here and there—a crew of nearly two thousand—the public address system constantly blaring out bugle calls, the shrill of boatswain's whistles, and unintelligible orders to 'hear this' or 'hear that.'" By afternoon he was already at

The seventh USS *Enterprise*. When he first saw her, Seaman Alvin Kernan described the aircraft carrier as "beautifully shaped despite her size." *U.S. Naval Institute Photo Archive*

work, chipping paint off the three-foot links of the ship's anchor chain. It was hard work, particularly in the warm Hawaiian climate, and Kernan was glad when it was over so he could join the ordnance gang in his squadron to begin "learning the ropes." Being an inexperienced striker, he was paired up with a veteran petty officer, and together they were responsible for three of the Devastator torpedo bombers—belting ammunition, fuzing bombs, moving torpedoes around on special hydraulic trucks, changing bomb racks, and loading bombs and torpedoes onto the aircraft.

His squadron was required to supply men for the flight deck crews, and, before long, Kernan was manhandling aircraft on the windswept deck, wearing a dark blue T-shirt and a canvas helmet dyed to match. His days began before dawn and ended after dark, pushing aircraft at a dead run from one spot to another in a seemingly endless choreography of launch and recovery. In years to come, catapults and tractors would come to carrier flight decks, but in 1941 the planes took to the air by the power of their engines and were moved about the deck by the muscles of men like Alvin Kernan. It was very hard work, less tedious than painting anchor chains but physically demanding. And so very important: as events would later prove, battles would be won or lost by the relative skills of the flight deck crews on each side's carriers.

The long hours of training were paying off for *Enterprise*. Though barely three years old, the ship already had a good reputation as a "hard worker," where discipline and training allowed few excuses, and results were paramount. In the fleet, ships competed for the coveted efficiency award, to earn the right to paint a large "E" on their superstructures. *Enterprise*'s growing efficiency and her formal name soon earned her the nickname "Big E."

At the end of November 1941, *Enterprise* left Pearl Harbor to deliver aircraft to Wake Island, accompanied by a task force of three heavy cruisers and six destroyers. Although the war in Europe seemed a long way off, and isolationists in the United States had so far managed to keep America out of the struggle against Hitler, the admiral in charge of this task force, William F. Halsey, was convinced that war was coming to the Pacific, probably sooner rather than later. They were hardly under way when he issued orders warning that the task group was to consider itself "in wartime conditions" and that any unidentified ship or aircraft approaching the force was to be destroyed.

Halsey was more than a little prescient. Before the task force could get back to Pearl Harbor, Japanese aircraft and midget submarines attacked the air and naval bases there, sinking or disabling nineteen ships (including all eight battleships), destroying 188 aircraft and damaging another 159, and killing more than twenty-four hundred. *Enterprise* had been scheduled to arrive at Pearl Harbor on 6 December, but bad weather slowed the task force, causing her to miss the attack on the morning of the seventh. The feisty Halsey tried to find the Japanese force, but it was probably just as well that his reconnaissance aircraft came up empty—good reputation or not, the Big E would not likely have fared well against the six Japanese carriers that had carried out the surprise attack.

Needing fuel, the U.S. task force entered Pearl Harbor late on the eighth. In the fading light, Kernan peered out from one of Big E's catwalks at the eerie scene. Many fires still burned, and a heavy cloud of smoke blanketed what had been a beautiful tropical paradise the last time he had seen it. Great quantities of heavy black oil covered the surface of the water, and the smell of burned paint and hot steel filled his nostrils as the ship made her way through the channel, now made narrower by the protruding stern of a battleship grounded in the mud on one side. Off the port side Kernan saw the devastation on Ford Island, where the hulks of aircraft smoldered and the roofs of hangars lay collapsed inside shattered walls. In the foreground were the remnants of Battleship Row, where the carcasses of once formidable ships lay broken, twisted, capsized, and sunk.

There was something so horribly depressing and yet positively prophetic in that scene, as the unscathed aircraft carrier passed by the broken battleships. For the next several years, it would be the aircraft carriers far more than the battleships that would decide the outcome of the raging conflict in the Pacific. While submarines and troop-laden amphibious ships would play major roles as well, and countless destroyers and various other ships would fight ferociously in what would prove to be the greatest sea war in history, it would be the carriers that would strike the most telling blows against the Japanese navy, and it would be *Enterprise* who would become the most famous carrier in the war.

Kernan later recalled that on this second night of the war, he and his shipmates worried that a follow-up attack might catch them helpless here in the confines of Pearl Harbor. So there was a sense of relief when, before dawn, "the lines were cast off, and the *Enterprise* began to edge her way out of the harbor, down the channel, through the nets, and into blue water, picking up speed as she went, the sun rising, the water beginning to hiss alongside, and the smell of burning oil, charred paint, bodies, and defeat left far behind. The planes came aboard and the war had begun."

There would be many moments of sheer terror and adrenaline-laden excitement in the next few years as *Enterprise* led the way across the Pacific in battle after battle, ever closer to the home islands of Japan and to ultimate victory. But those moments were few in comparison to the many hours of wartime routine that blended days into weeks into months of hard work and tedium. Kernan and his shipmates learned that war is the worst combination of endless work and gnawing fear, a strange brew of boredom and terror that makes life seem terribly difficult, yet frighteningly tenuous and so precious. Alvin Kernan, and legions of other young men like him, suffered this existence, answering the call to arms in their nation's hour of need to ensure the survival of the American way of life.

In the immediate aftermath of the devastating attack on Pearl Harbor, there would not be much to cheer about for America and its allies. The Japanese seemed unstoppable as they chalked up victory after victory, spreading the boundaries of their empire farther and farther out until half the Pacific was under their control. For the first few months of the war, *Enterprise* conducted several raids on the Japanese-controlled Gilbert and Marshall Islands. These attacks were more symbolic than tactically or strategically significant.

For Seaman Kernan, every spare hour initially was spent in the ship's interior pounding away with a chipping hammer. At Pearl Harbor the Navy learned the hard way that paint and linoleum serve as fuels for fire and produce a heavy toxic smoke, so one of the early tasks for *Enterprise*'s crew was to strip both from the decks, bulkheads, and overheads. Kernan and others spent countless hours chipping and scraping until the ship's spaces were down to bare metal. The result, according to Kernan, was "depressing, as if the ship had already been burned out."

His days became cycles of red, white, and blue: the red lights of the berthing compartment during predawn reveilles and late-night taps; the blinding white light of the tropical sun as it beat down on the flight deck during air operations; and the blue of the battle lanterns during general quarters whenever danger—real or suspected—lurked close by.

Then, in early April 1942, things suddenly changed. *Enterprise* left Pearl Harbor on the eighth, but instead of heading southward as before, she and her escort of four destroyers and an oiler turned northwest. Scuttlebutt began to circulate that something important was about to happen, but when word arrived that the Americans holding out for months against the Japanese onslaught at Bataan in the Philippines had at last surrendered, morale plummeted.

For three days Big E and her escorts steamed farther north, the weather turning colder and bleaker as they went, and morale continued to deteriorate. Then, just before 0600 on the twelfth, a lookout reported another aircraft carrier approaching from the east.

Kernan and his squadron mates peered through the gray mist as the other carrier and her escorts—two cruisers, four destroyers, and another oiler—closed on the *Enterprise* group. Beneath leaden skies colors were subdued, but it soon became clear that the aircraft strapped to the approaching carrier's deck were not blue like those on *Enterprise,* but were brown and much larger, with twin engines. Someone identified them as Army Air Corps B-25 bombers. Someone else speculated that the mission must be to deliver them somewhere, perhaps the Aleutian Islands, near Alaska.

But soon it became clear that truth, for once, had outdistanced scuttlebutt. The glare of a signal lamp's beam pierced the gray atmosphere with a brief but powerful message: THIS FORCE IS BOUND FOR TOKYO.

Morale instantly skyrocketed. Shouts reverberated through the steel passageways and men slapped each other heartily on the back as the word spread. *Enterprise*'s general announcing system crackled to life with details of the mission. The other carrier was *Hornet,* and the two carrier task groups were headed to a point a mere five hundred miles from Japan where the B-25s would be launched to strike at Tokyo and other targets in the Japanese homeland. The bombers would fly on to land in China. It was a daring plan, not only because it required two of the U.S. Navy's very few carriers to penetrate deeply into enemy-controlled waters, but also because the Army pilots would have so little deck space from which to launch their bombers. The first B-25 to take off, piloted by the mission commander, Lieutenant Colonel James Doolittle, would have only about three hundred feet of "airfield" from which his bomber would either become airborne or drop into the cold waters of the North Pacific.

For the next several days the force steamed westward, covering nearly four hundred miles per day. Then, at 0315 on 18 April 1942, *Enterprise*'s surface search radar picked up several contacts ten miles ahead. Admiral Halsey ordered the force to turn north until the contacts faded; then he turned the force westward again. The possibility of detection was increasing with each mile they steamed westward, but each mile also meant an extra gallon of fuel for the Army aviators to fly their dangerous mission. So the force pressed on.

Several hours later, an *Enterprise* reconnaissance plane flew low over Big E and dropped a beanbag onto the flight deck. A yellow-shirted member of the flight deck crew scooped it up and dashed to the bridge. The scribbled message attached to the beanbag reported that the pilot had spotted Japanese patrol craft fifty miles ahead. Worse, the pilot was certain the enemy had spotted him.

Still the Navy task force pressed ahead, buying more miles that the bombers would not have to fly. The tension was palpable as anxious eyes peered into the gray gloom. Soon, masts could be seen among the great gray troughs of the sea ahead. The American task force was about one hundred miles short of the intended launch point, but the risk had become too great. It was time to launch.

The moment of truth had arrived as both *Enterprise* and *Hornet* turned into the wind. Big E's aircraft, along with the cruiser *Nashville,* engaged the Japanese ships while *Hornet* set about the task of launching her unusual payload. Never before had Army bombers been launched on a combat mission from the relatively tiny airfield provided by a Navy carrier.

No one had any illusions about the mission. It was certainly not going to win the war, nor would it have much tactical significance in the grand scheme of things. But at that moment in the war, the American people needed to strike back, to deliver a blow—no matter how small—against this enemy that for the last few months had seemed unstoppable, had chalked up all the victories, had humiliated the United States of America. So every Sailor watching was focused on those olive drab bombers, virtually willing them into the air.

From his perch on *Enterprise*'s flight deck, Kernan had a "ringside seat" from which he could watch history being made. He remembered the cold and windy morning as "near gale-force winds, gray and blue everywhere, with high dark green waves and the real taste and smell of the northern ocean." But the wind would be an ally as *Hornet* turned into the gale to launch the giant bombers. "So powerful was the wind added to the full speed of the ship—about seventy-five knots combined—that the B-25s needed only to get about thirty-knots' speed to float off the deck like some great kites, only slowly moving ahead of the ship, which seemed to remain almost stationary below them." Kernan remembered cheering loudly with his shipmates through "patriotic tears" as one after another the entire squadron took to the air.

Later that same day, the men in the coding room were listening to Radio Tokyo's afternoon propaganda broadcast (in English) when, suddenly, excited Japanese voices could be heard in the background and the broadcast went off the air. The U.S. bombers had arrived.

Kernan and the other Big E crew members were justifiably proud of their role in this first strike at the enemy's vitals. Though it would be a long time before U.S. forces could again hit the Japanese homeland, this early

An Army B-25 bomber takes off from the deck of USS *Hornet* headed for the very heart of the Japanese empire. *Naval Historical Center*

attack served its intended purpose. American morale received a badly needed boost and Japanese pride had been seriously injured—so much so that it altered their strategic thinking and caused them subsequently to make some costly decisions.

Enterprise remained on the offensive for the rest of the war, taking part in most of the major engagements, often playing a pivotal role. She was one of the three carriers that defeated a vastly superior Japanese force at Midway, literally turning the tide of the war. She fought off Guadalcanal and participated in the occupation of the Gilberts and Marshalls. She struck at the powerful Japanese bastion at Truk and dealt a devastating blow to Japanese naval aviation at the Battle of the Philippine Sea. Her aircraft struck at the Bonin Islands, Palau, Nansei Shoto, Formosa, Indochina, Hong Kong, Canton, Iwo Jima, and Okinawa. And in February 1945, she once again struck Tokyo, this time with her own aircraft at a range that permitted them to return.

Sadly, fate would deny her the victorious entry of the U.S. fleet into Tokyo Bay for the Japanese surrender. Struck by a kamikaze off the coast of Japan late in the war, she had sustained serious damage and was undergoing repairs at Puget Sound Navy Yard when the war ended.

Alvin Kernan also survived the war, though he tempted fate by becoming a gunner in the rear seat of a torpedo bomber. He took part in the first night-fighter action in history and was awarded the Navy Cross. After the war, he learned that Big E was slated to be scrapped and that a campaign had been launched to raise enough money to save her as a museum ship. "I thought about it but decided not to contribute because I couldn't bear to think of her sitting around in some backwater, being exploited in unworthy ways, invaded by hordes of tourists with no sense of her greatness. Better by far, I thought, to leave her to memory of those who had served on her when she was fully alive, vibrating under full steam at thirty-two knots, the aircraft turning up, guns firing, heeling over so sharply that the hangar deck took on water to avoid the bombs." Others must have agreed with Kernan. *Enterprise VII* made her rendezvous with the cutter's torch early in 1959. No longer pulsing with the life of a crew, she gave up the ghost and became, once again, the piles of steel and Douglas fir from which she had been built.

But in a gigantic graving dock at Newport News, Virginia, the spirit of the Big E was being revived as *Enterprise VIII* began to take shape. In 1961, a commissioning ceremony bestowed the now-hallowed name of *Enterprise* on the world's first nuclear-powered aircraft carrier. In the decades to follow, this great ship would carry on the "Big E" tradition in the confrontation with the Soviet Navy during the Cuban missile crisis in 1962, six combat deployments to Southeast Asia during the Vietnam War, the protection of Kuwaiti tankers in the Persian Gulf and launching of strikes against Iranian naval units in 1988, support for the NATO intervention in Bosnia, enforcement of the no-fly zones over Iraq after the Persian Gulf War of 1991, and the attack on al Qaeda and Taliban targets in Afghanistan in the early days of the War on Terrorism. She still steams today.

What's in a Name?

The U.S. Navy's tradition of carrying on the names of some of its ships has resulted in the name *Enterprise* being linked to much of the nation's history, so much so that the name has carried over into American popular culture. When Gene Roddenberry conceived the highly successful television program *Star Trek,* he chose the name *Enterprise* for the starship that would travel "where no man has gone before." The first space shuttle in the NASA space program, several racing yachts, and one of the Goodyear blimps have all been named *Enterprise.*

There is a story—probably apocryphal—that tells of a Soviet agent overhearing a conversation between two American Sailors during the Cold War, then reporting back to Moscow that the U.S. Navy had developed a new defense system for its aircraft carriers that protected them from incoming missiles. As the story goes, the agent had heard the Americans discussing the "*Enterprise*'s protective shields." Of course, the Sailors were referring to television's starship *Enterprise,* not the U.S. Navy's aircraft carrier!

Other ship names—for example, *Wasp, Independence, Constellation, The Sullivans, Bonhomme Richard,* and *Intrepid,* some of which feature in this heritage story—have also appeared and reappeared at critical moments in our past. But sometimes—as with the fourth, fifth, and sixth *Enterprises*—the roles of these ships do not catch the public's fancy, nor do they earn much ink in the history books. But with each new incarnation, whether a sailing sloop with an assortment of cannons or a nuclear-powered submarine with ballistic missiles capable of striking virtually anywhere in the world, the mission remains the same: stand ready to protect the nation, by mere presence or by force of arms. It is a legacy that has been handed down from ship to ship, Sailor to Sailor, for more than two centuries, and it will likely continue for centuries to come.

Don't Tread on Me **5**

On 31 May 2002, Secretary of the Navy Gordon England directed that until the War on Terrorism is won, a more symbolic flag would replace the Union Jack. A red-and-white-striped flag bearing a rattlesnake and the words "Don't Tread on Me" now flies from the jackstaff of every Navy ship in port. In the words of Secretary England, "The temporary substitution of this Jack represents an historic reminder of the nation's and Navy's origin and [its] will to persevere and triumph."

That flag is an appropriate symbol for the struggle at hand, warning those who would challenge the American ideal and attempt to curtail our liberty that such actions bear consequences similar to those encountered should one step on a rattlesnake.

That flag is also appropriate because of the widespread belief that the same one had been flown by some ships of the fledgling Continental Navy when it first stood up to the might of Great Britain in the American Revolution.

Throughout its history, the U.S. Navy has often faced formidable odds, seemingly down and out at first, but coming back with the ferocity of a rattlesnake strike to ultimately prevail, proving that one should think twice before treading on a rattlesnake or before stepping on the liberty of America.

Weevee

Doris—"Dorie" to his shipmates—Miller had enlisted in the Navy to earn money for his family. The year was 1939, and opportunities were limited for African-Americans ("Negroes" in those days). He became a mess attendant third class, serving in USS *Pyro,* an ammunition ship, and later transferring to the battleship USS *West Virginia*—"Weevee" to her crew—at Pearl Harbor, Hawaii.

A big man who had played fullback on his high school football team in Waco, Texas, Miller also earned the title of heavyweight boxing champion in *West Virginia.* Because of his obvious physical strength, he was assigned as an ammunition handler in the antiaircraft battery magazine amidships for his battle station.

On the morning of 7 December 1941, Miller crawled out of his rack at 0600 to grab some early breakfast and then attend to his morning duties. Normally, those duties included waking Ensign Edmond Jacoby, but today was Sunday, and the ensign was sleeping in, so Miller went to the junior officer's wardroom where he had been assigned as a mess attendant. It was quiet in the wardroom—just two officers had shown up for breakfast—so Miller began collecting laundry. He had been sorting among the piles of uniforms for more than an hour when, to his surprise, general quarters was sounded. General quarters drills were usually conducted during weekdays or on an occasional Saturday, but he could not remember ever having one in port on a Sunday.

As he headed along the long passageway leading to his magazine battle station, Miller felt the ship shudder violently and heard men shouting that the Japanese were attacking. The reality hit him like a left hook when he arrived at his battle station to find that it had been destroyed by a torpedo hit. He could feel the ship beginning to list as she took on water. Unsure of where to go or what to do, he was relieved when a chief petty officer told him to carry wounded men to the nearest battle-dressing station. Hefting wounded shipmates onto his broad shoulders, Miller made several trips, wading through water and slipping on oil as he struggled "uphill" along the sloping deck, until Lieutenant Commander Doir Johnson ordered Miller to follow him to the bridge.

The two men dashed up the steep ladders leading to Weevee's towering bridge. When they stepped out into daylight for the first time, Miller saw Ensign Jacoby, now fully awake, and a number of other officers trying desperately to establish some kind of order in the midst of all the confusion. Miller wondered where the captain was.

Peering out through one of the shattered bridge windows, he saw an unbelievable scene of great chaos and devastation. Japanese aircraft swooped about like a flock of angry birds, darting among the towering pillars of smoke that rose from the decks of stricken ships into the pristine blue of the Hawaiian sky. The harbor water was striped with the wakes of inbound torpedoes and cluttered with struggling Sailors. He saw other men lolling in the water who would struggle no more. Ugly clogs of black oil floated among the huge ships in Battleship Row, some of it burning, some of it waiting to absorb those who had no choice but dive into it as raging fires engulfed their ships. He stared, momentarily mesmerized, as USS *Oklahoma*—moored directly ahead—listed farther and farther to port until, to his horror, she turned turtle, her glistening, barnacle-encrusted hull suddenly facing the sky. He wondered how many men were now trapped inside the inverted ship.

Looking away from the awful sight, Miller saw his captain and realized why he had not taken charge. Captain Mervyn Bennion was lying across the sill of the signal bridge door on the starboard side. He had been cut down by a jagged piece of shrapnel from an exploding bomb on nearby *Tennessee,* his abdomen badly torn. It seemed apparent he was not going to survive. Ensign Victor Delano was kneeling near the captain, trying to ease

USS *West Virginia* ("Weevee") and USS *Tennessee* after the Japanese attack on Pearl Harbor. *U.S. Naval Institute Photo Archive*

his pain by holding a can of ether to Bennion's nose, hoping to make him pass out. Despite his pain and the ether, the captain kept asking how the battle was going, what was the status of his ship? Delano lied to his captain, knowing the truth would merely add to the dying man's misery.

Weevee too was perilously close to death. Like *Oklahoma*, she had been listing heavily to port and might well have suffered the same fate had not the senior gunnery officer, Lieutenant Claude Ricketts, gone to damage control central and taken it upon himself to counter-flood. This caused the big battleship to settle into the mud of the harbor bottom, relatively upright. Ricketts was now on the bridge, and in the words of a witness, "served as a pillar of strength."

Dorie Miller and several other men moved their captain to a safer spot behind the conning tower. Then Ensign Delano recruited Miller and two other Sailors to man two .50-caliber antiaircraft machine guns forward of the conning tower. Because Negro Sailors were always assigned as ammunition handlers, never gunners, Delano assumed the other two Sailors would do the shooting and Miller would pass them belts of ammunition. But a moment later he discovered that Miller was firing one of the guns as though he had been doing it his entire life. Whipping the gun about with great agility, he fired hundreds of rounds at the marauding Japanese planes. Miller later said: "It wasn't hard. I just pulled the trigger and she worked fine. I had watched the others with these guns. I guess I fired her for about fifteen minutes. I think I got one of those Jap planes. They were diving pretty close to us."

By then, most of the battleship that remained above water was engulfed in flames, and much of her hull was filled with water and oil. Captain Bennion had died, and it was apparent that little else could be done for *West Virginia*. From down in central control the word was passed to abandon ship. The encroaching fires cut off Miller, Delano, Ricketts, and the others on the bridge. Seeing their plight, a seaman from the deck below aimed a fire hose their way and managed to keep the flames away long enough for them to climb down a line that another shipmate had tossed up to them.

Before long, Miller and Weevee's other survivors had left the stricken ship, and it seemed "the old girl had breathed her last," as a grizzled old chief said, tears cutting winding paths through the soot on his blackened face.

After the Japanese aircraft returned to the six aircraft carriers that had launched them on their surprise attack, Pearl Harbor was a shambles. Nineteen ships were sunk or heavily damaged, including battleships *Arizona, Oklahoma, California, Nevada, Maryland, Tennessee, Pennsylvania,* and *West Virginia*. Ninety-two naval aircraft were destroyed and 31 damaged.

The Army lost 96 aircraft, with another 128 damaged. Casualties were enormous: 2,008 Sailors killed and 710 wounded; 109 Marines killed and 69 wounded; 218 Soldiers killed and 364 wounded; and 68 civilians killed and 35 wounded.

On the evening of 8 December, an American task force that had been at sea during the attack returned to Pearl Harbor. Admiral William F. Halsey, embarked in the carrier *Enterprise,* watched from the carrier's bridge wing as the ship made her way up the channel. A pall of smoke hung over the harbor, and the surface of the water was coated with an ugly blanket of fuel oil. The blackened skeletons of burned-out buildings lined the shore, the smells of death and destruction were everywhere and strong, but perhaps the worst sight of all was the broken remains of Battleship Row where the concentrated power of the Pacific Fleet had once resided. *Arizona,* or what little of her that remained, still burned. Little more than *California*'s super-structure showed above the black water. *West Virginia* was a scorched hulk, and *Oklahoma*'s underbelly turned skyward was the most unsettling sight of all. Staring at the devastation with a fierce intensity carved into his rugged features, Halsey was heard to snarl, "Before we're through with them, the Japanese language will be spoken only in hell!"

The Japanese had dared to tread upon the U.S. fleet. Now the rattlesnake was poised to strike.

Midwatch in Surigao Strait

On board the destroyer *McDermut,* Torpedoman's Mate Third Class Roy West sat at his battle station on the ship's torpedo mount amidships waiting for something to happen. He watched as a bit more perspiration than the 80-degree night would normally have drawn traced glistening paths down the face of the man nearest him. The tension had been building ever since the word had come down that the Japanese were coming up Surigao Strait and *McDermut* had received her battle instructions from the squadron commodore.

Roy West and the other men manning the torpedo mount did not know the details of the battle plan, but they did know the Japanese were expected to come up through the strait to the south of them and that *McDermut* and the other four ships of Destroyer Squadron 54 would attack with torpedoes when, and if, they came. The captain had seemed pretty certain that the Japanese would come when he spoke to the crew earlier over the ship's general announcing system, briefly explaining what was expected to hap-pen and exhorting each man to do his best in the coming battle.

At about 2200, the ship had been ordered to "Condition I Easy," which meant that all battle stations would be manned but that certain designated doors, hatches, and scuttles could be briefly opened and shut to allow the men limited movement to make head calls or to deliver coffee and sandwiches. All around the ship the men passed the time according to individual needs. Some were very quiet, silently praying, while others joked loudly. A few invoked the seafarer's ancient rite of complaining, and some ventured to predict what the night would bring. Letters, pictures of wives, girlfriends, and dogs, and decks of playing cards emerged from denim pockets, and more cigarettes than usual flared in the ship's interior spaces where there were no munitions.

At *McDermut*'s torpedo mount amidships, West listened as a young man nearby talked about the many virtues of his mother, and he watched as another man nervously fingered a small silver cross. One of the men, who consistently wore an air of bravado as though it were part of his Navy uniform, caught Roy's eye and grinned at him as if to say that all was routine and normal. But tiny strands of spittle between the man's lips said more about what was going on inside than did the forced grin.

The life jackets and helmets that always seemed a burdensome nuisance during drills now brought a mixed sense of foreboding and comfort as the minutes ticked slowly by. West had the almost constant, unsettling feeling of having just stepped in front of a speeding automobile, waiting helplessly while the vehicle careened toward him, tires screeching as the few feet of asphalt between them rapidly disappeared.

And still nothing happened.

Roy West and his shipmates were about to fight in one part of the largest naval battle in history at a place called Leyte Gulf in the Philippines. It was the night of 24–25 October 1944, and a lot had happened since the attack on Pearl Harbor in December 1941. The U.S. Navy had fought a long and arduous campaign across the Pacific, at places like Midway, Guadalcanal, and the Philippine Sea.

Dorie Miller had served in two more ships since *West Virginia* had gone to the bottom of Pearl Harbor. For his valor, the boxer-turned-gunner had received the Navy Cross, second only to the Medal of Honor. At the presentation ceremony on 27 May 1942, Admiral Chester Nimitz, Commander in Chief of the Pacific Fleet, proved prescient when he said, "This marks the first time in this conflict that such high tribute has been made in the Pacific Fleet to a member of his race and I'm sure that the future will see others similarly honored for brave acts." Indeed, many more Sailors of every race had shown their mettle as the Navy had beaten back a fanatical and capable enemy across the vast reaches of the Pacific.

Petty Officer Doris Miller receives the Navy Cross from Admiral Chester Nimitz, Commander in Chief, Pacific, 27 May 1942. *U.S. Naval Institute Photo Archive*

The victories came with price tags—many of them hefty. Assigned to the newly constructed escort carrier USS *Liscome Bay* in the spring of 1943, Dorie Miller was serving in her during Operation Galvanic, the seizure of Makin and Tarawa atolls in the Gilbert Islands the following November. At 0510 on 24 November 1943, a Japanese submarine fired a torpedo into the carrier's stern. The aircraft bomb magazine detonated a few moments later, sinking the warship within minutes. Six hundred forty-six Sailors went down with the ship, Dorie Miller among them.

Sometime after 0200, Roy West and the other men at *McDermut*'s torpedo stations sensed that the ship was no longer pacing monotonously at her patrol station but had changed course and speed. A quick look at the gyro repeater confirmed they were moving south. West heard someone nearby say, "This is it." He felt the soft rustling of butterfly wings somewhere deep in his stomach.

Torpedoman's Mate Third Class Richard Parker's battle station was on the port bridge wing, along with the torpedo officer, Lieutenant (junior grade) Dan Lewis, who was running the port torpedo director. From their vantage point, Parker and Lewis had more information about what was happening, and Parker began passing the "gouge" over the sound-powered phone system to the others at the various torpedo stations. West, whose battle station was gyro setter for torpedo mount number two, looked at the mount captain, Torpedoman's Mate Second Class Harold Ivey, as reports came in describing American PT boat attacks against the oncoming Japanese force. Several times the word *battleship* was used, and each time West and Ivey exchanged quick looks.

After a few more minutes, the luxury—or curse—of idleness dissipated as things began to happen rapidly. Evidently, *McDermut* was closing on the enemy because a torpedo firing solution began to take shape. The men on both mounts began quickly matching pointers with the information coming down from the port torpedo director, cranking in gyro angle, alternately engaging and disengaging spindles, and occasionally taking a quick swipe at the beads of perspiration running down their faces. West concentrated hard as the glowing dials before him spun in a jerky dance of whirling numbers. Trying to ignore the thumping cadence of his heart, he worked the cranks just as he had done hundreds of times before in training for this moment.

The destroyer heeled to port as her rudder went over, and she came quickly right about 40 degrees. As she steadied up, West knew his ship must be directly paralleling the target's approach course, on the reciprocal, because there was suddenly no gyro error to correct. Assuming the enemy would continue on his present course and speed, this meant *McDermut* had a near perfect firing solution and an optimum chance for success. It also meant the Japanese ships were closer to Roy West than they had ever been before, and they were probably coming directly at him at a relative speed of nearly fifty knots.

For nearly two hours in the subterranean darkness of USS *Remey*'s CIC, the squadron commodore, Captain J. G. Coward, had been monitoring reports from the PT boats farther south in the strait. Despite the excited confusion in the reports, one thing was clear: there was a sizable Japanese force headed up Surigao Strait.

When it appeared that the Japanese had passed the last section of PTs, Coward sent a message to Admiral Jesse Oldendorf saying he was taking his destroyers down the strait. *Remey* led two other tin cans down the eastern side of the strait, while *McDermut* and *Monssen* proceeded southward along the western side.

Before long, radar revealed what no human eye could see. Like tiny green ghosts, several faint contacts flared, then faded on the screen, bearing 184 degrees, range thirty-eight thousand yards. Believing that he could better control his destroyers in a night battle from the bridge, Captain Coward left CIC and emerged into the humid night air. It was darker there than it had been in *Remey*'s CIC.

Soon a report came from CIC that seven enemy ships could be discerned on the radar. From the relative sizes of the pips, the radar men evaluated them as two battleships, a cruiser, and four destroyers. As the American destroyers raced headlong toward the contacts, excited voices called out the diminishing radar ranges. Radio speakers crackled with reports in a chorus as indiscernible to the untrained ear as that heard by the uninitiated at an opera.

"SKUNKS BEARING ONE EIGHT FOUR DISTANCE FIFTEEN MILES, OVER."

"STANDBY TO EXECUTE SPEED FOUR. JACK TAR AND GREYHOUND ONE, ACKNOWLEDGE."

"THIS IS JACK TAR, WILCO."

"THIS IS GREYHOUND ONE, WILCO."

"THIS IS BLUE GUARDIAN, I AM COMING LEFT TO ZERO NINER ZERO TO FIRE FISH."

And so on.

As the two sections of destroyers converged on the Japanese column, Coward assigned targets to his ships. Five U.S. destroyers, with a total displacement of about 12,500 tons, were about to engage two battleships, a heavy cruiser, and four destroyers, whose tonnage topped a hundred thousand. Undeterred by this unsettling fact, the American destroyers pressed in for the attack.

In *McDermut,* now charging down the western side of Surigao Strait, Richard Parker passed the word over the sound-powered phone circuit that the three tin cans on the other side of the strait were launching torpedoes at the Japanese.

From his perch atop the torpedo tubes amidships, Roy West peered out over the port side of the ship, trying to see if he could make out anything on the eastern side of the strait. His eyes probed the inky darkness as he heard the command to release spindles.

Suddenly, there was a burst of light in the sky above *McDermut* as a Japanese star shell ignited. The brightly burning flare hanging from the shrouds of its miniature parachute seemed fixed in the sky above them as it cast an eerie gray-white light on the sea. West glanced about and saw *Monssen* revealed in the ghostly pallor, and he hoped that neither destroyer was as visible to the Japanese. From somewhere ahead, a green searchlight began sweeping the sea, and West knew he was in the thick of things.

A moment later, the command to "commence firing" came down from the bridge, and West could feel the expulsion of the five torpedoes beneath him as they leaped from the ship into the boiling sea. Both of *McDermut*'s quintuple mounts fired full salvoes. Ten "fish" swam off into the night in pursuit of Japanese steel. *Monssen* also fired a full salvo so that ten more torpedoes were making Surigao Strait a very dangerous place to be.

West and the other torpedo men quickly secured their mounts and gathered around Chief Virgil Rollins, who was peering at a stopwatch in the subdued red glow of his flashlight. As the group waited anxiously for the expected run time of the torpedoes to expire, they could feel *McDermut* heeling sharply over as she came about to dash back up the strait. The wind swept across her decks as she came hard to starboard, and the whole world seemed to be spinning out of control. Suddenly, West could see the faces of his shipmates in a ghastly green light and knew that the searchlight had found them. He felt the concussion of a nearby detonation and was astonished to see a large column of water rise up out of the sea off the port side. Several more rounds exploded so close aboard that *McDermut*'s weather decks were drenched in a shower of warm salt water.

Before the realization of what was happening could cause him to panic, West heard Chief Rollins—who was still watching his stopwatch—in a calm voice, say, "It's about time for something to happen." And something did.

As if cued by Rollins's words, a huge fireball erupted from the darkness to the south of them. Before the sound of the explosion could reach them, two more detonations flared from the sea in same direction. It was a beautiful and a horrid sight, conjuring a strange mix of fear, awe, and elation in West. He could hardly tear his eyes away, but the continued sound of explosions much closer to him wrested his attention once again as his ship weaved her way north in a frantic dash for survival.

As the final hour of the midwatch began, the flames of burning ships marred the natural darkness of Surigao Strait, and the ominous rumblings of hostile gunfire and exploding ships broke the stillness that normally would have reigned in these wee hours of the night. And there was more to come.

Roy West and the other torpedo men remained clustered together near *McDermut*'s torpedo tubes as the destroyer charged northward. Japanese shells were no longer falling close aboard; there was little to do besides bask in the exhilaration that often follows when one has survived the dangers of combat.

Then, one of the torpedo men said, "Would you look at that?" His voice was full of wonderment. "Over there. Off the starboard side. In the sky."

West peered in the direction indicated and saw several crimson streaks of light flash across the sky from north to south like meteors. Several more followed almost immediately. A throaty rumble, like distant thunder, felt more than heard, rolled in from the north. "The heavies are shooting," someone said.

The "heavies" were U.S. battleships and cruisers that Admiral Oldendorf had positioned horizontally across the northern end of Surigao Strait, their heavy guns lined up with a clear shot down the strait.

An old saying often heard around the Navy warns "paybacks are hell." The phrase probably has its origins in money lending, where high interest rates can make the paying back of the sum borrowed a painful experience. But in the Navy it has come to be used in a wide variety of situations. For example, a Sailor who asks a shipmate to swap duty days might have to agree to do two for one. Or even if there is an even swap, fate may intervene, involving the arrival of bad weather or a surprise inspection or some other unexpected situation, making the newly acquired duty day much worse than the one originally scheduled.

"Paybacks are hell" also has a larger meaning that involves great events and proves that seeming victories can later have serious consequences. An example of this is the 9/11 terrorist attacks on the World Trade Center and the Pentagon. What must at first have seemed a great victory to Osama bin Laden and his followers quickly resulted in the loss of the terrorist training haven in Afghanistan as well as a worldwide War on Terrorism that has had many serious consequences for those who once celebrated those 9/11 attacks.

This night in October 1944, the Imperial Japanese Navy was about to learn that paybacks could indeed be hell. Among those battleships waiting at the northern end of Surigao Strait was USS *West Virginia*!

In fact, all but one of the battlewagons there that night had been at Pearl Harbor nearly three years earlier. *Pennsylvania, Maryland,* and *Tennessee* had all been heavily damaged in the Japanese surprise attack, and both *California* and "Weevee" had been sunk and later resurrected from the bottom of Pearl Harbor. These ships had a score to settle.

And settle it they did. When the first Japanese ship had closed to within twenty-eight thousand yards, the American fire control radars locked on target, and Oldendorf ordered "commence firing." With a tremendous roar, some of the most powerful artillery pieces in the world breathed fire into the night and hurled gargantuan projectiles—some of them weighing more than a ton each—at an enemy sensed but, as yet, unseen.

The log entries for *West Virginia* on the night of 24 October 1944 read:

0332: Received orders from Commander Battle Line to open fire at 28,000 yards.

0333: 4,000 yards to go; gunnery officer reports range 30,000 and has solution with large target.

0351: Cruisers on right flank have opened fire. Gunnery Officer says he has had same big target for a long time and that it is an enemy. Commanding Officer ordered commence firing.

0352: First eight-gun salvo at 22,800 yards, AP [armor piercing] projectiles.

0353: Could hear Gunnery Officer chuckle and announce that first salvo hit. Watched the second salvo through glasses and saw explosions when it landed.

0354: Our salvos very regular at about 40 seconds interval. Other BBs [battleships] opened after our second or third salvo.

0358: Gunnery Officer reports target is stopped and [radar] pip is getting small.

0402: BBs of Battle Line turned 150 degrees on signal to course 270. Ordered cease firing. Have to think about small amount of ammunition on board. CIC reports targets turned left and reversed course.

0411: Pip reported to bloom and then fade.

0412: Target disappeared. Can see ships burning. One is a big fire.

This rather laconic account of the gunfire phase of the Battle of Surigao Strait captures the essence of what occurred. What it does not describe is the awesome power of those many ships delivering terrible devastation in the form of heavy-caliber seagoing artillery. What it merely hints at—by the mention of the gunnery officer's chuckling—is the high level of emotion felt by the men delivering those blows. What it refers to as a "pip" blooming and then fading is actually the catastrophic loss of a giant ship and the hundreds of men crewing her. What it does not record is the irony of the moment, as this great battleship, once burned and sunk in the humiliation of a successful surprise attack, later resurrected, now struck back in retribution.

As the sun rose next morning, several columns of thick black smoke towered into the brightening sky like remnants of the black shroud that had engulfed Surigao Strait the night before. The morning light revealed clusters of men clinging to debris littering the waters of the strait and large smears of oil stretching for miles. As U.S. destroyers moved in to pick up the Japanese survivors, most swam away or disappeared beneath the oily water, shunning rescue in one last great act of defiance.

Far to the north, in Leyte Gulf, American Sailors in the amphibious ships that had brought the invading troops to the Philippines had spent the night watching in fascination and some dread as the flashes of gunfire had reflected off the clouds to the south of them. They need not have worried. The scorecard for this battle was an impressive one, and notably one-sided.

The Japanese fleet that had come up from the south to disrupt the amphibious landing had been annihilated. The Japanese had lost two battleships, three cruisers, and four destroyers as a result of this last of the great gun and torpedo battles. By comparison, one American destroyer and several PT boats had been damaged in the action. One of the PTs was sunk, but no other U.S. ships had been lost.

Exact personnel casualty figures for the Japanese are unknown, but they were in the thousands. The Americans had lost but 39 men, with another 114 wounded.

Two years, ten months, and seventeen days before, the Japanese had dared to tread on the toes of a sleeping giant. On that night in Surigao Strait, they learned the true meaning behind those four words on that early Navy Jack: *Don't Tread on Me.*

The Most Bold and Daring Act of the Age

Almost a century and a half before that epic clash in Surigao Strait, another group of aggressors in another part of the world would learn that treading on the toes of the United States could bring an unexpected reaction. The story begins in tragedy and ends in triumph and is one that will never be forgotten as long as there is a U.S. Navy.

"Had Homer written an epic poem on the subject, he would have shown that every step in the chain of events was caused by a deeply laid and cleverly conceived conspiracy of the gods to bring fame to Stephen Decatur and we would agree that poor Bainbridge had been but a plaything in their hands." Holloway H. Frost wrote these words in his book titled *We Build a Navy,* published by the U.S. Naval Institute in 1929. Evidently, Frost—a naval officer himself—was trying to put a "spin" on a tragic event to make it just a bit more palatable. Frost was referring to one of the lowest points in the Navy's history, which occurred in those early years when the newly established service was just getting its sea legs.

This "conspiracy of the gods" unfolded in 1803 when USS *Philadelphia,* one of the young Navy's few frigates, arrived in the Mediterranean

Sea to make a show of force against the marauding vessels of the Barbary States (Morocco, Algiers, Tunis, and Tripoli), which had been preying on American merchant shipping engaged in trade in the Mediterranean. While attempting to blockade the port city of Tripoli, *Philadelphia*'s captain, William Bainbridge, gave chase to a native vessel that was attempting to get into the harbor. Not only did the latter have a considerably shallower draft than her American adversary, the Arab sailors were also very familiar with their home waters. With all sail set, Bainbridge took his frigate in close to the shore, trying to cut off the blockade runner. With neither a native pilot nor an accurate chart, it was a risky venture. Bainbridge had taken the precaution of stationing three leadsmen to test the depth, but the ship was moving along at a brisk eight knots, thus allowing very little reaction time when the men began singing out rapidly decreasing depth readings. Before Bainbridge could respond to the warnings of rapidly shoaling water, there was a terrible grating noise and the ship slammed to a halt, throwing many of her crew off their feet. *Philadelphia* had run her whole length well up the sloping shoal, leaving her bow four feet out of the water above her normal waterline. It was 1130 on the worst day of William Bainbridge's life.

Frantic efforts to free the ship ensued—removing the foremast, jettisoning the water stores, moving some of her cannon aft, even throwing some of the guns into the sea—but to no avail. The ship was hard aground. Worse, nine Tripolitan gunboats had emerged from the harbor and were fast approaching. Before long, the enemy craft were firing on the helpless ship.

Four hours passed, with the situation not improving in the least. Bainbridge at last called his officers to a council of war, and they concluded that there was no choice but to surrender the ship. In the words of Midshipman Henry Wadsworth, the decision was based on the desire to "save the lives of the brave crew." But many of the "brave crew" did not agree and exhorted Bainbridge to reconsider. There seemed no hope of getting the ship free. Because of her list he could not bring his remaining cannon to bear on the enemy, and the latter continued to fire into his ship at will. Bainbridge concluded that refusing to surrender would simply result in the pointless loss of 307 Sailors, and the ship would still fall into the hands of the enemy. He issued the painful order to a nearby Sailor to strike *Philadelphia*'s colors. The man refused to carry out the order, even when threatened with severe punishment. Finally, one of the midshipmen seized the halyard holding the nation's flag aloft and hauled it down. *Philadelphia*'s crew was taken prisoner and were further humiliated when a storm several days later freed the ship from the shoal and permitted the Tripolitans to bring the ship safely into Tripoli harbor. The United States of America had truly been trod upon.

William Bainbridge would later command another ship (USS *Constitution,* "Old Ironsides," no less) and bring great glory to himself and his nation by defeating a powerful British frigate in a hard-fought battle during the War of 1812. But for now, it was Stephen Decatur who would rise to the occasion.

At the time of *Philadelphia*'s capture, Lieutenant Decatur was serving as commander of the twelve-gun schooner *Enterprise.* Decatur paid a visit to Commodore Edward Preble, the officer in charge of all U.S. ships in the Mediterranean, and proposed a daring plan. Impressed with the young lieutenant's thinking and spirit, Preble gave his approval.

Decatur returned to his ship and mustered the crew. He told them that he intended to sail into the harbor at Tripoli and destroy *Philadelphia* rather than let her remain in enemy hands. When he asked for volunteers for the dangerous mission, *every man stepped forward.* Knowing that the likelihood for hand-to-hand combat was high, Decatur chose sixty-two of the fiercest, strongest Sailors and Marines.

Some time before, *Enterprise* had captured a Tripolitan sixty-four-ton ketch named *Mastico*; she had been renamed *Intrepid* and taken into service. Because she looked like—indeed had been—a Tripolitan vessel, the Americans believed they might be able to sail her into the harbor without being challenged. To complete the ruse, a Sailor named Salvador Catalano—who looked the part and spoke Arabic fluently—was designated to masquerade as *Intrepid*'s captain.

With Preble sending them off with a prayer—"May God prosper you in this enterprise"—and one of the midshipmen leaving behind a letter to his mother—"Dear Mother, I sail for Tripoli"—the intrepid crew of *Intrepid* got under way.

Thwarted from their mission for nearly two weeks by a ferocious storm, the crew endured the severe hardships of terrible overcrowding, spoiled food, and the exhaustion of battling mountainous waves and the continuous manning of the pumps to keep the ship from foundering. Rats and other vermin added to the hardships and made it a most miserable time.

Finally, the winds abated and the seas calmed. Exhausted by their ordeal but as determined as ever, most of *Intrepid*'s crew hid themselves below decks as Catalano steered the little vessel for Tripoli's harbor; Decatur and several others disguised as native traders remained on deck. By the time they were well into the harbor, the night had turned blissfully calm. A light breeze blew toward the shore—ideal for this part of the mission, not so good for their hoped-for escape. A crescent moon showered a thin light over the dark waters, helping them to navigate but making them more visible to their adversaries.

As they approached *Philadelphia,* they could see cannons looming ominously through her open gun ports. To be discovered at this point would be a disaster, for if the Tripolitans touched off those big guns, *Intrepid* and her crew would quickly cease to exist.

A few lanterns flickered on the frigate, and Decatur could make out several turbaned heads moving about just beyond the rail. He was relieved to see that they were not hurrying. The sound of wavelets lapping at the big ship's solid hull drifted across the water, and a slight luffing of *Intrepid*'s large sail seemed much louder than it actually was.

Suddenly the wind failed them, and they drifted to a halt, still about twenty yards from the frigate, still peering into the bores of those cannons. A lookout in *Philadelphia* called out in Arabic, telling them to bear off. Catalano responded, telling the Tripolitan that he was a trader from Malta, he had lost his anchor in the recent storm, and he wished to tie up alongside the big ship just for the night.

There was a moment when not a single breath was taken aboard *Intrepid* as the Americans waited for the reply. A few indistinguishable words drifted across the water, then a number of men climbed down from the frigate's deck into a small boat. They rowed around to *Philadelphia*'s bow, took a line that had been lowered, and began rowing toward *Intrepid.* Not wanting the Arabs to get too close, Decatur quickly dispatched his own boat and the two met just a few yards from *Intrepid.* Once the line had been brought on board, the Americans began hauling in.

The gap between the two vessels narrowed as *Intrepid* moved slowly forward. Decatur was relieved when he could look up and no longer see down the bores of *Philadelphia*'s cannons. As the ribbon of water separating the ships grew very thin, another line accommodatingly dropped from the frigate's stern. All was going exceedingly well.

As the two ships drew together, someone on the main deck of the frigate noticed that their smaller visitor had an anchor on her forecastle! Suddenly, an alarmed voice cried out: "Americani!"

Frenzied shouts and the rapid rustling of bare feet on wooden decks could be heard in *Philadelphia* as the Americans frantically pulled on the lines to close the few remaining feet. Then Decatur gave the order—"Away boarders!"—and the men began swarming aboard.

Some of the Tripolitans ran below decks, many dove overboard, and others stood their ground and bravely fought. It was a grisly fight. Decatur had ordered that no firearms be used, so the night air was filled with the clash of cutlasses against scimitars and the cries of cleaved men.

Within ten minutes, there was no more opposition. About twenty Tripolitans lay dead, the rest having fled. The Americans moved quickly through the ship, focused on their main mission of setting fires at key points. They spread tar, lint, and gunpowder about and, on Decatur's signal, they simultaneously tossed lighted candles into their handiwork. There was a virtual explosion as the ship ignited. It happened so quickly that several men were nearly trapped below by the rapidly spreading flames.

The Americans quickly dropped over the side to *Intrepid*'s waiting deck and began shoving off. They had some difficulty freeing themselves, and *Intrepid*'s sails began to burn as gusts of flame roared out of the frigate's gun ports and steaming tar poured down from the great conflagration above. *Philadelphia*'s rigging began burning through, and as lines and stays parted, they flew about like burning whips, some of them coming to rest across *Intrepid*'s own rigging. To make matters worse, several shore batteries opened up, one of them scoring a hit through *Intrepid*'s topsail.

Managing to free themselves at last, the Americans began pulling at their sweeps to distance themselves from the roaring fire that by now was illuminating the whole harbor and much of the surrounding city. The shore batteries continued to hammer away at the fleeing ship from the large waterfront castle nearby, but they could not find their mark. As if in one last great act of defiance, *Philadelphia*'s loaded cannons suddenly cooked off in the great heat, and some of her rounds actually struck the castle walls from which the shore batteries had been firing.

A welcome breeze sprang up and soon *Intrepid* was sailing into the outer harbor, her bow pointed toward the open sea. On their starboard quarter, *Philadelphia* burned in one giant flame like the magnified fire of a single match. Then the fire reached her magazine, and like a volcanic eruption, a massive explosion lifted the great hull into the air and brought it down again, shattered and no longer recognizable as a ship.

Decatur and his men paused at the mouth of the harbor and looked back in awe at what they had done. Then *Intrepid* caught a freshening wind and headed off to rejoin the rest of the U.S. fleet, bringing back a piece of restored honor and every man who had left on the mission. Miraculously, not a single American Sailor or Marine had been killed or even seriously wounded. When word of the feat reached British Admiral Horatio Nelson—the most respected naval hero of the time—he was reported to have remarked that the burning of *Philadelphia* was "the most bold and daring act of the age."

Boarding the Philadelphia.

Sailors boldly entered the enemy harbor at Tripoli to board the captured *Philadelphia* and set her on fire. When word of the feat reached British Admiral Horatio Nelson—the most respected naval hero of the time—he was reported to have remarked that the burning of *Philadelphia* was "the most bold and daring act of the age." *Naval Historical Center*

An Ongoing Tradition

The examples cited here are but a few of the many in the U.S. Navy's history when foolish culprits have dared to tread on this nation's honor, and Sailors have had the duty—and the commitment—to seek appropriate retribution. Revenge may not be sweet, as the old proverb goes, but there are times when might must be met with might in order to maintain credibility and to remain a potent deterrent. Al Qaeda dealt the nation a serious blow when they took down the World Trade Center and struck the Pentagon on 11 September 2001, but the subsequent loss of the terrorist training haven in Afghanistan, as well as the ongoing worldwide War on Terrorism, has once again sent the message to those who might consider stepping on the American rattlesnake; they would be wise indeed to heed the warning: Don't Tread on Me.

Don't Give Up the Ship   6

In September 1813, a group of American Sailors led by American Master Commandant Oliver Hazard Perry built a fleet from scratch and took it into battle against the British on Lake Erie. They were a polyglot group—in many ways representative of the new and growing nation of various racial and ethnic backgrounds. One in four was black, and alongside the few experienced seamen and untrained militiamen were local Indians and a Russian who spoke not a word of English.

Perry's flagship, USS Lawrence, *was built from green timber hewn out of the local forests and was named for Captain James Lawrence, who had lost his life during an earlier battle between his ship, USS* Chesapeake, *and the Royal Navy's HMS* Shannon. *Lawrence's inspiring words—spoken as he was carried below, mortally wounded—had been "Don't give up the ship," so Perry had these words sewn in bright white letters onto a navy blue field to create a unique flag to carry into battle.*

Inspired by this flag, the American Sailors were victorious on Lake Erie, causing Perry to send a famous dispatch: "We have met the enemy; and they are ours. Two ships, two brigs, one schooner, and one sloop."

It was a momentous victory of great strategic significance and, along with a similar victory on Lake Champlain by Sailors led by Thomas Macdonough, helped bring an end to the war.

Today, Perry's flag is on display at the U.S. Naval Academy, and through the ages, those inspiring words—Don't give up the ship—have guided Sailors through times of terrible crisis. Although U.S. Navy ships have been lost in battle and to natural catastrophes in the years since those Great Lakes battles of the War of 1812, many others have been saved by intrepid Sailors who, in the face of great adversity, have met the challenges head-on and simply refused to give up their ships.

One Crew in One Moment in Time

In January 2000, USS *The Sullivans* arrived in Aden, Yemen, to take on fuel. This *Arleigh Burke*–class guided-missile destroyer was not the first ship to stop in the port city near the southern tip of the Arabian Peninsula.

Aden's location at the juncture of the Red Sea and the Gulf of Aden, west of the Arabian Sea, makes it a natural fueling stop for vessels transiting these waters.

The ship got her rather unusual name because she commemorates the name of not just one Sailor, as is the more common practice, but *five*. Five brothers, all serving in the same ship during World War II, were lost in a single, terrible night when USS *Juneau* went down in the Battle of Guadalcanal.

An earlier ship named for the Sullivan brothers, a *Fletcher*-class destroyer, served in World War II and the Korean War and played a key role in the Cuban missile crisis of 1962. That ship earned nine battle stars for her service.

The newer *The Sullivans* lay at the Aden facility gulping fuel just two days after the new millennium had begun, her crew unaware that this new century would be marked by a new kind of war, and that at that very moment, evil forces were gathering to do her serious harm.

Not far away, a small boat shoved off from the shore, full of explosives. The boat looked like any number of other local craft, but this one was manned by several fanatics with ties to a group most Americans had never heard of—al Qaeda, an Islamic extremist organization. These men were determined to die for their cause and to take an American warship with them.

As the boat moved out across the shimmering water, she behaved sluggishly, and soon her gunwales were awash. Fanatical these men were; brilliant they were not! They had miscalculated the effect all those explosives would have on the small craft, and in minutes they found themselves sinking into the warm waters of Aden's harbor. The bad luck that had taken all five Sullivan brothers back in 1942 did not haunt their namesake on this day. USS *The Sullivans* was spared the intended attack; in fact, her crew would not even be aware until much later that they had been targeted.

Ten months later, the al Qaeda fanatics were ready to try again. USS *Cole* steamed into the harbor at Aden on 12 October 2000 to refuel. Like *The Sullivans,* she was an *Arleigh Burke*–class guided-missile destroyer. Like her predecessor, her crew had no idea they were the intended target of an attack.

This time the fanatics stayed afloat and made their way across the blindingly bright waters, headed for the American warship. It would be another year before 9/11 would waken the "sleeping giant" of America to the reality of the war that had been declared against it, so the men in this boat had the great advantage of surprise on their side. Waving to the crew on the main deck of the large destroyer, the men steered right for her exposed port side. It was 1118 on the day before the Navy's 224th birthday.

Command Master Chief James Parlier and Damage Controlman First Class Ernesto Garcia, the Repair Division Work Center Supervisor, emerged from *Cole*'s training room, where they had just concluded a Morale, Welfare, and Recreation Committee meeting, when they suddenly felt the deck move beneath their feet. The lights momentarily flickered off and on, and a television fell from its shelf. It was fortunate that Parlier had been at the meeting in the after portion of the ship; unbeknownst to him, a two-ton reefer had just crashed clear through a bulkhead, destroying his office.

Hull Maintenance Technician Second Class Chris Regal was standing in an after passageway near the flight deck when he was abruptly slammed to the deck. Nearly knocked unconscious, he was aware of a great pressure change inside the ship. Shaking his head like a boxer who has just taken a jolting left hook, he climbed to his feet and began running toward the source of the detonation.

Petty Officer Third Class Tayinikia Campbell, a twenty-four-year-old hospital corpsman from Latta, South Carolina, had joined the Navy six years earlier, right out of high school. Because she was the junior corpsman in *Cole,* in addition to not being very big, the crew had christened her "Baby Doc." She was in sick bay, working with her striker Seaman Eben Sanchez, when the doors blew open "like someone had kicked them in," and thick black smoke poured into sick bay. Campbell and Sanchez could hear voices frantically calling, "We need Doc," and the two of them ran down the passageway toward the calls. Finding injured shipmates all about, they set up a makeshift aid station there in the passageway and began treating the many wounded. The longest day in Baby Doc's life had just begun.

The fanatics had driven their boat into *Cole*'s port side amidships. This time they had done all their homework—the shaped charge of powerful explosives had detonated with great force, tearing a forty-by-forty-foot hole in the destroyer's side, smashing in bulkheads, and tearing deck plating as though it were made of paper. Smoke filled her passageways, and water was already pouring into her engineering spaces. Dozens of *Cole*'s crew had been killed or injured in the blast. In an instant, the many ranks, ratings, and other distinctions in the complex crew of this billion-dollar ship were of little relevance. As a *Navy Times* article would later observe, just three jobs mattered now, and every able-bodied crew member would soon be performing one of them: caring for the injured, providing security against further attack, and saving the ship.

The ship was already listing to port, a sure sign she was suffering major flooding. All power was lost; torn electrical cables dangled from overheads, arcing and sparking dangerously close to fuel that gushed out of

The 12 October 2000 terrorist attack on USS *Cole* as she was refueling in Aden harbor tore a forty-by-forty-foot hole in the destroyer's port side. *U.S. Navy (Lyle G. Becker)*

ripped fuel tanks and coated everything in its path. A portion of the deck in the mess decks area had been rolled up like the lid of an opened sardine can—protruding from the roll, four boots could be seen. One badly injured Sailor was placed on a door as a makeshift stretcher for evacuation. Injured Sailors tended to shipmates who were more seriously injured. Others opened canisters of fire-fighting foam concentrate and poured the yellow liquid onto the fuel-covered decks in hopes of preventing ignition.

In the oil lab one deck below the chief's mess, Gas Turbine Technician Mechanical First Class Margaret Lopez could see daylight through a jagged hole in the ship's side. Water streamed in through the hole and choking smoke made breathing difficult. She had been seriously burned over twenty percent of her body. Looking about she soon realized that she and another Sailor were trapped in the space; crushed bulkheads had sealed them in.

Helping her shipmate, she waded into the flowing water and fuel and got both of them out through the jagged hole and into the gulf waters. She then swam back into the ship in search of a missing shipmate. Exploring the internal wreckage, she was unable to find him and eventually went back out into the harbor and swam alongside the side of the ship until some Sailors on the main deck hauled her aboard.

Shortly after the explosion, Hull Maintenance Technician First Class Michael Hayes made his way to the mess decks area—or what was left of it. With several other shipmates, he ventured into the surreal world of death and destruction, stepping over a puddle of boiling water to get there. In his fifteen years in the Navy, he had never seen anything like this. It was pitch dark except for the strobing lights of arcing electrical wires. Smoke filled the compartment, muffling sound and softening what images there were as though they were part of a dream sequence in a movie. There was an acrid taste in his mouth that he had experienced many times before in training, but there was something different about it this time.

Hayes donned a damage control helmet with a light on it so he could see through the haze. He did not need his years of experience and training in damage control to tell that the ship was in bad shape. The damage to this area was extensive, making almost unrecognizable what had been a familiar area where he and his shipmates had shared meals and talked about the things Sailors always talk about when deployed to far-off parts of the world. Struggling through the massive wreckage, he began to sort among the human beings who were scattered about, passing by those who were obviously gone and tending to the injured. Some Sailors were trapped beneath equipment, so Hayes made his way to a repair locker and returned with several crowbars to dislodge the equipment and extract the victims. With a number of others, including Ensign Kyle Turner—whom Hayes would later describe as being "everywhere"—he helped carry or drag many of the injured to the relative safety of adjoining passageways.

Petty Officers Regal and Garcia had teamed up and were moving toward the source of smoke that filled the portside passageway. The lights were out, but emergency battle lanterns lit their way. In the half-light, Regal nearly bumped into an electrical panel that was sparking a deadly warning; Garcia saw it in time and shoved his shipmate away from the danger. When they reached the mess decks, they saw that there was no deck left on the port side. Both men entered the space and began the hardest work of their lives.

Regal formed a team of Sailors and moved forward to see how far the damage extended and to render assistance to those who might be trapped up there. Garcia remained on the shattered mess deck, helping a chief petty officer out of a hole he had fallen into and then comforting a Sailor while others used a "jaws of life" to extract her from twisted wreckage. Regal returned from his foray forward, and he and others muscled a partition away from a number of injured chiefs who were trapped by it in their mess. Although injured himself, Chief Boatswain's Mate Eric Kafka immediately began helping those more seriously wounded.

At makeshift triage stations Baby Doc, Sanchez, Parlier (whose rating had been hospital corpsman before he became command master chief), and *Cole*'s independent duty corpsman, Chief Clifford "Doc" Moser, worked frantically to save the worst cases while directing the efforts of the uninjured and less-injured Sailors who worked on broken bones and jaws, bleeding wounds, crushed arms and legs, and various other injuries. Makeshift splints were rigged, shirts were made into bandages, and words of encouragement were whispered into shipmates' ears.

Those who were not caring for the wounded were caring for their ship, doing everything in their power to save her. The destroyer had been dealt a devastating blow, and she was in grave danger of going to the bottom. As an indicator of how serious the situation was, divers would later report that a sixty-foot crater had been carved out of the bottom by the powerful blast. But it was the gaping hole in the ship's side that was the potential mortal wound unless these Sailors could contain the damage and stop the reverse bleeding as tons of water poured in.

Using the tried and true methods of damage control they had been trained in since boot camp, Sailors shored up weakened bulkheads, filled holes, and set up barriers to prevent progressive flooding. Because they had

HM3 Tayinikia "Baby Doc" Campbell, along with the other corpsmen in USS *Cole,* set up makeshift triage stations to care for the many wounded. *U.S. Navy Photo. Courtesy of* All Hands *magazine*

no power to the pumps, they set up portable pumps where possible. Other Sailors formed a "bucket brigade" by lining up and passing scrub buckets, wastebaskets, and garbage pails from one to another to remove the water.

When all the wounded had been cleared from the mess decks area, Hayes and Garcia teamed up in Auxiliary Machinery Room #1 to repair a ruptured pipe that was allowing fuel and water to pour into the ship's bleed air system. When that was done, the two moved to Auxiliary Machinery Room #2 to control the flooding there.

For hours, the battle to save *Cole* went on. Many of these young people had grown up thinking of "blood, sweat, and tears" as a rock group from an earlier time; now, as they tended to horrific injuries, labored in oppressive heat to accomplish gargantuan tasks, and said farewell to fallen shipmates, those words had new meaning.

As the sun began to disappear below the horizon, *Cole*'s skipper, Commander Kirk Lippold, met with the crew on the fantail. Standing before him were Sailors covered with oil, soot, all manner of dirt, and blood—some their own, some their shipmates'. Their faces showed they were utterly drained by their ordeal, yet all knew this trial was not over. Lippold's words are unrecorded, but they were the words between a captain and his crew, trying to express the inexpressible, spoken from deep within a human soul to other souls who have experienced the unthinkable, who have witnessed the unconscionable, who have learned within a few hours what is worst and

Damage Controlman First Class (SW) Ernesto Garcia labored in the mangled mess decks area of the *Cole,* helping injured shipmates and clearing away tangles of debris. *U.S. Navy Photo. Courtesy of* All Hands *magazine*

what is best in mankind. He later summed it up by describing these men and women as "one crew in one moment in time who rose to a challenge no crew should ever have to face."

The next few days were exhausting ones for the crew of USS *Cole*. With little time for food, rest, or even much reflection, they worked constantly to keep their ship afloat and to restore the vital functions that would make their ship the living organism she had been before the attack. Through a gargantuan effort, the men and women of this stricken ship resuscitated her by calling upon their training, their sense of duty, their upbringing, their anger, and most of all, their devotion to each other. They rigged pumps and kept them running in a constant battle with the intrusive sea. They removed debris and cleaned up fuel. They defanged the snakes of electrical cabling that dangled dangerously from the overheads. They built makeshift bridges across gaping holes and cut away jagged metal.

By Saturday night, two and a half days after the attack, most were convinced that the battle was being won, that *Cole* would stay afloat and not give her enemies the satisfaction of seeing her surrender to the devastation they had unleashed. Then the ship suffered a major setback that once again put the matter in grave doubt and threatened the loss of an American warship to enemy action, the first in a very long time.

The seal around the starboard propeller shaft in Auxiliary Machinery Room #2 began to give way, and water was flowing into the space faster than the pumps could evict it. The sound of a bulkhead giving way could be heard, and it was evident they were not going to be able to save Aux #2. All that could be done was to remove the dewatering equipment and drop the hatches, sealing off the space to prevent the water from advancing any farther.

But pressure was now building on the adjacent main engine room. The day before, Chris Regal and Michael Hayes had reinforced the seal around the starboard propeller shaft. For two hours they had pounded wooden wedges and fibrous oakum into the seal to prevent the passage of water. But now the makeshift seal was succumbing to the pressures of the water in Aux #2, and the water was now pouring into Main Engine Room #2 at a furious rate.

To accommodate the powerful gas turbine engines that serve as the source of propulsion for these modern ships, the engine rooms need to be very large. Too many spaces had been flooded already, and if that huge space succumbed as well, the battle would be over. So much added water surely would take *Cole* to the bottom.

Portable pumps are a wonderful invention, and they had done much to help save the ship. But in Main #2, the distance from the engine room up to the main deck and then over the side was too great; these small pumps did not have enough power to lift the water such a distance. Lining them up in tandem did not work, and all other attempted solutions had failed. The situation was becoming desperate. The water was winning, and time was running out.

And then, a desperate plan was put into effect. Recognizing that the only way the pumps could work would be to shorten the vertical distance the water had to travel, someone suggested cutting a hole in the side of the ship, just above the waterline. Through this hole could be passed a discharge hose and then the water would not have to travel all the way up to the main deck before it could be returned to the harbor. It was a good plan except for one frightening fact. Because so much fuel had been spilled in the catastrophe, there was great concern that the sparks from a cutting torch might ignite it. They might be jumping from the proverbial frying pan into a very real fire.

Despite the frightening possibilities, five brave Sailors descended into Main #2 armed with a cutting torch. Damage Controlman First Class Robert Morger, Machinery Repairman Second Class Rick Harrison, and Damage Controlman Third Class William Merchen joined Michael Hayes and Chris Regal to make the dangerous foray. They waded through four feet of water coated with fuel as they made their way to the starboard side of the engine room. With the help of the others, Regal climbed up the listing bulkhead and, bracing himself against an angle iron, lit the cutting torch. There were some tense moments as he began cutting into the hull and sparks danced about like fireflies on a summer's night.

But their luck held. No fire started, and soon Regal had cut a four-inch hole into the hull, large enough to pass a fire hose through. Before long, water was being discharged out of Main #2 and back into Aden harbor, from which it had come.

The crew's ordeal was far from over, but this seemed to be the pivotal point; by Sunday, it seemed certain that *Cole* was going to survive. It would be a full week before all the bodies could be removed from the wreckage— the crew chose to leave *Cole*'s soot-covered ensign flying day and night until the last shipmate was recovered.

It would be two weeks before the ship left Aden's harbor under tow to be loaded onto a heavy-lift ship for the long trip home. During that time, twelve of *Cole*'s Sailors reenlisted in the Navy.

After an extended yard period, the destroyer came back to the fleet, fully repaired and ready for the challenges that lay ahead. By then, the whole nation—wakened by the attacks on 9/11—knew what *Cole*'s Sailors already understood: the nation was at war.

Hull Maintenance Technician Second Class (SW) Christopher Regal and several of his shipmates helped save *Cole* by cutting a hole in her side. *U.S. Navy Photo. Courtesy of* All Hands *magazine*

Cole was able to come back to fight another day because her crew refused to give up their ship. In the aftermath of that cataclysmic day, the ship's executive officer, Lieutenant Commander Chris Peterschmidt, told an *All Hands* journalist that when he and the captain "found our spirits lagging, we looked around at all these other Sailors who were very undeterred by what was happening. And that in itself gave us strength."

Master Chief Parlier reinforced his executive officer's words by paying his shipmates the ultimate compliment when he said, "I'm really proud of these Sailors—I'd go anywhere with them."

In just a few hours, Parlier, Moser, Sanchez, and "Baby Doc" Campbell had seen things most hospital corpsmen never see in an entire career. They had treated terrible injuries and had done so in blazing heat, with limited facilities, and not knowing if more attacks were on the way. With the experience behind her, Campbell later spoke the words common to those who have seen death and destruction up close: "Nothing can surprise me now," she said.

Despite the terrible things he had experienced and the great challenges he had faced, Michael Hayes summed up the experience by saying, "It's a privilege to serve our country and a privilege to serve God."

As images of the gaping hole in *Cole*'s side flashed around the world, most who saw it were shocked, although some of America's enemies certainly rejoiced. As Americans back home began hearing the news that an American warship had been attacked, most were outraged, many were saddened, and some were frightened. But few understood that this ship was literally in danger of being lost; that, were it not for her determined crew who refused to give up, a U.S. warship would have gone to the bottom.

It seems somewhat inappropriate to ponder such things as politics and world image in the context of death and injury to our fellow human beings. But in the grand scheme of things, they do matter. Images of a damaged naval vessel were bad enough, but a sunken ship would have been far worse, encouraging America's enemies all the more and possibly shaking the faith of some who looked to the United States for strength and encouragement.

Most strategists believe that the outcome of the War on Terrorism will be determined by many things, but chief among them will be which side has the greater will to prevail. If *Cole*'s Sailors are any indication of the American will, the outcome is not in doubt.

Crisis on Yankee Station

Unless one consulted a nautical chart, it would be difficult to tell that "Yankee Station" was a place. It looked pretty much like many other pieces of ocean in many parts of the world when the aircraft carrier USS *Forrestal* arrived there in July 1967. Blue water stretched to three horizons and, on clear days when the frequent squalls did not get in the way, a distant coastline was visible to the west.

But it was a place nonetheless—a place in the Gulf of Tonkin, west of the South China Sea, where U.S. warships went to strike at enemy targets in North Vietnam. A place where aviation ordnancemen hefted live bombs and rockets to the wings and underbellies of attack aircraft, where enemy surface-to-air missiles were just over the horizon, where aviators too often did not return from sorties.

When *Forrestal* joined the carriers *Oriskany* and *Bonhomme Richard* on Yankee Station, U.S. forces had been fighting the war in Vietnam for two years. Sailors were by then conducting "brown-water" operations in the rivers and along the coasts of South Vietnam; hospital corpsmen were in the Central Highlands alongside their Marine brothers; SeaBees were building naval bases in key tactical positions; SEALs were conducting covert operations; and naval advisors of all rates and ranks were all over the war-torn country helping to build the South Vietnamese navy out of the remnants left behind by the defeated French.

At the time of her arrival for her first combat tour, *Forrestal* was one of the largest ships in the world. Manned by five thousand Sailors, she was more than 1,000 feet long, as tall as a twenty-five-story building, and displaced more than eighty thousand tons. At four acres, her flight deck was longer than three football fields laid end-to-end, and she was 252 feet wide at her broadest point.

Yet she was a tiny airfield. All those impressive measurements meant little to Gerald Farrier and the other aircraft handlers who constantly struggled to move nearly one hundred big airplanes around on the crowded flight deck. With so many aircraft on board, it was an ongoing challenge to position the planes so they could be launched, recovered, refueled, rearmed, repaired, and otherwise maintained. Moving about *Forrestal*'s flight and hangar decks, one felt not her vastness, but her confinement.

Farrier had left his home in Batesville, Arkansas, fourteen years before to serve in the U.S. Navy. His career had so far been a successful one. He had risen steadily as an aviation boatswain's mate and, at the age of thirty-one, he was a chief petty officer with serious responsibilities. Among his many duties in *Forrestal,* he was in charge of Repair Eight, the highly trained team of Sailors who would respond in case of a plane crash, a fire, or some other emergency on the flight deck. He was responsible not only for multi-million-dollar aircraft but for the lives of his shipmates as well. On 29 July, just five days after *Forrestal*'s arrival on Yankee Station, that responsibility was about to become very real.

Preparing for a major strike against targets in North Vietnam, many fully fueled and armed aircraft had been crowded into position on *Forrestal*'s flight deck. Strapped into one of those aircraft, an A-4 Skyhawk, was a young lieutenant, John McCain—a future U.S. senator and presidential candidate.

Not far away, wearing the blue shirt that identified him as a plane handler, Gary Shaver sat aboard one of the small tractors that scurried about the flight deck, positioning aircraft and starting their engines when it was time for them to prepare to launch. Suffering from a broken hand, he had been assigned lighter duty than usual.

At 1052, stray voltage from an electrical charge used to start the engine of an F-4 Phantom across the flight deck ignited a Zuni rocket attached to the fighter's port wing. The rocket roared across the flight deck and struck the belly fuel tank of McCain's A-4. It tore open the fuel tank, spilling and igniting two hundred gallons of aviation gasoline that quickly spread across the flight deck. Two bombs that had been attached to McCain's aircraft also fell to the deck.

In an instant, an inferno had erupted, engulfing McCain's plane and spreading rapidly across the flight deck. McCain scrambled out of the cockpit and onto the plane's nose. Crawling out along the refueling probe, he leaped ten feet to the burning deck below, then rolled through a wall of flames as his flight suit caught fire. He quickly put out the flames and then, shaking from adrenaline, he went to help another pilot whose flight suit had also burst into flames.

Shaver grabbed a fire extinguisher from his tractor and, struggling with his broken hand, began spraying the spreading flames. An instant later, he saw Chief Farrier grab another portable fire extinguisher and run headlong into the conflagration, fighting back the flames as he tried to get to the trapped pilots. The chief began spraying one of the 1,000-pound bombs that had dropped from McCain's aircraft onto the flight deck and was now engulfed in flames. As Shaver's small extinguisher ran out, he watched in awe from twenty feet away as Farrier ignored the danger around him and tried to prevent the bomb from detonating. As Shaver remembered it, Farrier "looked at me and waved his arm as if to say 'get the hell out of here.' Before I could move, there was an explosion and Chief Farrier was gone."

Through the ship's PLAT system, fire can be seen erupting on the deck of the aircraft carrier USS *Forrestal*. Sailors can be seen running toward the fire to fight it. *U.S. Naval Institute Photo Archive*

Flames engulf the entire after half of *Forrestal*'s flight deck. Exploding ordnance tore holes in the deck, and flaming fuel poured down into the ship's interior spaces. Only through the crew's great courage and determination not to give up their ship was *Forrestal* saved from destruction. *U.S. Naval Institute Photo Archive*

The ship's PLAT system confirms what Shaver witnessed. There, in stark black and white imaging, is Chief Farrier charging headlong into the fire, spraying his extinguisher, undeterred by the raging flames and the imminent danger of explosion, putting the lives of his shipmates before his own. And in a blinding flash that momentarily overwhelms the PLAT system, this courageous Sailor is committed to the ages, personifying the Navy's creed of honor, courage, and commitment in a manner that is both sobering and awe-inspiring. "It takes one's breath away," said one observer.

Pieces of shrapnel from the exploded bomb tore into McCain's legs and chest. But he was among the more fortunate; other pilots and flight deck personnel, as well as most of the men in Repair Eight, were lost in that early detonation, the first of many explosions that day as the fire spread out of control across the after half of the huge aircraft carrier. With the experts of Repair Eight gone, it fell upon amateurs to continue the fight. Sailors with little or no prior training stepped up to man the hoses and fight back the inferno that now threatened to destroy the ship. Planes burned everywhere, pilots ejected from them, and men jumped off the flight deck to escape the flames. More bombs cooked off, tearing great craters into the flight deck and allowing flaming fuel to pour down into the spaces below. Rockets and missiles ignited and streaked across the deck, cutting a deadly swath among the firefighters and slamming into other aircraft. A huge column of black smoke climbed into the sky, visible for many miles. There could be little doubt that *Forrestal* was in mortal danger.

But the carrier's crew was not about to let their ship succumb. The same PLAT system that captured Chief Farrier's selfless heroism also shows Sailors running *toward* the wall of flames despite the showers of shrapnel and large flying chunks of burning wreckage from a massive detonation just seconds before.

A third round of detonations cleared the deck of men and destroyed much of the firefighting gear, yet moments later more Sailors appeared to fight the inferno. Ignoring the chain reaction of exploding fuel tanks and ordnance, men wrestled with hoses, rolled hot bombs across jagged decks, and muscled aircraft over the side before their fuel tanks could ignite. One Sailor plugged a hole in a plane's fuel tank with his finger to keep the fuel from spilling out as a group of men rolled the aircraft toward the side for jettisoning. Below decks, men lit off pumps, set up fire barriers, searched for the missing, rescued fallen shipmates, and performed first aid despite the clouds of choking smoke and the cascades of burning fuel pouring down through holes in the decks above. In a display of incredible professionalism and courage, the men in the port after steering compartment were cut off beyond rescue but continued to keep their equipment working and maintained their composure on the sound-powered phone lines until they died.

For thirteen hours, *Forrestal*'s crew fought the conflagration until the last fire was out. By great courage, exemplary sacrifice, and sheer determination, they had saved their ship. At a cost of 134 lives and hundreds of injuries, *Forrestal* would serve the Navy for many years to come. With most of her after flight deck gone and charred wreckage strewn over much of the ship, she left Yankee Station under her own power and returned to her homeport in Norfolk for extensive repairs. She would return to duty and make another seventeen major deployments to the Mediterranean and Arabian Seas, participating in a number of important operations, including Earnest Will (keeping the sea-lanes open in the Persian Gulf during the Iran-Iraq War) and Provide Comfort (deterring Iraqi attacks against the Kurds in 1991).

Many who survived confided that they were certain they would have to abandon ship before the day was over. The loss of Repair Eight so early on had been a near-fatal blow. The ship had been saved primarily by the willingness of so many volunteers to carry on when shipmates had fallen or disappeared before their very eyes, to pick up the hoses that had been dropped by men burned beyond recognition, to jettison heated ordnance over the side despite the tremendous risk, to stand up to smoke and flames when running away was still an option.

The Navy learned some valuable lessons that day. Despite their great courage and sacrifice, some of these untrained men had made costly errors—such as washing foam away with water, allowing fires to reignite—that could have been avoided had they received adequate training beforehand. Never again would a ship sail in harm's way with just part of her crew trained in firefighting. After the *Forrestal* fire, the Navy decreed that every Sailor, from seaman to admiral, would be trained in firefighting before going to the fleet.

Today, the survivors of the *Forrestal* fire look back with mixed emotions. Many have difficulty recounting the experience: Charlie Rodgers, a yeoman who worked in a ready room below the hangar bay, recalls watch-

Chief Petty Officer Gerald Farrier charged headlong into the fire on *Forrestal*, armed with just a fire extinguisher, determined to save his shipmates. Today the Navy's firefighting school in Norfolk, Virginia, bears this heroic Sailor's name. *Courtesy of USS* Forrestal *Association*

ing the events on the PLAT system, saying, "I can't tell you how I felt," as he chokes back tears. Gary Shaver, who saw Chief Farrier run "full gate to what was to become our hell on earth," remembers with awe that "there was never a look of fear or doubt in [Farrier's] eyes as he fought the growing fire. Only the look of determination to do his job!" Today, the firefighting school in Norfolk, Virginia, bears the name of that courageous chief who paid the ultimate price trying to save his ship and his shipmates.

Shaver, McCain, Rodgers, and the others who survived that terrible day on Yankee Station many years ago carry with them the memories of lost shipmates and the responsibility of living a good life—something that was denied Farrier and 133 others. They also carry with them a wisdom not granted to all, an understanding that fate sometimes deals us difficult hands and the only way to prevail—or, in some cases, simply to survive—is to find in ourselves the kind of courage and determination that Sailors commemorate in their traditional saying: *Don't Give Up the Ship.*

Another Tradition

There have been many other occasions when Sailors have carried on the tradition of not giving up their ship. From patrol craft to capital ships, courageous, committed Sailors have heeded the words spoken by a dying man in the War of 1812.

In World War II, the aircraft carrier *Franklin,* operating closer to the Japanese homeland than any other U.S. carrier, suffered incredible damage when a single Japanese plane came through the cloud cover on a low-level bombing run and hit the ship with two armor-piercing bombs. One struck the flight deck centerline, penetrating to the hangar deck, which it devastated. The bomb also ignited fires through the second and third decks and knocked out the CIC and air plot. The second bomb hit aft and tore through two decks, spawning fires that detonated ammunition, bombs, and rockets.

Franklin, within fifty miles of the Japanese mainland, lay dead in the water, with a 13-degree starboard list, all radio communications lost, and enveloped in flames. Seven hundred and twenty-four crew members were killed and another 265 were wounded. Many others were either blown overboard or driven over the side by the raging fires. Remaining were 710 Sailors who, by sheer valor and tenacity, miraculously saved the ship. *Franklin* had the dubious distinction of being the most heavily damaged aircraft carrier in the entire war, yet she remained afloat and eventually proceeded under her own power to Pearl Harbor for repairs.

While there are numerous examples of Sailors who have not given up their ships, there is another tradition in the U.S. Navy that has never been articulated in the same way as Captain Lawrence's inspiring words, but it could just as easily be emblazoned on a flag for posterity: Don't Give Up the Sailor.

In 1939, USS *Squalus,* the eleventh in the new *Sargo* class of submarines, was conducting sea trials off New England when her main engine air induction valve failed and water poured into the boat's after engine room. The submarine rapidly sank stern first to the bottom, coming to rest keel down in sixty fathoms of water. During the disaster, twenty-six men were trapped and died in the flooded after portion of the ship. This left thirty-three men alive in the forward compartments of the submarine. The survivors sent up a marker buoy and then began releasing red smoke flares to the surface in an attempt to signal their distress.

USS *Sculpin,* another *Sargo*-class submarine sent to the area later that morning, spotted one of the smoke signals at 1241 that afternoon and marked the spot with a buoy. She was joined in the afternoon by a number of other vessels that had been sent to find a way to rescue the Sailors trapped in the crippled sub. Divers and submarine experts, including the Experimental Diving Unit from Washington, D.C., also converged on the location.

During this preparatory period, the thirty-three survivors spent a cold night trapped inside *Squalus* and began to suffer from the effects of chlorine gas seeping out of the battery compartment. Despite the knowledge that never before had the victims of a submarine sinking ever been saved from such a depth, no one in *Squalus* caved in, and discipline, if not spirits, remained high.

Ashore, the wives and families of the *Squalus* Sailors awaited news. A Morse-code message tapped out from the sunken submarine—"condition satisfactory but cold"—was interpreted most hopefully. Interviews with relatives nearby and at distant locations were published and broadcast by reporters. One group of newsmen rented a boat for the fifteen-hour journey to the scene and back and learned that not all the crew had survived. When they brought this news back, the impact on the wives and relatives was devastating.

The would-be rescuers had three options. One was to pump out the flooded compartments to bring the *Squalus* to the surface; this was risky because the reason for the sinking was still unknown. The second option was to have the men come to the surface using their individual Momsen Lungs (at that time, the lungs were a recently invented rescue device for situations similar to this); but the sub's depth was greater than the 207 feet for which the lungs had been tested. Also, the men were extremely cold and undoubtedly weak from the foul air and tension. The decision was made to take the third option, which was to use a revised version of a diving bell, also invented by Commander Charles B. Momsen, to descend to the sub and attach to her deck above one of the hatches. A few of the trapped men could then climb up into the bell and be transported to the surface. It would take several trips under uncertain conditions to get them all out, but it seemed the best plan available.

At 1130, the dramatic rescue operation began, and at 1247 direct contact was established with the trapped crew. With the bell positioned over the submarine's hatch, the first group of men climbed up into the tiny chamber. The bell was hauled to the surface and, for this first group, the ordeal was over. Those who waited below must have felt a powerful urge to rush up into the safety of the rescue chamber when the hatch opened each time; but naval discipline—both admirable and necessary—prevailed, and the evacuation was both orderly and logical, with those in the worst shape and more junior in rank going before the others. Over the next six hours, twenty-five survivors reached the surface in three trips. After serious difficulty with tangled cables threatened to prevent the rescue of the remaining seven survivors, the fourth trip finally rescued them just after midnight. All thirty-three were recovered.

Determined salvage operations later raised *Squalus,* and she was towed into the Portsmouth Navy Yard on 13 September 1939. Following an investigation into the cause of the disaster, the boat was formally decommissioned on 15 November, then recommissioned with the new name *Sailfish* on 9 February 1940, in time to serve in World War II. During her twelve war patrols, *Sailfish* sank seven Japanese ships, including the escort carrier *Chuyo,* for a total of more than forty thousand tons. *Sailfish* was awarded the Presidential Unit Citation.

It was a remarkable achievement. The Navy had not given up on either its Sailors or its ship. James Lawrence and Oliver Hazard Perry would have been proud.

Part III

A Unique Profession

It should be clear from the preceding chapters that serving as a Sailor in the U.S. Navy—whether for two years or thirty—is a truly unique experience. It is a bit of an understatement to say that men and women who serve in the Navy see, hear, say, and do things they would otherwise never have done. In the remaining chapters, we will see why, no matter what else a person may do in his or her life, those years spent in the Navy will always be remembered as unique.

Transitions

7

As with all things that rely on technology, navies have evolved over the years. Oars have given way to sails, which have given way to steam propulsion, which has in turn given way to gas turbines and nuclear reactors. Weapons have evolved from boarding parties and rams to guns, missiles, and supersonic aircraft. That which remains the same throughout all this change is the Sailor who dares to venture into the unknown when new challenges emerge and who uses this ever-changing technology to defend the nation and, when necessary, to achieve victory at sea and to project power ashore.

Contrasts

Gunner's Mate Second Class Joseph Palisano stood on the deck of the destroyer USS *Paul F. Foster* at 0441, 17 January 1991, peering into the predawn darkness that blanketed the Persian Gulf. Suddenly, there was a deafening roar as a Tomahawk missile leaped into the black sky, momentarily turning night into the brightest noonday glare. Like a shooting star, the reflection from the flaming engine traced a path across the dark waters as the weapon soared off in search of its assigned target. In seconds, it was gone, leaving Palisano once again enshrouded in darkness to ponder what he and his shipmates had just done. To no one in particular, he remarked: "There it goes. We just started a war!"

Although one might argue it was the Iraqi tyrant Saddam Hussein who had actually started the war when he sent his armies into an unprovoked invasion of neighboring Kuwait, Palisano was correct that his ship had just fired one of the opening salvos of what had been dubbed Operation Desert Storm, the war to liberate Kuwait.

The largest naval armada since World War II had gathered in the Middle East to strike at the very heart of Iraq; even the capital city of Baghdad was among the many targets that would be hit in the devastating assault. Three aircraft carriers—*Saratoga, John F. Kennedy,* and *America*—launched their strike aircraft from the northern Red Sea. Across the Arabian Peninsula, in the Persian Gulf—where some had deemed it impossible to conduct carrier operations—*Midway* and *Ranger* proved the skeptics wrong and fired off sortie after sortie. Battleship *Missouri* (upon whose decks the Japanese had surrendered to end World War II nearly half a century before) and her sister *Wisconsin* were there again to fire in anger.

This time, however, it was not gigantic 16-inch guns that served as their main batteries, but a barrage of state-of-the-art guided missiles. They were joined by *Aegis* cruisers *San Jacinto* and *Bunker Hill* and destroyers *Paul F. Foster, Leftwich,* and *Fife,* and together they fired 48 Tomahawks in the first hour. That was just the beginning: in the first two days of the war alone, 216 Tomahawks and 1,100 combat sorties from the carriers had been launched against Saddam Hussein's Iraq.

One of the vessels of this powerful striking force made history in those early hours of the war. Like many other ships in the armada, USS *Louisville* had come a long way to fight. Her voyage had been more than 14,000 miles at high speed. But unlike most of the other vessels, she had made the transit *underwater*. *Louisville* was the fourth ship to bear the name: Her predecessors had been an ironclad steamer that fought in the battle of Vicksburg during the Civil War, a troop transport that carried thousands of Soldiers to Europe during World War I, and a World War II cruiser who fought in several engagements, including the Battle of Leyte Gulf that destroyed the Japanese navy. But this *Louisville* was the first to be a submarine. And on 19 January, she became the first submarine in history to launch a Tomahawk missile in actual combat.

This massive assault from the sea crippled the enemy's infrastructure and weakened their will and ability to fight. After the air war, the ground war began and was over in just a few days. Kuwait was liberated, and Saddam Hussein's bid for mastery in the Persian Gulf region had been thwarted. While this spectacular victory was achieved by a joint effort of all U.S. armed forces with the assistance of a coalition of foreign allies, the U.S. Navy's role was unquestionably vital to the outcome. Without control of the surrounding seas and the power projected from those waters, the war would have been a different one indeed, if it could have been fought at all.

The ships, aircraft, and submarines that accomplished this liberation were representatives of the pinnacle of naval power at the time, incorporating state-of-the-art technology that was a far cry from the sailing frigates who had fought the despots of Morocco, Algiers, Tunis, and Tripoli nearly two centuries earlier. Even though Sailors from both eras answered orders with a traditional "aye-aye" and knew the value of a half-hitch, much had changed since the twelve-gun *Enterprise* had captured a Tripolitan ship in a ferocious action off Malta and a party of courageous Sailors had sailed the tiny ketch *Intrepid* into Tripoli's harbor to destroy the enemy fleet berthed

A Tomahawk cruise missile, as viewed through the periscope of the submarine launching it. USS *Louisville* was the first submarine in history to launch a Tomahawk in combat. *Naval Historical Center*

there on what turned out to be a suicide mission. Those tiny wooden vessels following the whims of North African winds in the early 1800s bore little resemblance to the great steel ships plying Middle Eastern waters in 1991. The contrast between hundred-yard cannons and Tomahawks flying hundreds of miles into Iraq is almost beyond comprehension. And those brave men in *Intrepid* who made that last sortie into Tripoli harbor would no doubt have gratefully welcomed the assistance of a flock of strike aircraft or a missile-firing submarine.

The U.S. Navy of the late-twentieth and early-twenty-first centuries is unquestionably the most powerful world has ever seen. But it did not come to be that way without the imagination, innovation, and outright genius of some brilliant inventors and the courage of Sailors who, using those inventions, dared to go where no one had gone before.

Peter Williams

Seaman Peter Williams would not have been cast as a hero in a Hollywood movie. His slender build, mousy brown beard, and gray eyes were not features that made him stand out in a crowd. But he had proved himself a capable seaman during his first voyage shortly after the Civil War began. He was a quick study and had already learned a healthy respect for the sea. His ship had been seriously damaged in an Atlantic winter storm and was undergoing repairs in the Brooklyn Navy Yard when Williams heard of a strange new kind of ship being built nearby. The rumors had been spreading along the waterfront for some time, and although he was no naval architect and not among the most experienced Sailors in the Union Navy, Williams knew enough about ships to know how they worked. What he was hearing about this vessel did not seem possible.

It was a blustery January afternoon in 1862 when the young Sailor decided to have a look for himself. A chilling wind nipped at his ears as he made his way along the waterfront. A wad of tobacco bulged his left cheek, and he was careful to spit to leeward as he walked. On his right, tall masts skewered the bright blue sky, and to his left, soot-covered brick buildings housed the industrial shops and chandlers' lofts of the Navy Yard. The pungent smell of burning coal wafted on the wind, and across a narrow band of water he could see Cob Dock, a man-made island created over the years by dumping the cobblestone ballast from ships that came in for overhaul.

He was stopped at a gate by an old watchman, an attempt to maintain the secrecy that had long before been compromised. There had even been stories in the newspapers about the strange new vessel that had been designed by the colorful and sometimes difficult John Ericsson. Williams had some difficulty getting past the old watchman, but he succeeded after his persistent (but untrue) assurances that he was a member of the new ship's crew. As he passed by the watchman, the old man said, "Next time bring me a pass so that if you are a spy and blow up the ship, I'll have something to fall back on." So much for priorities.

Williams snaked his way among piles of metal plating, then got his first look at the mystery ship he had heard so much about. What he saw was even more amazing than what he had heard. Stretched out before him was an extremely low, flat deck—indeed so low that he could barely see any freeboard—broken only by a very large cylinder directly amidships and a much smaller projection closer to one end of the vessel. None of the things Williams associated with a ship seemed to be there. No majestic hull rising out of the water to support decks cluttered with weapons, capstans, and the like. No towering masts reaching for the heavens, nor webs of lines to awe and confuse a landsman.

Though the ship was teeming with busy people, no one challenged his presence, so Williams boldly went aboard and gave himself a tour. He discovered that the large cylinder amidships was a revolving turret about twenty feet in diameter and nine feet high, housing two 11-inch guns. It was the first time such a design had ever been used in a warship. Williams, whose naval experience had primarily been as a helmsman on vessels with rows of cannons along their sides, had more than once heard a gunner's mate say, "You seamen aim the ship and we'll fire the guns." He was awed by this new invention that allowed the guns to be trained in any direction— the single exception being dead ahead because of the projection near the bow, which Williams learned was the pilothouse.

As a professional helmsman, Williams was most interested in that pilothouse. It stood just four feet above the deck and reminded him of a log cabin because it had been constructed of nine-inch square logs that were notched and bolted on the ends. Inside, Williams noted there was room for no more than three men. He would later describe it as a "chicken coop."

As he moved about the strange vessel, he learned that there were two steam-powered engines, one to propel the ship through the water and the other to rotate the turret. Heavy iron plating encased the entire ship, which made Williams feel uneasy about her seaworthiness but reassured him when he thought about riding her into combat.

Williams met an older Sailor named George Geer who told Williams that he was a first-class fireman. He made sure Williams knew that he was *not* one of the "coal-heavers" who would stoke the engines when the ship was under way. His job was to attend to the more complicated aspects of keeping pressure up and steam flowing. Geer explained that the ship's name was *Monitor*; two pistons in one cylinder drove her engines, and she had a forced-air ventilation system that fed air to the boilers and actually moved air throughout the ship for the crew. The smoke from the engines was vented through gratings in the deck aft of the turret, and a detachable stack could be mounted over the gratings to funnel the smoke upward when the ship was not in battle. Peter Williams left the ship very impressed.

As he passed through the gate for the second time, the old watchman reminded him, "Next time bring me something in writing." Continuing his earlier lie, Williams said, "I'm her quartermaster." As he headed back through the shipyard, he realized that he liked the sound of that.

Rampage

Far to the south, near Norfolk, Virginia, another strange vessel was taking shape. She too was clad in iron, and she too had no masts, sails, or associated rigging. She was CSS *Virginia,* and she had been created on the hull of USS *Merrimack,* a steam-and-sail-powered frigate that had been seized when Confederate forces captured Gosport Navy Yard a year earlier. The retreating Union Sailors had set her afire before they were driven out, and her masts and rigging had been destroyed, but her hull and engines remained relatively intact. Unlike *Monitor,* taking shape to the north, *Virginia* had no rotating turret; instead, she had a more conventional array of ten guns aligned along the length of the hull, their muzzles protruding from the armor that was angled upward at a 35-degree slope. Like an ancient Greek galley, she also had a ram protruding from her bow, just below the waterline.

Virginia had been under construction since the previous summer, and by the first thaw of 1862, her commander, Franklin Buchanan, the first superintendent of the U.S. Naval Academy before he left the Union Navy to fight for the Confederacy, decided it was time for the iron ship to go to war, even though the yard workers still had things to do. On 8 March, with clouds of black smoke initially belching from her untried engines, she moved slowly away from the shore and then gained momentum as her great weight began moving down the Elizabeth River, headed for nearby Hampton Roads where a Union fleet had taken up blockade duty. She glistened in the sun because her crew had greased her topsides with pork fat to help deflect enemy shot and to make boarding her more difficult. As the cumbersome but fearsome-looking vessel made her way down the river at six knots—her top speed—crowds waved and cheered from the banks. The Confederate Navy had been the underdog to the more powerful Union Navy since the war had begun, and it seemed at this moment all of that was about to change.

Out in the more open waters of Hampton Roads, the wooden Union ships were at Saturday routine, the laundry fluttering from their rigging, drying in the midday sun. Scuttlebutt had been warning of a great iron monster for so long that few took it seriously when reports began to circulate that something was coming out of the river.

On board USS *Congress,* a sailing frigate of fifty guns lying directly across the roads from the mouth of the Elizabeth River, Quartermaster John Leroy had been peering southward through a telescope for several minutes when he turned to a nearby officer and said: "I wish you would take the glass and have a look over there, Sir. I believe that *thing* is a-comin' down at last."

As *Virginia* emerged from the river, all eyes in Hampton Roads were fixed upon her. Among those watching was a young lieutenant named T. McKeen Buchanan, *Congress*'s paymaster and brother of *Virginia*'s captain—such are the terrible ironies of a civil war. Curiosity, awe, and dread seemed to be the prevailing emotions among the onlookers. Seaman Frederick Curtis, captain of Number 8 gun in *Congress,* later recalled, "Not a word was spoken, and the silence that prevailed was awful." Those who watched the iron monster come out of its lair remembered it as looking like a "barracks building on water," "a long, low barn," a "crocodile," and "an iron-plated coffin."

Virginia closed on *Congress.* According to the latter's surgeon, the ship waited until the ironclad's "plating and ports" could be clearly seen and then "tried her with a solid shot from one of the stern guns, the projectile glancing off her forward casemate like a drop of water from a duck's back. . . . This opened our eyes." The doctor had little time left for observation because *Virginia* replied with a broadside of grapeshot, "killing and wounding quite a number on board the *Congress.*"

There was a deafening roar as *Congress* fired a thirty-two-gun broadside at her attacker. A Soldier on the nearby shore could hear the great blast of the guns but was amazed when the shower of projectiles "rattled on the armored *Merrimack* [*Virginia*] without the least injury."

One of *Virginia*'s shells made a direct hit on *Congress*'s Number 7 gun. Seaman Curtis "felt something warm, and the next instant I found myself lying on the deck beside a number of my shipmates." The cannon next to him had been blown off its carriage, "sweeping the men about it back into a heap, bruised and bleeding. The shell struck right in back of me and took my left-hand man."

Quartermaster Leroy, who had first spotted *Virginia,* lost both legs in that first broadside and was carried below, bleeding profusely. He did not live long, but in his last few minutes of life he urged the men to fight on, telling them to "stand by our ship."

The Confederate ironclad moved away, and the men on *Congress*'s deck began to cheer, thinking that *Virginia* had given up. But the Confederate was simply heading for the next target, *Cumberland,* a thirty-gun sailing sloop of war. Furthermore, what those cheering men did not yet realize was that *Congress* was burning in her main hold, sick bay, and below the wardroom, dangerously close to the after powder magazine.

As CSS *Virginia* headed for USS *Cumberland,* shore batteries and smaller Union gunboats pounded her with numerous direct hits. But as one dismayed Union officer described it, they either exploded harmlessly against the iron sides or ricocheted into the water "like India rubber balls."

The Confederate ironclad CSS *Virginia* (formerly USS *Merrimack*) attacking the wooden-hulled USS *Congress* in Hampton Roads, Virginia, during the American Civil War. *Naval Historical Center*

Virginia raked her new adversary with her guns and then rammed her. The ram broke off as the ironclad backed away, but the gaping hole left in the wooden ship quickly filled with a torrent of water. In the Confederate captain's admiring words: "She commenced sinking, gallantly firing her guns as long as they were above water. She went down bravely with her colors flying."

Attempting to get under way to join the battle, the forty-gun frigate *Minnesota* ran aground and was now a helpless target for the rampaging ironclad and several Confederate gunboats who had joined the fray. But the light of day was fading, and *Virginia*'s Captain Buchanan decided to retire for the night, saving the remainder of the destruction for the next day.

Sometime after midnight, the raging fires reached *Congress*'s magazine and a huge explosion destroyed the ship. It had been a bad day for the Union Navy, and the next day promised to be more of the same. It seemed apparent that no wooden ship was going to be able to stand up to the Confederate ironclad. When word reached Washington of the day's events, President Abraham Lincoln met with his cabinet. Secretary of War Edwin Stanton feared that the ironclad might be on her way up the Chesapeake Bay to attack Washington itself. He warned that the "monster" will "change the whole character of the war; she will destroy every naval vessel; she will . . . come up the Potomac and disperse Congress, destroy the Capitol and public buildings."

But Secretary of the Navy Gideon Welles had other thoughts on the matter. He told Lincoln and the cabinet that all was not lost, that help was on the way. On 6 March, two days before *Virginia* had gone on her rampage in Hampton Roads, USS *Monitor* had left Brooklyn Navy Yard and headed south for the Norfolk area. She was due to arrive the next day, Sunday, 9 March 1862, a day that would make naval history and change surface warfare forever.

Cheese Box on a Raft

During the voyage down the East Coast, Peter Williams had reason to wonder if he had made a serious mistake when he managed to land a berth in USS *Monitor* as one of her crew of fifty-eight. He had quickly earned the confidence of her captain, Lieutenant John Worden, and had been designated as one of the strange new ship's helmsmen. He was steering the ship when she encountered heavy seas in the stormy Atlantic. With her extremely low freeboard, *Monitor* was nearly swamped as water poured over and into her. Crashing waves knocked down her smokestack, and the ventilator drive belts began to malfunction when the intruding water soaked them. Only heroic efforts by the engineers had managed to repair them before the crew suffocated from the mounting fumes inside the iron hull.

On the helm, Williams peered out through one of the narrow slits that served as windows, studying the angry sea, trying to read patterns among the chaos. He fought the ship's apparent desire to slip down into the inviting troughs that seemed like havens beneath the raging mountains of the swells. Williams knew that once in a trough, *Monitor* would be seductively rocked from side to side until she could no longer right herself and might then turn turtle and disappear beneath the waves into an eternal peace. His experience as a seaman told him that safety could be found only on the broad backs of those monstrous swells, that he must keep her head into the sea, perpendicular to the seductive troughs, to climb up the formidable slopes and then career down the far side like a sled racing down a snow-covered slope.

At one point, water came driving into the pilothouse through the narrow slits with such force that it knocked Williams down, away from the helm. He struggled to his feet, seized the spinning wheel, and fought the heaving seas for control of the ship. "You *will,* will you?" he said to his ship as he struggled to keep her out of the trough. "Well, you *won't*! You're going to do it *my* way." His arms ached as he fought with the tons of water pushing against the rudder. Despite her seeming reluctance to do what was best for her, Williams had already developed an "exasperated affection" for this iron monster. Back in New York, he had knocked a man down for calling her a "filthy old tub."

By the great efforts of Williams and his shipmates—many of whom had bailed water with buckets for long, exhausting hours—*Monitor* survived. In the evening of 8 March, the "cheese box on a raft"—as some had aptly dubbed her—rounded the tip of the Delmarva peninsula, heading into calmer waters. Safe from the raging sea at last, *Monitor* and her crew were now headed into a storm of another sort.

As they steamed up the channel, they could hear the distant booming of gunfire, and soon they could see a Union frigate burning. It became clear that there would not be much time to recover; these exhausted Sailors were going to have to find the strength to fight in the morning.

Duel of Iron

All night long, *Monitor*'s crew made preparations for the coming battle. There was a lot to do, both in the aftermath of the arduous voyage and in getting ready to face *Virginia*. As they worked, it suddenly occurred to Williams that the next day would be the first time the crew had ever fired the guns; there had been no time in the hasty preparations and the harrowing voyage to exercise the crew at battle stations. His even more sobering thought was that *Virginia*'s crew had already had experience working *their* guns—fresh experience indeed! The burning wreck of *Congress* was evidence enough of that.

After many hours of exhausting work, Williams found time for a quick nap just before dawn. He rolled himself into a blanket and dropped to the deck. Gazing up at the constellations above, he breathed in the fresh night air—it was like a tonic after so many hours in *Monitor*'s stifling interior—and wondered, before sleep overtook him, what the day would bring.

At dawn, Williams got up, shook the stiffness out of his limbs, and set about a final inspection of *Monitor*'s steering gear. Finding everything in order, he joined his messmates for breakfast.

He was relieved that the cooks had chosen to open one of those "newfangled" tin cans that kept meat fresh. It was so much better than the dehydrated vegetables they sometimes ate after soaking them in water for an hour. He was grateful that the hardtack was fresh and had not yet molded nor been infested. It was a good breakfast and a good start to a day that would soon prove to be like no other before.

As he ate, Williams watched a group of engineers messing nearby. He wondered how they did it, how they endured the conditions below decks. It was confining and stifling enough in his tiny pilothouse, but at least he did have the slits through which to see the outside world and to get an occasional breath of fresh air. Those men who worked among the tangles of piping and in the coal bins were in a class of their own. His friend George Geer had told him of the hell below decks when the ship was under way. Under optimum conditions, the coal heavers had to shovel nearly six hundred pounds of anthracite into the fireboxes. Their sweat produced steam at a pressure of twenty-six pounds per square inch and at a temperature of 240 degrees Fahrenheit. The pipes had no insulation and were 230 degrees to the touch. In a letter to a friend, a Sailor wrote: "When we beat to quarters, my place is in the boiler room—hot steam pipes all around me and I know the gas inside would admire to get at me for the work I've made it do; it hisses out sometimes as if to say, 'Look out young man, you got me in a tight place right now, but it may be my turn someday.'"

Williams knew it was not all disadvantage working in that hellish world. Geer told him they always had plenty of hot coffee down there. Nonetheless, Williams was glad to be a helmsman and not an engineer.

At about half past seven, excited voices reported that *Virginia* was under way and heading straight for helpless *Minnesota,* the latter still hard aground. *Monitor*'s crew raced to their stations, closing hatches behind them, removing the stack, and placing protective covers over her running lights. Within minutes, she was steaming toward her Confederate counterpart.

To those watching from shore, it was evident that *Virginia* was much larger and more heavily armed than *Monitor,* and many anticipated seeing a quick end to this Union newcomer. On board *Virginia,* her chief engineer was astonished to see "a black object that looked like . . . a barrelhead afloat with a cheese box on top of it" come out from behind *Minnesota* and head right for them.

Peter Williams was at the helm as *Monitor* positioned herself between *Minnesota* and *Virginia.* Also crammed into the tiny space were the captain and Samuel Howard, who was acting master of the bark *Amanda.* The latter, being familiar with the waters of Hampton Roads and a brave man, had volunteered to serve as pilot for the Union ironclad.

Paymaster William Keeler had no assigned battle station, so he positioned himself in the turret in case he could be of assistance there. He watched in awe as the men loaded 175-pound projectiles into the big guns. Once they were loaded, Keeler noted that "the most profound silence reigned." Sealed inside the armored turret, unable to see out with the gun ports closed, the men seemed almost to freeze in place as they waited for the battle to begin. Keeler thought, "If there had been a coward heart there, its throb would have been audible, so intense was the stillness." Although he admitted no fear, Keeler did ponder their circumstance as he waited, noting that "ours was an untried experiment and the enemy's first fire might make it a coffin for us all."

At last the awful silence was broken. Keeler could hear the "infernal howl" of *Virginia*'s shells as they passed over *Monitor* on their way to *Minnesota*. The speaking tube between the turret and the pilothouse was not working, so the ship's executive officer, Lieutenant Samuel Greene, told Keeler to "ask the Captain if I shall fire." Relaying through Daniel Toffey, the ship's clerk, the question was passed, and Captain Worden's reply was, "Tell Mr. Greene *not* to fire till I give the word." He also told his executive officer "to be cool and deliberate, to take sure aim and not waste a shot."

Worden calmly passed his conning orders to Williams, who expertly spun the helm in response. He maneuvered *Monitor* toward *Virginia,* closing the range, "approaching her on her starboard bow, on a course nearly at right angles with her line of keel, saving my fire until near enough that every shot might take effect." When *Monitor* was sufficiently close, Worden stopped the engine and gave the order to commence firing.

Inside USS *Monitor*'s gun turret. Paymaster William Keeler noted that before the battle began: "The most profound silence reigned. If there had been a coward heart there, its throb would have been audible." *Naval Historical Center*

The executive officer "triced up the port, ran out the gun, and, taking deliberate aim, pulled the lockstring." At that moment, naval warfare was indeed changed forever.

The two ironclads went at each other with a determined fury. *Monitor*'s first shot struck her adversary at the waterline, and *Virginia* responded with a broadside that would have destroyed a wooden ship of the same size. To the great relief of Greene and the other Sailors inside the revolving cheese box, "the turret and other parts of the ship were heavily struck, but the shots did not penetrate; the tower was intact, and it continued to revolve."

The two ships spiraled about one another, trading shots for quite some time, with neither able to strike a fatal blow. Their suits of armor withstood the terrible punishment each was attempting to inflict upon the other. One witness on the nearby shore later remembered, "Gun after gun was fired by the *Monitor* which was returned with whole broadsides by the rebels with no more effect, apparently, than so many pebblestones thrown by a child." Inside the ironclads, the shots striking the metal did not *sound* like pebblestones; the din inside both vessels was almost unbearable as striking shot reverberated throughout their echo-chamber hulls.

Ironclads USS *Monitor* and CSS *Virginia* dueling in Hampton Roads. Inside the ships, the din was almost unbearable as shot bounced off their armored sides. *U.S. Naval Institute Photo Archive*

The spirals grew ever tighter until the two ships were next to each other, firing at point-blank range. And still the shots glanced off *Monitor*'s whirling turret and off *Virginia*'s sloping sides, causing no more than dents and the awful clatter. It was clear that each had met her match, yet neither was able to prevail.

As the battle wore on indecisively, Williams continued working *Monitor*'s helm in response to Worden's calm orders. At one point as they maneuvered around *Virginia*'s stern, Williams could see the enemy ship by looking over Worden's shoulder through the forward window slit. He realized he was looking right into the muzzle of the Confederate's stern gun just twenty yards away. Worden was saying to Williams, "Keep her with a very little port helm, a very little," when, suddenly, there was a great flash and a thunderous crash as an enemy shell slammed into the pilothouse. Williams was thrown from the helm and found himself on his hands and knees. The top of the pilothouse was partially torn off, and the light that poured in from above momentarily blinded Williams. Miraculously, the young helmsman was not seriously injured. His captain, however, was less fortunate. Worden had taken much of the blast full in the face, and his eyes were filled with smoke and burning powder. He staggered back, his hands to his face, and cried: "My eyes. I am blind!" With blood pouring down his face, Worden was taken to his cabin.

Trembling violently, his ears ringing from the concussion, Williams climbed to his feet and grasped the spokes of *Monitor*'s helm. To his relief, the ship responded when he moved the wheel. Locating *Virginia* through one of the slits, he steadied his ship and began maneuvering her into position as he had seen Worden doing. For a time, until the executive officer could get to the pilothouse and take command, Williams was in sole command of the ironclad's movements.

By this time, the two iron contestants had fought for several hours, with neither ship suffering disabling damage. No one had been killed on either ship; only Worden was seriously injured. *Virginia* had fought a battle with enemy ships the day before; *Monitor* had fought a battle with the forces of nature that day as well. The result was that the men in both ships were exhausted. The two vessels had expended great amounts of coal and ammunition. It was time for this undecided but historic battle to end. *Virginia* headed for Sewell's Point and *Monitor* returned to her anchorage.

Aftermath

Both sides would claim victory in this first clash of the ironclads. In truth, it was, by most objective assessments, a draw. Northerners could rightfully claim that *Monitor* had prevented *Virginia* from succeeding in her mission to destroy *Minnesota* and the other Union ships in Hampton Roads, and there certainly was a measure of victory in that. George Geer wrote a short letter to his wife after the battle that reveals maddeningly little about the battle itself—telling her she can read about it in the newspapers—but he makes it clear how the Union leadership felt about the outcome: "Our ship is crowded with Generals and Officers of all grades both army and Navy. They are wild with joy and say if any of us come to the Fort we can have all we want free, as we have saved 100s of lives and millions of property to [*sic*] the Government."

Circumstances would prevent these two ships from having a rematch. *Virginia* would survive just another two months. On 11 May, with Norfolk about to fall to Union forces, Confederate Sailors destroyed her to keep her from falling into enemy hands. *Monitor* lasted until the end of that same year, when she was lost in a storm off Cape Hatteras on New Year's Eve as she headed south to participate in blockade operations. Fourteen men were lost as she succumbed to twenty-foot waves and high winds.

George Geer and Peter Williams were still part of *Monitor*'s crew when she went to the bottom of the Atlantic, but they were not among those lost. Geer left the Navy several years later, eventually using his skills as an engineer to make a good living in civilian life. Quartermaster Williams remained in the Navy and was eventually promoted to acting master's mate. For his courageous performance as *Monitor*'s helmsman, he was awarded the Medal of Honor.

Lieutenant John Worden recovered from his wounds and commanded another ironclad in action the following year. When President Lincoln heard that Worden was recuperating in a friend's home in Washington, the president hurried to the house. Worden, his eyes still bandaged, heard Lincoln's voice, and said, "Mr. President, you do me great honor by this visit." Lincoln paused a moment, then said, "Sir, *I* am the one who is honored."

Although those two ships would never fight one another again, on that day in April 1862 the age of the ironclad had dawned. Many more ships would fight in the Civil War with steam-powered engines, forced-air ventilation, revolving turrets, and other new inventions. These vessels would soon take control of the seas away from the beautiful wooden sailing ships with their webs of lines and clusters of billowing canvas. By the time America would fight her next major war—the Spanish-American War just thirty-six years later—the two major engagements of that clash would be fought by cruisers and battleships made of steel slugging it out with breech-loading, rifled guns in rotating turrets. The day *Monitor* fought *Virginia* (ex-*Merrimack*) marked the beginning of a revolution and the end of an era.

Below

The duel of the ironclads was not all that was new to naval warfare during the American Civil War. Two years after the historic battle in Hampton Roads, on the night of 17 February 1864, USS *Housatonic,* a steam-powered sloop, was positioned about five miles southeast of Fort Sumter at Charleston, South Carolina, as part of the Federal blockade of the Confederacy. It was a clear night, bathed in bright moonlight, and the seas were calm. Thus, it was no surprise when one of *Housatonic*'s lookouts spotted something in the water that "looked like a log." Flotsam in these waters was not unusual, but an object moving toward his ship faster than the prevailing current was something worth the lookout's attention. After sounding the alarm, the lookout and several other Sailors opened fire with small arms, but to no effect. The "log" made contact with the ship's starboard side and a large explosion ripped off *Houstonic*'s starboard quarter. Although just five Union Sailors were killed, the ship was fatally wounded, and she quickly went to the bottom.

The "log" had been CSS *Hunley.* With her 90-pound spar torpedo, she had earned the distinction of being the first submarine to sink an enemy vessel. It would prove to be a costly victory for the history makers, however; for reasons not entirely clear, *Hunley* disappeared on her way back from the attack, taking her entire crew of nine to their deaths.

Hunley's brave crew were not the only casualties. Other crews had paid the ultimate price while testing the strange new vessel; even her designer, H. L. Hunley, was lost on one of these test dives.

Essentially a converted boiler about forty feet long and four feet wide, she was powered by a hand crank that turned a screw propeller when manned by most of her crew. Ballast tanks at either end of the vessel provided buoyancy and permitted her to submerge. Weights attached to her underside could be detached from the inside if necessary. She could stay submerged for about half an hour before needing to come up to replenish air through breathing tubes. The crew used a burning candle to warn when oxygen was running out.

This primitive technology was just a little more sophisticated than that used in an earlier submarine built during the American Revolution a century earlier. Named the *Turtle,* she was a one-man submarine that looked like an upright egg and used a foot pedal to flood the bilges in order to submerge. A hand pump could eject the water to bring the sub back up. Like *Hunley,* she relied on a hand crank for propulsion and had detachable weights. Unlike the Confederate version, *Turtle* did not have a very effective means of weapon delivery. She carried a keg of powder that was to be attached to the underside of an enemy vessel and subsequently detonated by a timing device.

Ezra Lee, a sergeant in Washington's Continental Army, volunteered to take *Turtle* out in New York harbor to attack the anchored British flagship. He successfully maneuvered the submarine into position but was unable to attach the powder keg before being discovered by the enemy. Pursued by an enemy boat, Lee cut the keg loose as he withdrew. It exploded spectacularly but harmlessly among the ships in the anchorage. Although *Turtle* was unable to attack the Royal Navy successfully, many of the British ships hoisted their anchors and moved farther downstream as a result of Lee's attempt.

From those early ventures beneath the sea came one of the most formidable weapons in the history of warfare. Before the nineteenth century had come to a close, John Holland had designed a workable submarine, and by 1900 the U.S. Navy had its first, appropriately named USS *Holland.* Before the beginning of World War I, the Navy had twenty-five subs in service. Because these early craft were so small, they were called "boats" rather than ships, and the term has stuck to this day, even though USS *Louisville,* the submarine who first fired a Tomahawk missile into Iraq, is 360 feet long and displaces more than seven thousand tons. Submarines nearly changed the outcome of World War I, and they played a vital role in the U.S. victory in the Pacific during World War II. Nuclear-powered submarines were likewise key components of the U.S. victory in the Cold War, though none ever fired a shot.

Today, submarines continue to be a principal component of America's nuclear deterrence strategy, while expanding their roles in tactical missile attack and support of Special Forces operations. They are manned by

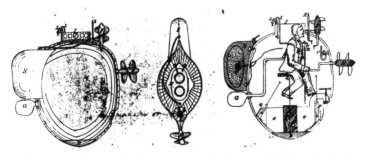

Design drawings of *Turtle,* the first operational submarine. She attacked a British ship in New York harbor during the American Revolution. *U.S. Naval Institute Photo Archive*

Sailors who routinely descend into regions once considered off-limits to mankind. Like the surface above, the undersea regions of the world are now the dominion of the U.S. Navy because of Sailors who dared to go into the unknown.

Above

In March 1898, Assistant Secretary of the Navy Theodore Roosevelt wrote to Secretary of the Navy John D. Long about some experiments that were being conducted with a device he called an "aerodrome." He informed Long that "the machine has worked," and then advised, "It seems to me worthwhile for this government to try whether [or not] it will work on a large enough scale to be of use in the event of war." The Navy and the Army formed a board to investigate the matter and concluded there was merit in Roosevelt's suggestion. The Navy Bureau of Construction and Repair, on the other hand, concluded that the "apparatus," as they called it, "pertain[ed] strictly to the land service and not to the Navy." How wrong they were!

Although these lighter-than-air aerodromes would never play a major role in naval warfare, other flying machines, pioneered by the likes of the Wright brothers, would prove that earlier board's decision to be a bit hasty. Later members of that same Navy board gave this new idea the chances it needed, once again changing naval warfare forever.

A little more than forty years after the initial Wright brothers' flight, the Battle of Midway would prove to be the decisive turning point in the largest war the world had ever seen, and the entire engagement was decided by fleets that never laid eyes on one another—except from the air. Instead of Roosevelt's "aerodromes," the flying machines at Midway were dive-bombers, fighter aircraft, and torpedo bombers, and they were launched from ships far out at sea. Naval air had become the predominant weapon for war at sea in just a few decades.

Conservative impediments were overcome by larger events and by the vision and courage of some Sailors who sensed that a revolution was upon them and who decided their only choice was to join or get out of the way. One such Sailor was Captain Washington Irving Chambers. Noting in 1910 that the Germans—who were rapidly becoming a world power—were planning to launch an airplane from a ship, he decided that the U.S. Navy should make the attempt first. Unable to get funding from the Navy Department, he persuaded a wealthy publisher to contribute one thousand dollars to the project. He then persuaded a pilot by the name of Eugene Ely to make the attempt. On 14 November, Ely took off from a specially constructed platform that had been erected on the bow of cruiser *Birmingham*—then anchored in Hampton Roads, Virginia—and then landed near a row of beach houses on shore.

Two months later, on 18 January 1911, Ely again piloted an aircraft for the Navy, but this time he successfully *landed* on a platform that had been erected on the afterdeck of USS *Pennsylvania* in San Francisco Bay. An hour later, he took off again and landed safely ashore. Besides the primitive aircraft he was flying, Ely depended upon a series of lines attached to sandbags as the arresting gear to facilitate his landing on the ship, and he used a bicycle inner tube wrapped around his waist as a life preserver. Rudimentary as it might have been, this experiment proved the viability of aircraft carrier operations and marked the beginning of the most sweeping change to naval warfare that had ever occurred.

Innovative and courageous Sailors from seamen to admirals carried forth the work that Ely had started. Over a relatively short period of time, the primitive experiments on *Birmingham* and *Pennsylvania* were transformed into a powerful instrument of naval warfare, conducted with astounding efficiency and reliability despite the great dangers involved. Those who have ever witnessed flight operations on an American aircraft carrier are consistently awed by the precise choreography of so many people doing so many things with such powerful machines amidst so much noise and surrounded by so much potential death and destruction. From the aircraft handlers in their yellow shirts to the refueling teams in purple, from the red-shirted ordnance loaders to the pilots in g-suits, and so on, it is a ballet of sorts, in which the performers are artists in their prime, and every successful performance deserves a standing ovation.

Many Sailors paid with their lives for this boldness, but their sacrifices have given the Navy another powerful arm to project its power over the seas and into the littoral regions of the earth. Whether striking targets in the once-forbidden regions of mountainous Afghanistan or flying deterrent patrols in the airspace between Communist China and Taiwan, U.S. naval aircraft play a vital role in both war and diplomacy: putting muscle behind words and ideals and applying measured force, when necessary, to protect America's interests in virtually any corner of the world.

Beyond

One Sailor's adventure into the unknown began rather ignominiously, yet ended in glory. He had served in the destroyer *Cogswell* during World War II and then entered flight school after the war, earning his wings in 1947. A gifted aviator, he attended Navy Test Pilot School, subsequently helping the Navy develop an in-flight refueling system and conducting early trials on the first angled carrier deck. He later flew test flights in the F3H Demon, F8U Crusader, F4D Skyray, F11F Tigercat, and the F5D Skylancer. But all of these contributions would pale in light of his historic flight on 5 May 1961.

Strapped into his aircraft waiting for launch after several delays, he suddenly realized that he had a problem. Speaking into his radio headset, he reported, "Man, I've got to pee!"

"You what?" came the response.

"You heard me. I've got to pee."

Alan Shepard was sitting atop a Redstone rocket, strapped into a space capsule named *Freedom 7,* waiting to make history by being the first American to go into outer space, when he realized that despite all the scientific innovations and technological wonders that had gone into preparing for this moment, no one had thought of this need.

Shepard was told that no time had been factored in to the launch sequence to allow him to leave the space capsule. By this time, he was getting truly desperate, and he said he was going to have to let go. The aeronautical engineers were afraid that if he did so, the liquid inside his flight suit might short-circuit some of the many electrical leads that were attached. The mission seemed in serious jeopardy.

It was Shepard himself who came up with a low-tech solution. He said over the radio to fellow astronaut Gordo Cooper in mission control, "Tell 'em to turn the power off!" It seemed like a possible solution that would allow him to urinate without shorting out any of the leads, so Cooper checked with the engineers. With a less than convincing shrug, they gave their assent. Laughing at the absurdity of the situation, Cooper told the man who was about to make history: "Okay, Alan. Power's off. Go to it."

Lying on his back in the capsule, with his face to the heavens, about to challenge the forces and laws of nature by literally reaching for the stars, Alan Shepard gave in to a basic law of nature that neither he nor any of the brilliant minds that had designed the mission could defy. Soon a pool of liquid formed at his back, soaked up by the heavy undergarment he was wearing. Power was restored, and the flow of oxygen in his suit began drying the unwanted puddle.

Then, at Shepard's urging—"Let's light this candle!"—the huge rocket was ignited. Like Peter Williams and his shipmates who changed the way their Navy did business, and Ezra Lee and the other submarine pioneers who took their Navy into the depths of the sea, and Eugene Ely and countless other aviators who braved great dangers to lift their Navy into the skies, Alan Shepard took his Navy into the "final frontier," the vast reaches of outer space. Climbing to an altitude of 116 miles, and flying at speeds greater than 5,000 miles per hour, *Freedom 7* left the bonds of Mother Earth and entered the weightless world of outer space. Flying down the Atlantic Missile Range for 302 miles, the space capsule reentered the atmosphere and landed in the ocean to be recovered by the carrier USS *Champlain.*

It was an astounding accomplishment that would lead the way to a landing on the Moon just eight years later. The first human to walk on the surface of

America's first man in space, Alan Shepard, is recovered from his space capsule by fellow Sailors from USS *Champlain. U.S. Naval Institute Photo Archive*

the Moon was Neil Armstrong, a former Sailor. Shepard would also eventually land on the Moon, as would a number of other Sailors. Today, the Navy's presence in space is less human but no less vital to the missions of the operating forces. Satellites provide vital support in communications, navigation, weather forecasting, and intelligence. Many modern naval weapon systems rely upon technology developed as part of the space program, and some receive actual targeting data from space systems.

Alan Shepard and the other space pioneers changed the Navy (and the world) through their courageous steps beyond the norm. They were carrying on the same tradition that had motivated a young man to go beyond the familiar and the comfortable, to want to take the helm of a "cheese box on a raft," and steer her into the history books.

War Words   8

Like most specialized subjects, warfare has a vocabulary of its own. Among the most used—and misused—terms dealing with war are strategy *and* tactics.

Highfill

When Vernon Highfill reported to the aircraft carrier USS *Lexington,* he had no way of knowing that he would soon be in the midst of one of the earliest and most significant battles of World War II.

Highfill found himself in a strange new world unlike anything he had experienced before. The big flat deck on top of the ship, where airplanes took off and landed, was an amazing and unforgiving place whose big aircraft moved about in unpredictable ways, their spinning propellers a constant hazard to anyone who "skylarked" for even a moment. The hangar bay was a vast cavern of open space, yet it was so packed with aircraft that walking through it was a constant exercise of bobbing and weaving to avoid the many potential dangers, not the least of which were the many bombs, torpedoes, and belts of machine-gun ammunition.

Soon after he reported aboard, a petty officer showed Highfill around the engineering spaces where the young fireman would spend most of his time. Like the flight and hangar decks above, this too was a strange world, where daylight and darkness had no effect, where boilers bigger than some of the houses back home roared like man-made volcanoes, where the smells of lubricating oil, steam, and sweat filled the pressurized air.

During the tour, Highfill learned about the opening to a small crawl space that ran vertically alongside the ship's smoke stack. It was almost like a second skin surrounding the big tube that ran from the boilers straight up through many decks to expel the hot gasses of combustion to the atmosphere. This small space, he was told, was there to allow firemen like him to clean and perform other maintenance tasks on the stack. Highfill was in no hurry to take on that duty.

When they got to the forward engine room where Highfill would be standing his watches among the whining turbines, the petty officer pointed out that there were eight inches of steel armor surrounding the space and that the ship's fire-main pumps could pump thirty-six thousand gallons a minute; in a world of so many combustibles, this was all comforting information. *Lexington* seemed a good place to be if one had to go to war with the Japanese.

Coral Sea

In May 1942, Japanese and U.S. fleets converged in the waters of the Pacific bounded by the Solomon Islands, Australia, and New Guinea—an area known as the Coral Sea. The Japanese had come to these waters to invade Port Moresby on the southeastern side of New Guinea. The Americans were there because they had successfully broken the Japanese code and, knowing the enemy's intentions, were determined to stop them. If the Allies lost Port Moresby, that would give the Japanese a very favorable position from which they could cut off sea communications between the United States and Australia and might well threaten Australia itself.

At this point in World War II, the U.S. Navy had but five aircraft carriers available in the Pacific. Two—*Enterprise* and *Hornet*—had been sent on the morale-building mission of attacking Tokyo using Army B-25 bombers launched from *Hornet*'s deck, and *Saratoga* was being refitted in a shipyard on the U.S. West Coast. That left only *Yorktown* and *Lexington*. Admiral Chester Nimitz, Commander in Chief of the Pacific Fleet, decided to commit them to stopping the Japanese capture of Port Moresby.

For the invasion, the Japanese had assigned two of their most powerful carriers—*Zuikaku* and *Shokaku,* both veterans of the attack on Pearl Harbor—as the muscle for a main striking force. They also sent a smaller aircraft carrier, *Shoho,* along with four cruisers as an escort force for the ships bringing the invading troops.

As it developed, this initial major engagement of U.S. and Japanese naval forces would become the first naval battle in history in which the ships of the two opposing fleets would never see one another. This new way of fighting at sea, brought about by the development of naval aviation, would become the model for most of the major battles for the remainder of the Pacific War. Besides the "firsts" and its strategic importance, this battle would also be characterized as one of much confusion.

As the forces converged in the Coral Sea, foul weather joined them, making air reconnaissance exceedingly difficult. The opponents moved about in the Coral Sea like blind boxers—a lot of punch, but unable to deliver it.

The Japanese were the first to make contact; on 7 May one of their scout planes reported seeing a U.S. carrier and a cruiser. Determined to take advantage of this fortunate discovery and thus strike first, Admiral Takeo Takagi launched all of his attack aircraft from *Zuikaku* and *Shokaku.*

But the scout pilot had been mistaken. What had seemed to him to be a cruiser and a carrier were actually an oiler—USS *Neosho*—and a destroyer—USS *Sims.* The two U.S. ships never had a chance and were overwhelmed by the Japanese air armada. *Sims* was sunk, and *Neosho* was left a floating derelict. Their terrible loss was not in vain, however. The mistaken identity had preoccupied the Japanese and prevented their aircraft from discovering and attacking the much more vital U.S. carriers.

Meanwhile, American scout planes had discovered several Japanese cruisers, and they too had mistakenly identified them as aircraft carriers. This time it was the Americans who took the bait and launched a full strike. Their mistake was somewhat offset when, en route to the attack, they discovered the Japanese escort carrier *Shoho* and hit her with thirteen bombs and seven torpedoes, sending her to the bottom. Sinking a Japanese aircraft carrier, even a small one like *Shoho,* was uplifting to the Americans after the months of Japanese successes that followed Pearl Harbor. The U.S. flight commander happily radioed back, "Scratch one flattop!"

The confusion continued on into the afternoon, with the bad weather causing further misidentifications, some chaotic fighter engagements in the air, and several Japanese pilots actually trying to land on *Lexington.* As night fell, the ships faded into the cover of darkness, with the score one oiler and one destroyer lost by the Americans versus one Japanese escort aircraft carrier sunk. In the cold calculus of war, where units are given relative values, it seemed the U.S. Navy was winning this first carrier battle.

The next day, 8 May, the scorecard would change significantly. Locating one another's carrier forces at last, both the Japanese and the Americans launched nearly simultaneous strikes. Although each side's forces were nearly equal in strength, the Japanese aircraft were generally superior, and their pilots at this point in the war had more experience. To further tilt the tactical advantage toward the Japanese, their carriers were operating under a partial cloud cover, while the U.S. ships were completely exposed under bright blue skies in their part of the Coral Sea.

When the U.S. aircraft arrived, the carrier *Zuikaku* headed into a passing rainsquall, where she was adequately hidden from her attackers. *Shokaku* was not so fortunate. American dive-bombers screamed down out of the sky and managed to score three hits. Though she would live to fight another day, the *Shokaku* was sufficiently damaged to put her out of action, and her returning aircraft were forced to land on the undamaged *Zuikaku.* With so many aircraft crowded on board, *Zuikaku* was no longer able to conduct air operations and was, therefore, effectively out of action as well. Both carriers would ultimately head back to Japanese home waters for repairs and reallocation of aircraft.

While the U.S. pilots were attacking the enemy carriers, their Japanese counterparts were simultaneously hitting the American flattops. A single bomb struck *Yorktown* causing serious but not fatal damage.

As Japanese aircraft swarmed about *Lexington,* torpedo bombers came in on both bows, flying into a hail of gunfire from the carrier's more than one hundred antiaircraft guns of various calibers. Red and white tracers filled the sky on the port side as men fighting for their lives poured out a curtain of rounds into the path of the approaching enemy. Those up forward could see "fish" dropping from the underbellies of the bombers, and *Lexington*'s captain ordered a starboard turn in an attempt to minimize the target profile of his ship by presenting her narrower stern to the oncoming torpedoes. Dive-bombers dropped out of the sun. One of their bombs nicked the tube containing the lanyard used to operate the ship's siren from the bridge so that an eerie wail joined the din of hammering weapons and swooping aircraft. Several of the Japanese aircraft were shot down, but nothing could stop the torpedoes. Shortly after the delivering aircraft were either destroyed or fading from sight, two of the deadly fish slammed into *Lexington*'s port side.

Manning his station near a screaming turbine down in the forward engine room, Fireman Vernon Highfill felt that "hell broke loose" when the reverberations of the torpedo explosions rattled everything around him. Remembering what the petty officer had told him about the armor and those powerful fire-main pumps helped him remain calm.

But things were more serious than Highfill believed. Within minutes, the big carrier was listing 7 degrees to port as water rushed in from the sea and filled a number of compartments below the waterline. Three fires were burning, and numerous pieces of vital equipment were inoperable, including the aircraft elevators used to hoist the planes from the hangar deck to the flight deck. Damage control parties went to work fighting back the fires, shifting fuel from port-side tanks to starboard, and jury-rigging inoperable equipment. Soon they had the wounded ship—and her airfield perched on top—on an even keel, and she was able to recover her returning air wing. It seemed that despite the serious damage, she would survive. In reporting the ship's status to the captain, the damage control officer quipped, "I would suggest, sir, that if you have to take any more torpedoes, you take 'em on the *starboard* side." But it would not be more torpedoes that would put *Lexington* in more jeopardy.

Ruptured fuel lines caused vapors to settle into the lower parts of the ship; these eventually ignited, causing powerful explosions that were followed by raging fires. Her Sailors fought hard to save "Lady Lex," as she was affectionately called. Stan Johnston, a war correspondent riding the carrier at the time, described the ensuing struggle: "Many of [the Sailors] who fought on with such downright guts, and completely without heroics, and without compensation (the satisfaction of shooting back) that battle brings, had been in the Navy for only a few months. They were choking and burning as they strove, unseen, deep inside the smoke-filled galleries of the lower decks. They were aware every second that the *Lexington*'s own ammunition stores might shatter her at any moment sending them to the bottom with her. Yet they never faltered; they battled on unselfishly."

The fires grew worse, communications within the ship deteriorated, and fire mains ruptured. Fireman Highfill was still at his station when suddenly the lights went out, plunging him into complete darkness until the beams of battle lanterns and waving flashlights here and there cut through the smoky air. His strange world beneath the waterline had just gotten stranger. Then he heard the ventilation blowers winding down as electrical power began to fail, and he immediately felt the temperature begin to soar. Soon, some of the men were passing out from the infernal heat. Someone reported that the temperature had climbed to 157 degrees. Highfill "ate lots of salt tablets and drank a lot of water but that did not help much. So I took off all my clothes except my pants, trying to keep cool." He watched as large blisters of paint formed on a nearby bulkhead, obviously caused by the intense heat of a fire in the next compartment.

Fires were raging above and all around Highfill's engine room, and smoke billowed about in great suffocating clouds. Before long, steering control from the bridge was lost, and *Lexington* began yawing back and forth unpredictably, becoming a danger to her escorting destroyers, some of whom were trying to close in to render assistance.

On the bridge, Captain Frederick Sherman was informed that only one sound-powered phone line to main control was still working, and it was growing weak. He knew once that last line of communication was lost, he would have no way of telling the men in the engineering spaces to leave. He also knew that without being told to abandon their stations, those men would stay there, hemmed in by red-hot bulkheads, until they perished.

He ordered the boilers and turbines shut down and the men out of the engineering spaces. The Sailor manning the sound-powered phone on the bridge relayed the captain's order but received no acknowledgment. For several tense seconds, Sherman feared the worst, but then a great hissing roar signaled that the boiler's safety valves had been lifted, and he knew that his order had been received.

Vernon Highfill heard the word passed to leave the engine room, but he soon realized that his intended escape route was blocked. Then he remembered the narrow space that ran between the main tube and the outside skin of the stack. Through choking smoke, Highfill made his way to that space and squeezed in. Climbing upward as quickly as he could, he soon emerged into the open air at the top of the stack. Climbing down from the stack, he "saw a hole in the flight deck big enough to put a house in." Exhausted, he dropped to the deck and marveled at being alive.

But it was now apparent that Lady Lex would *not* live. With the ship dead in the water and fires raging out of control, Captain Sherman reluctantly gave the order that no captain ever wants to give: "Abandon ship."

To the inexperienced and the uninformed, the act of abandoning ship probably conjures up visions of men simply jumping over the side or climbing down lines to lifeboats. But that would be simply "every man for himself." To be sure, when ships are in their death throes and panic is lurking close at hand, there are those who do just that. But on *Lexington* at this dark moment, a higher calling prevailed for many of her crew. Because the gen-

Sailors from USS *Lexington* abandon ship during the Battle of the Coral Sea during World War II. *U.S. Naval Institute Photo Archive*

eral announcing system was no longer functioning, many Sailors had not gotten the word to leave the ship. Still manning their stations, they were in grave danger of being left behind. Others were injured or overcome by heat and smoke. In the "shipmate" tradition that is as old as seafaring itself, *Lexington* Sailors returned to the hell raging inside the ship to find buddies and strangers. At great risk to themselves, those who were able-bodied carried their injured shipmates through dark, debris-laden, smoke-filled passageways. As they got the wounded to relative safety, many again went back into the chaos below to find others who might be trapped and lead them to safety as well. A young mess steward made repeated trips despite the second-degree burns he suffered each time he went back. One Sailor saw the executive officer, Commander Seligman, "continually being blown through doors and out of scuttles like a cork out of a champagne bottle" as he kept hunting for men still lost below. In the radio shack, would-be rescuers burst in, ready to assist those in need, only to find a young radioman busily cleaning the dust off the now-dormant radio sets.

Knotted lines, cargo nets, and bedsheets tied together were suspended from the flight and hangar decks, and men were streaming down them in good order. Others jumped or dove as though they were back at their hometown swimming holes.

In a few hours, Fireman Highfill, Commander Seligman, the dusting radioman, and hundreds of other men were crowded onto escort ships, watching the final moments of their ship. In the gathering darkness, the burning ship lit the sea and sky. Exploding ammunition and aircraft fuel tanks periodically flared like some great fireworks display.

Admiral Frank Fletcher, the officer in tactical command, worried that *Lexington* would serve as a beacon to aid the enemy in locating his fleet, so he made the painful decision to send her to the bottom as quickly as possible. He ordered one of the destroyers to torpedo her and then ordered the task force to depart the area.

Lady Lex did not give up easily as multiple torpedoes bit into her sides, but eventually she settled quietly into the sea just as the evening watch was being set on the surviving ships. The great fires winked out until all was dark as nature intended. Then there was a final explosion that was felt on the departing ships miles away, and *Lexington* plunged to the bottom of the Coral Sea.

In writing his official report, Captain Sherman recorded that 216 men of a total complement of 2,951 had been lost with the ship. He added that both the ship and the crew had "performed gloriously." He also noted that *Lexington*'s demise was "more fitting than the usual fate of the eventual scrap heap or succumbing to the perils of the sea."

The Battle of the Coral Sea was over. As the Japanese and American forces withdrew from these waters, the fighting had temporarily ended, but the reckoning had just begun. Each side had scored victories; both had suffered losses. For those who had perished, the war was over, but for those whose task it remained to fight on, there was a long road of struggle and sacrifice ahead. One of the tasks of the living was to determine the significance of this first major battle and to decide how to take best advantage of it. As events would prove, it would be the U.S. Navy who would do the better job.

The Vocabulary of War

Like most specialized subjects, warfare has a vocabulary of its own. The word *logistics,* for example, describes an element of warfare that is often overlooked by the casual observer but absolutely essential to the achievement of victory. Logistics is supplying forces with the crucial things they need to fight effectively—food, fuel, clothing, ammunition, repair parts, and so forth. Another term, *metrics,* has more recently entered the vocabulary of war and describes those elements—numbers of casualties and rounds expended, for example—by which effectiveness is measured. But among those specialized words, *strategy* and *tactics*—terms often used to describe the planning, the classifying, and the differentiating of various actions and their significance in war—are among the most frequently used, yet their meanings are often not fully understood by those who use them. For example, the Battle of the Coral Sea in World War II is often described as a *strategic* victory for the U.S. Navy and a *tactical* victory for the Japanese. But what does that mean?

Although these terms are similar and overlap in their meanings, there are notable differences, nevertheless, that are valuable when plans for wars and battles are made and those engagements are assessed in their aftermath.

Both strategy and tactics deal with using available military forces to accomplish objectives—that is, what it is that you want to achieve by the use of force. An overly simple but helpful way of describing the two terms is to think of strategy as pertaining to the *war* as a whole and tactics to the *battles* that are part of the war. Another simplification is that strategy can be thought of as *the plan* and tactics are the ways that plan *is executed.* Neither of these descriptions is completely accurate, however, and both fail to account for the variations and the overlaps sometimes encountered in the usage of these two words. For example, the planning for a major battle may be described as strategic, rather than tactical.

Much of the difference between the two depends upon size and scale. Strategy often involves larger components (such as fleets) and usually is more long-term in duration (years, months, weeks). Tactics are smaller in scale (involving individual ships, for example) and shorter in duration (days, hours, minutes). Strategy can be employed in both war and peace, but tactics are generally linked to combat operations. Strategy is usually carried out by military commanders of high rank, while tactics can be employed by virtually anyone in contact with an enemy, from admirals to petty officers.

In the case of the Battle of the Coral Sea, the Pacific Fleet commander, Admiral Nimitz, made the decision to send his available carriers to Australian waters to prevent the Japanese from invading Port Moresby on the southeastern side of New Guinea, knowing that the Allies' loss of Port Moresby would give the Japanese a favorable geographic advantage and put Australia in serious jeopardy.

That was a *strategic* decision made by a high-ranking officer involving large forces—two carriers and their escorts, a large percentage of all forces then available in the Pacific Theater—over a relatively long period of time (in the vast reaches of the Pacific it can take weeks to reposition forces). Once Admiral Nimitz had planned his strategy, he then turned operational command over to his subordinate commanders to devise the tactics that would accomplish the objective of preventing the Japanese from taking Port Moresby.

During the actual battle on 8 May, the Japanese took advantage of the weather by hiding under the available clouds so that U.S. pilots would have difficulty spotting them, and *Zuikaku* was able to avoid damage by hiding in a passing rainsquall. Because the weather was clear around the U.S. carriers, the Japanese dive-bombers were able to dive on the carriers with the sun behind them, making it difficult for the American Sailors manning the antiaircraft guns to see them. These actions were *tactical* in nature, some made by captains (the commanding officers of the carriers) and some made by lieutenants (the dive-bomber pilots).

When Japanese torpedo bombers came skimming in at low altitude, *Lexington*'s captain ordered a starboard turn to minimize the target profile of his ship. To thwart that maneuver, the Japanese pilots came in on both bows, so that if their target changed course in either direction, she would present a broadside aspect to their torpedoes, increasing the likelihood of a hit. These were decisions made in the heat of battle that were designed to give a tactical advantage.

Coupled with courage and skill, the tactics employed during the battle by the ship captains, pilots, gunners, and others had much to do with the survival or the loss of the individual units. When the smoke had cleared and the fleet commanders had withdrawn their forces, the score in a purely tactical sense seemed to favor the Japanese. They had lost only a light air-craft carrier compared to the U.S. loss of a full-sized attack carrier, as well as a destroyer and an oiler.

But in the greater strategic sense, the Americans actually fared better than the Japanese. The elation evident in the flight commander's report, "Scratch one flattop!" when U.S. pilots were able to sink the light carrier *Shoho* was appropriate not only in the heat of the moment, but also because the loss of the air support that *Shoho* was tasked with supplying to the invading forces caused the Japanese commander to turn his task force around, abandoning the attack on the Port Moresby. Because taking Port Moresby was a major objective of the Japanese—the primary reason for the Battle of the Coral Sea—the loss of *Shoho* was a victory of *strategic* importance for the Americans. Going back to the earlier simplistic definitions of strategy and tactics, the *battle* had gone in favor of the Japanese, but the effect on the *war* had favored the Americans. Viewed this way, the assessment that the battle had been a *tactical* victory for the Japanese navy and a *strategic* victory for the U.S. Navy is a reasonable assessment.

There was another strategic consideration as well. Because the carriers *Zuikaku* and *Shokaku* were temporarily put out of action at Coral Sea, they were not available for the next major battle at Midway. The number of carriers that faced off in that critical battle was three for the Americans and four for the Japanese, a much better matchup for the Americans than the three-to-six ratio it might have been. Because Midway proved to be a pivotal battle in the war, the Japanese suffered a defeat from which they never fully recovered. Thus, the relatively minor damage inflicted on *Zuikaku* and *Shokaku* had important strategic effects on the outcome of the war.

Strategy versus Tactics

At the Battle of Valcour Island during the American Revolution, the Americans employed good tactics to offset some of the advantages enjoyed by the British as they carried out their strategy of trying to split the colonies along the Hudson River corridor in New York. Although the British had a far superior force, the Americans placed their forces in Valcour Bay so they would have the upwind advantage. This caused the British ships sailing southward along Lake Champlain to have to come about and attack into the wind—no easy task for vessels powered by sails, especially those that were square-rigged. This was an excellent example of tactical positioning on the part of the Americans; it was enhanced by the crescent formation they used, which allowed them to concentrate their fire. They also cut spruce trees and rigged them along the sides of their vessels to make them blend in with the surrounding tree-lined shores and to provide some protection against small arms fire when the British got in close.

Despite these tactical enhancements, the American force was ultimately no match for the superior British fleet and the victory went to the latter. But just as at Coral Sea, the tactical victory for one side proved to be a strategic victory for the other.

The British strategy had been to come down the lake to the Hudson River and then proceed southward to New York, effectively cutting off New England from the rest of the colonies. But the presence of the American naval force at the southern end of Lake Champlain had forced the British commander to delay his advance. By the time the battle was over, winter had arrived, and the British commander decided to hold off any further advance until the following spring. This bought valuable time for the Americans and allowed them to gather the forces necessary to defeat the British at Saratoga the following year, which not only thwarted Britain's strategy of dividing the colonies, but also delivered a serious blow to British morale and convinced the French to enter the war as an American ally. While it would be several years before the full effects could be realized, that victory ultimately led to American independence. Clearly a strategic victory was realized despite a tactical defeat.

Strategy and tactics also had unexpected results in Vietnam in 1968. American forces were caught off guard in the early hours of the Tet Offensive, as Communist insurgents—the so-called Vietcong—rose up in many places all over South Vietnam during the celebration of the Vietnamese New Year and, in coordination with North Vietnamese forces, scored a number of tactical victories. They inflicted heavy casualties on American forces, managed to get several insurgents inside the walls of the American embassy compound, and seized the ancient and symbolic city of Hue.

American and South Vietnamese forces soon turned around these early tactical victories, however. The insurgents in the American embassy compound were killed before they could get into the embassy itself. Marines took back Hue City after a bloody siege. American naval forces operating on the rivers in the "brown-water" navy were credited with saving the strategically vital Mekong Delta in a series of battles along the twisting waterways. Army forces decimated the Vietcong, dealing them a defeat from which they would never recover; from that time forward, all serious opposition came from the North Vietnamese regulars coming into South Vietnam from strategic sanctuaries. Ultimately, it was clearly an overwhelming tactical victory for U.S. and South Vietnamese forces that, once they recovered from the initial surprise, fought courageously and effectively.

Further, Communist strategy had counted on a simultaneous uprising of the people of South Vietnam once the insurgent attacks had begun. This did not materialize. All things considered, it would seem that the American and the South Vietnamese forces had won both a strategic and a tactical victory in the aftermath of the Tet Offensive.

But this did not prove to be the case. The initial shock of the Communist attacks had so stunned the American people that what was actually a major victory was seen by many as a defeat. In the first days of the Tet Offensive, American media reported it as a major setback, which in many ways it had been. But in the weeks that followed, the resounding tactical victory for the Americans and their South Vietnamese allies was largely overlooked as the American media, the Congress, and the military leadership struggled to reassess the U.S. commitment in Southeast Asia. It was a classic case of perception overruling reality. With the American will shaken at home, a series of events over the next several years ultimately caused American military forces to come home from a war in which they had never lost a major battle, yet never achieved their overall strategic objective: the survival of South Vietnam as a democratic nation. Victory would be denied them because the Communist strategy of outwaiting their adversaries had prevailed.

While these examples demonstrate differences between strategy and tactics, they should not give the impression that the two are always at odds. Quite the opposite. In more cases than not, good tactics reinforce good strategy, so that important battles won ultimately lead to victory in war.

The Spanish-American War at the end of the nineteenth century illustrates the effects of good and bad strategy and tactics. In the events leading up to the war and in two major sea battles, strategic and tactical applications directly affected the outcome of the war as a whole.

Showing the Flag

For years, tensions had been building between the United States and Spain, mostly over the Spanish-owned island of Cuba, just a few miles off the coast of Florida. Cuban revolutionaries had long been trying to overthrow their Spanish overlords, and various U.S. interests were at stake. As the struggle between the two sides raged on, American plantations there had been taken, an American schooner was seized as a gunrunner, two American tourists were shot as spies, and various other incidents kept tensions high.

In January 1898, USS *Maine* was dispatched to Cuba to send a message of American determination to the Spanish government and to protect American citizens then in Havana. The strategy of sending a warship to an area in crisis is often called "forward presence" or "showing the flag," and the battleship *Maine* was in many ways an ideal way to accomplish this. She was an imposing sight for her day. Her hull, boats, and anchors were a gleaming white, her superstructure, masts, and smokestacks a reddish brown, and her guns and searchlights a foreboding black. From her varnished mahogany pilothouse, her officers could send orders to the coal-fired boiler rooms via specially designed telegraphs. Two 10-inch guns were mounted in a turret forward that was offset to starboard, and two more 10-inch guns were mounted in an after turret, offset to port. With this arrangement, the guns could fire through an unobstructed arc of 180 degrees on their respective sides and through an additional arc of 64 degrees on the opposite sides. This main battery was supplemented by an array of more than twenty smaller guns of various calibers and functions and by four torpedo tubes.

Apprentice First Class Ambrose Ham was signal boy of the watch when *Maine* made landfall on 25 January 1898. He had originally been assigned as a crew member in the captain's gig, but another young Sailor had convinced

Battleship USS *Maine* was sent to Cuba in 1898 to send a message of American determination to the Spanish government and to protect American citizens in Havana. *U.S. Naval Institute Photo Archive*

him to trade assignments. After getting approval from his division officer, Lieutenant Jungen, Ham made the switch, a choice that would later save his life.

Tensions were high in *Maine* as she slowly steamed into Havana harbor, close aboard Morro Castle perched upon a high rock on the port side of the channel. Ordinary Seaman Frank Andrews wrote in a letter to his father: "As we steamed in under the guns of Morro we calculated how long it would take us to silence it. Our turret-gun crews were standing out of sight, of course, while the rest of the crew was around the deck. At the first shot from the Spanish they would have found their places."

Ambrose Ham remembered that "as we entered the harbor everything looked peaceful." But he heard another Sailor tell two friends, "We'll never get out of here alive."

Arriving at mooring buoy number four, about four hundred yards from a wharf near the city's customhouse, the ship's anchor chain was detached from the anchor, passed through a ring on the buoy, and then brought back aboard the battleship and secured. Colors were shifted and *Maine*'s crew settled in for a long stay.

Because of the high state of tension, the crew was not allowed to go ashore. Instead of the normal in-port watch, Captain Charles Dwight Sigsbee had ordered a quarter watch at night, so that a fourth of the crew was immediately available to man the guns should the need arise. Armed sentries manned the forecastle and poop deck during the hours of darkness, and the ship's gangways were guarded as well.

Ham noted that "time was beginning to drag." He longed to go back to his home in Schenectady, New York, and spent much of the time thinking about that. There was not much in the way of entertainment, and every evening at sundown he watched the Spanish sailors on nearby ships "run up the masts and chase the devils out of the gear blocks. Some years ago a Spanish sailing ship got into a gale and when they tried to take in sail the blocks would not work. The ship capsized."

For more than two weeks, the 358-man crew of USS *Maine* went about their routines, aware of their part in a tense international situation, yet unable to do anything other than show their flag and be ready for hostilities should they erupt. On the morning of 15 February, Ham was roused from a deep sleep at 0530 by the gravelly voice of a boatswain's mate announcing reveille. Ham rolled out of his hammock and began tricing it up, unaware that this was the day when the mind-numbing routine would finally end.

After a quick trip to the galley to get a cup of coffee, he joined his shipmates swabbing down the deck with fresh water from a lighter that had come alongside. The ship's medical officer had banned the use of the harbor's water because of the foul smell it gave off. Breakfast at 0730 was followed by the 0800–1200 watch as signal boy on the poop deck. Normally, Ham's primary duty was to be available for wig-wag (semaphore) communications with other naval vessels, but because no other U.S. warships were in the harbor, there was no one to communicate with. Instead, he had been directed to keep a sharp lookout for any suspicious activity in the vicinity of the ship. There was none; at noon another apprentice relieved him, and Ham went down to eat dinner.

Ham spent the afternoon polishing brightwork and repairing torn signal flags. At 1730, the bugle sounded for supper, and half an hour later he was sweeping down the decks. He then watched several Sailors dance while one of their shipmates played the accordion. When the bugler sounded the call for hammocks, Ham went below and slung his so that it would be ready when he got off watch at midnight. He returned to the poop deck for the evening watch and began his vigil once again, this time staring into the gathering darkness.

Time crawled by. At 2110, the bugler sounded taps, and the decks emptied as Sailors headed to their hammocks in the stifling compartments below. A friend remained to talk to Ham for a few minutes but, afraid of being caught on deck after taps, he soon went below. The harbor was smooth as glass. Several boats passed by a few hundred yards away, but otherwise all was quiet and still. Like countless Sailors before him and since, Ham noted that night watches were a time of quiet reflection, when homesickness reared its unwanted head, when the unoccupied mind went to places better left alone.

Just a little after 2130, Ham engaged Landsman Thomas J. Waters of Philadelphia in conversation as a way of getting his mind off the creeping pace of time. Shrouded in the protective cloak of darkness, the two men spoke of things they might not have in the glare of daylight: family left behind and hopeful plans for the future. The talk had dwindled, and Ham was about to turn away and head aft, when a great flame shot up, engulfing the forward part of the ship. He heard what sounded like a shot, then a great roar followed, and a flying piece of debris struck him in the face, knocking him senseless.

In that instant, many of Ham's shipmates had perished, including Ordinary Seaman Frank Andrews. A huge explosion had originated somewhere forward, on the port side, ripping open the ship and curling her main deck back upon itself. Debris rained down into the harbor for hundreds of yards around the stricken vessel.

Once he recovered his senses, Ham headed for his old station as a member of the gig crew. The young apprentice who had switched duty with

Ham was killed in the explosion, so Ham helped a handful of other Sailors lower the gig into the water. He noted with dismay how quickly the boat had reached the water, a clear indication that *Maine* was sinking. He positioned himself in the boat's bow and began helping to pull men from the harbor as the gig moved slowly through the water. After a time, the gig returned to the ship to rescue those stranded on her gradually disappearing poop deck. Parts of the ship were on fire, and Ham worried that the flames might reach one of the magazines and cause another deadly explosion.

As they pulled up alongside, they found, among others, Captain Sigsbee. "I won't leave," Sigsbee said, "until I'm sure everybody is off." The after portion of the poop deck, *Maine*'s highest remaining deck, was now at the same level as the gig's gunwale. As a Sailor handed the captain's dog, Peggy, to one of the men in the gig, Ham heard Lieutenant Commander Richard Wainwright, the ship's executive officer, whisper to Captain Sigsbee that the raging fire was very close to the forward magazine and that it might blow at any moment. Ham felt the nearly overwhelming urge to shout, "Let's get out of here," but he sat quietly in the bow holding tightly to the bowline that tethered the small boat to the sinking, burning ship.

At last, everyone from the poop deck was in the gig. Sigsbee, convinced that no one else remained on board, stepped into the boat and ordered the crew to shove off. Ham gratefully took in the bowline, aware that his hands ached from the tight grip he had used to hold it during those tense moments. Oars struck the water and the gig moved across the harbor toward a nearby American merchant vessel as *Maine* continued to burn furiously while she slowly disappeared into Havana's harbor.

The cause of the explosion has been debated to this day. One theory accuses the Spanish of using a mine to destroy the battleship. Another attributes the tragedy to a fire in a coal bunker that ignited a nearby magazine. Yet another theory lays the blame on the Cuban revolutionaries, explaining that, by making it appear as an act of Spanish aggression, the explosion would urge the United States into war with Spain and thereby ensure Cuba's freedom.

Along with divers who had inspected the sunken hulk of the American battleship, Ambrose Ham and the other survivors testified before a board of inquiry. The divers reported that some of the ship's hull plates had been bent inward, and the board concluded that this "could have been produced only by a mine situated under the bottom of the ship." An aroused nation clamored for war against Spain, and on 25 April Congress declared that a state of war had existed since the twenty-first.

One of the many missions of the Navy is to "show the flag"—that is, remind other nations of U.S. power through the presence of one or more American warships. This can be a relatively easy mission with minimal risks, or it can be one with very high stakes. Commodore Matthew Perry's peaceful opening of diplomatic and trade relations with Japan in 1853 stands in sharp contrast to what happened to USS *Cole* at Aden in 2000. In Havana in 1898, a strategic "showing of the flag" at a time of great tension had led to war. USS *Maine* had been the first casualty as she carried out her difficult mission.

For the remainder of the Spanish-American War, however, U.S. warships would be on the offensive, and a blend of effective tactics and simple courage would ensure that *Maine*'s sacrifice would be avenged.

You May Fire When Ready

On the other side of the world, another Sailor, Landsman John T. Tisdale, stood at ease aboard the cruiser USS *Olympia,* flagship of the Asiatic Squadron, listening intently as an officer read a dispatch from the Navy Department. "Proceed at once to Manila; engage and destroy the Spanish fleet, when and where you find them," the lieutenant read. Tisdale and his shipmates "went mad with joy." Several times they shouted "Remember the *Maine*" as they celebrated.

When dismissed, many of those not on watch gathered together and began work on a battle flag. They discovered that among the crew of the flagship there was a representative from each of the forty-five states of the union, so one man from each state wrote his name and that of his home state on the back of a star and it was then added to the blue field of the flag. Tisdale wrote "California" on his. Before taps, the flag was finished and there was much self-congratulation among all who had contributed.

The American strategy to eliminate the Spanish naval presence in the Far East was indicated in the dispatch from the Navy Department; it had come about largely because of the writings of Captain Alfred T. Mahan, who some years earlier had penned what would become a classic work on naval warfare, *The Influence of Sea Power upon History.* Among the many principles that Mahan described were: "passive defenses belong to the army," whereas navies must be used as a means of "offensive defense"; coastal defenses were for weak nations who could do no better; and "the enemy must be kept not only out of our ports, but far away from our coasts." Far away was no exaggeration in this case. Commodore George Dewey's Asiatic Squadron was more than seven thousand miles from the nearest American support base as his ships steamed from China toward the Philippine Islands to engage the Spanish fleet based there.

The American squadron tasked with carrying out this strategy consisted of the cruisers *Baltimore, Boston, Raleigh,* and *Olympia,* the gunboats *Concord* and *Petrel,* the revenue cutter *Hugh McCulloch,* and the coal transports ("colliers") *Nanshan* and *Zafiro.* The squadron was manned by nearly fifteen hundred men, displaced more than nineteen thousand tons, and carried more than one hundred guns that could fire a total broadside of thirty-seven hundred pounds. The cruisers, launched as a result of a shipbuilding program begun some ten years earlier, represented the main firepower. With their tall masts and crossed yards ready to take on sail should the need arise, and their large smoke stacks billowing black clouds of coal-fired smoke, they were monuments to a dying age and pioneers of the next.

The next morning the order to "clear for action" was passed. Barricades of canvas and iron were built up around the gun crews' stations, and heavy chains were rigged over awnings to provide additional protection to the ships' ammunition hoists. Although these ships were built primarily of steel, veterans of the then-recent Sino-Japanese War had told of terrible casualties resulting from flying wood splinters, so Dewey made the tactical decision to have hatch covers, spars, chests, and other removable wood items either safely stowed or jettisoned. Overzealous cooks even threw some of *Olympia*'s mess tables over the side before they were stopped. A lieutenant in *Baltimore* noted that a trail of wood "was strewn for fifty leagues [150 miles]" in the ships' wakes.

In *Olympia* the word was passed that the Sailor's wooden ditty boxes would have to be jettisoned as well. As evidenced by their celebrations the day before, Tisdale and his shipmates were eager to fight the Spanish and were even willing to sacrifice their lives if necessary. But giving up their ditty boxes seemed too much to ask. Here on this disciplined warship on the far side of the world, the ditty box was the one thing a Sailor could call his own, where he kept tokens of his former life, where he had some small ties to home. To the crew's everlasting gratitude, Commodore Dewey came to the rescue, urging *Olympia*'s commanding officer, Captain Charles Gridley, to allow the men to stow their boxes below the cruiser's protected deck rather than toss them into the South China Sea.

Tisdale soon learned that wood was not the only thing that had to go. As the squadron drew closer to the Philippines, the ships' barbers got busy shaving each Sailor's hair down close to the scalp because the surgeons warned that "hair is as dangerous as cloth in a wound."

That evening, *Olympia*'s band assembled and played a series of rousing pieces, including several Sousa marches and "Yankee Doodle." Tisdale enjoyed the concert, but he and his shipmates were most enthusiastic when the band struck up a popular song of the day, "There'll Be a Hot Time in the

Old Town Tonight!" That odd sensation of nervous excitement that often prevails as battle draws near had taken hold of many Sailors of the Asiatic Squadron, and they swayed rhythmically and slapped each other's backs as they sang along. Indeed, a "hot time" in the "old town" of Manila was just a few days away as the U.S. ships steamed onward, ever closer to the Philippine Islands and to a page in the history books.

In the meantime, Admiral Patricio Montojo y Pasaron prepared his fleet for battle with the approaching American squadron. When word of the outbreak of war had come, the Spanish admiral had moved his fleet out of Manila to the more remote Subic Bay some thirty miles to the north. Upon his arrival, however, Montojo discovered that defensive preparations there were hopelessly behind schedule. Noting that the water at Subic was more than forty meters deep, Montojo concluded that his crews would have a better chance of survival if sunk in the much shallower waters of Manila Bay. This combination of tactics and pessimism caused him to return to Manila Bay to make his stand there.

Dewey had been concerned about the possibility of Montojo moving to Subic. "With this strategic point effectively occupied," he later wrote, "no hostile commander-in-chief would think of passing it and leaving it as a menace to his lines of communication." So he was relieved to find Subic Bay empty when his squadron arrived on 30 April. Calling a council of war on board *Olympia,* Commodore Dewey told his commanders, "We shall enter Manila Bay tonight and you will follow the motions of the flagship, which will lead."

That night, the Asiatic Squadron approached the *Boca Grande*—"Big Mouth"—of Manila Bay. The Moon was low in the sky and mostly masked by towers of clouds built up by the tropical heat of the day. Flickers of lightning that danced among the clouds occasionally broke the darkness, and light showers doused the white duck uniforms of those on deck. Guns were loaded but breechblocks were left open to prevent accidental premature firing. As had always preceded battle in the days of sail, the decks were covered with sand to provide traction should blood and sweat make them slick.

Sure that guns mounted among the high rocks on either side guarded the entrance to the bay and that mines had been placed in locations unknown, tension among the crews of the U.S. ships ran high. Apprentice Seaman Wayne Longnecher felt this was "the hardest part of the fight . . . running the gauntlet of both mines and forts, not knowing which moment a mine or torpedo would send you through the deck above." He sardonically reflected on the fact that he was doing this for sixteen dollars a month.

The scene was reminiscent of an earlier time, when Dewey's Civil War hero, David Glasgow Farragut, had run past the guns of Confederate forts at

New Orleans and again at Mobile Bay, uttering his famous words, "Damn the torpedoes, full speed ahead." But those guns were firing furiously and, so far, these were silent.

Olympia passed unharmed into the bay, as did several of the other ships following in column behind, steering by the single dim light that had been mounted on each ship's stern. It seemed as though they might all pass unchallenged, but near the end of the column, accumulated soot in *McCulloch*'s smokestack ignited, and a bright column of flame erupted skyward, giving the Spanish gunners an unmistakable target. A battery from the nearby headland opened fire, and an artillery round passed over *McCulloch* and hit the water on her far side. She immediately returned fire with her 6-pounder, and *Boston, Raleigh,* and *Concord* opened up with their larger batteries. The deep rumble of gunfire rolled across the bay and the garish flashes briefly lit up the dark waters. But the exchange was short-lived. The Spanish battery fired only three more shots before a round from *Boston* silenced it. And the Asiatic Squadron proceeded on into Manila Bay without further molestation.

Once past the Spanish guns guarding the entrance, the American ships slowed to four knots. The bay was twenty-five miles across, and Dewey decided it made good tactical sense to make a slow transit so that it would be daylight when he engaged the enemy. His squadron had a finite amount of ammunition and no means of rapid resupply, so he could not afford to waste many shots firing blindly into the dark. With no enemy in sight and the great expanse of the bay before them, the word was passed for the men to remain on station but to stand easy. Tisdale, Longnecher, and the others tried to lie down on the deck to catch a little sleep, but the excitement of the moment and the gritty sand on the decks made that a difficult proposition.

Montojo had likewise made some tactical decisions. Knowing that the U.S. ships were more maneuverable than his, he chose to fight from an anchored position where he could control and consolidate his firepower. Not wanting to subject the city of Manila to the ravages of the battle, he had positioned his fleet at Cavite, an arsenal some five miles to the south of the city. While achieving his aim of sparing the city, this decision greatly reduced his available firepower, because there were just 34 land-based guns in the Cavite area compared with 226 guns of various types at Manila.

To prevent his ships from being vulnerable to torpedoes, Montojo had constructed a protective boom in front of his anchored ships, consisting of lighters filled with stones and water and held together in a continuous line by heavy chains. Unlike his American counterpart, Montojo had *not* ordered the wood stripped from his ships.

At 0400, a cold breakfast augmented by hot coffee was served to the American crews still at their battle stations. As they ate, a young Sailor in *Olympia* began to sing a somber rendition of "Just Before the Battle, Mother." One of his shipmates poured coffee on him, cutting the concert short.

Increasing speed to eight knots, the U.S. squadron approached Manila as the sun lightened the sky behind the city. Before long it was evident that only sail-driven merchant ships were moored at the city. No warships. Dewey turned his column southward and, as the ships paraded past the Manila waterfront, a few of the Spanish gun batteries opened fire on the squadron. One 9.4-inch shell passed uncomfortably close between the cruisers *Raleigh* and *Baltimore,* but none of the Spanish shots found their marks.

A sharp-eyed *Olympia* lookout peering southward through binoculars discerned through the morning mist a row of masts topped with bright red and yellow flags. His report was what Dewey had been waiting to hear. Here was the Spanish fleet, the object of his strategy.

"Monday morning quarterbacks" later pointed out that Dewey gave away a significant tactical advantage by moving his squadron in close to the Spanish fleet. His largest caliber guns had a greater range than any of the opponent's and, by remaining outside his enemy's reach, he could have fired upon the Spanish ships without any risk to his own. But Dewey felt that "in view of my limited ammunition supply, it was my plan not to open fire until we were within effective range, and then to fire as rapidly as possible with *all* of our guns."

The Asiatic Squadron moved in ever closer to their adversary. Even when the Spanish opened fire, Dewey withheld the order to commence firing. Like so many others, Landsman Tisdale found the tension of waiting, under fire, excruciating. "Our hearts threatened to burst from desire to respond. I sat upon the gun-seat repeating to the rhythm of the engine's throb, 'Hold your fire . . . hold your fire . . . hold your fire until the bugle sounds,' while my fingers grew numb upon the spark."

Tisdale, waiting at his station in *Olympia*'s after turret, was certainly justified in his anxiety, but there were even more difficult jobs to be accomplished under the circumstances. Because the ships were moving in so close to shore and in danger of running aground, a leadsman was required to stand at the ship's rail, far forward on the open deck, casting his line down into the water to measure the depth. This Sailor had to cast his line, let it hit bottom, retrieve it, and report both the depth and the type of bottom—while enemy shells roared through the air and crashed into the nearby water, lifting great geysers of water skyward!

When at last the U.S. ships had closed to within five thousand yards, Commodore Dewey calmly uttered the words to *Olympia*'s captain that would be remembered for all time: "You may fire when you are ready, Gridley."

According to *Olympia*'s official log, she commenced firing at 0535. Two-hundred-and-fifty-pound shells erupted from her forward battery and the cruiser shuddered from the eruption. Still in column, only *Olympia*'s forward guns were "unmasked" to allow firing at the enemy, and Tisdale still "chafed for the opportunity to fight back." Dewey's tactics soon remedied the problem. The commodore turned the column to starboard until it was steaming nearly parallel to the Spanish line of ships. Now Tisdale's after turret could be brought to bear on the enemy, as could every American gun that could be trained to port.

The American gunners did not hold back. Long before the phrase "shock and awe" would enter the American lexicon of war, the Asiatic Squadron let loose with all its fury, firing every available gun as quickly as possible to deluge the Spanish fleet with exploding shellfire. On his flagship *Reina Cristina,* Admiral Montojo watched as "the Americans fired most rapidly. There came upon us numberless projectiles."

Olympia led the way as the U.S. ships ran along the Spanish line, firing relentlessly as they passed. When they were beyond the enemy line, they executed a tactical "corpen" of 180 degrees, turning in column to preserve the order of ships for another run in the opposite direction. The guns were shifted to starboard for this run, and again a withering fire was brought to bear on the enemy. The Spanish fought back, even as their ships began to burn and splinter apart. They sortied several torpedo boat attacks, but these were driven back by the Americans' smaller guns; even the embarked Marines participated, firing their rifles at the charging boats.

The battle raged on for several passes. These tactical maneuvers ensured that the maximum force of the American guns was brought to bear on the stationary Spanish ships. By keeping his ships immobile, Montojo had traded maneuverability for stability and control. As the battle took shape it became evident that this decision also had made them easily identifiable targets. At last Montojo decided to go on the offensive. Whether he saw it as a tactical venture, designed to gain some military advantage, or as merely an act of defiance for honor's sake is not clear, but he ordered his flagship to get under way and to charge headlong at his tormentors. Apprentice Seaman Longnecher, peering out from his gun port in *Olympia,* could see the Spanish ship coming. "As the *Reina Cristina* came out from the yard to meet us, she planted a shell into the side right at my gun port. But it was spent and did not come all the way through before it burst." John Tisdale was impressed by the Spanish tenacity. He witnessed one of his af-

U.S. cruisers attack Spanish ships in Manila Bay in the first big battle of the Spanish-American War. *U.S. Naval Institute Photo Archive*

ter turret's 8-inch shells rip "through and through" the charging Spanish ship, yet "like an enraged panther she came at us as though to lash sides and fight us hand to hand with battle axes, as in the olden Spanish wars."

But the charge was in vain. On fire and badly mauled, *Reina Cristina* was forced to come about and limp back to her mooring. She was so badly damaged that Montojo soon ordered her abandoned. As she sank, he shifted his flag to another ship. *Reina Cristina*'s losses were catastrophic: 150 were killed and another 90 wounded. Five years later, she would be raised from the mud of Manila Bay; the skeletons of 80 men were discovered in her sick bay.

The battle raged on for another half hour, until the smoke became so thick that it was impossible to see what was happening. It was then that Dewey received a most unsettling report. Word came from Captain Gridley that *Olympia* had just fifteen rounds of her heavy-caliber munitions remaining—a mere five minutes' worth of fighting. With the battle undecided as far as he could tell, and in light of this alarming report, Dewey ordered the Asiatic Squadron to withdraw, much to the mixed relief and consternation of the crews. They could not help but be glad for the rest, yet they were "fired up for victory," as one lieutenant observed.

Moving out of range, Dewey called his captains to *Olympia* for a meeting. He ordered a hot meal for the crews while these officers conferred. Word spread that Dewey had stopped the fight expressly for the purpose of having breakfast. Not a few of the men expressed their dismay and disapproval for that decision. One gunner was heard to say: "For God's sake, Captain, don't let us stop now. To hell with breakfast!"

While the many ate and passed scuttlebutt, the few conferred. Dewey soon learned that the report on low ammunition was in error. He also learned that there had been just six Americans wounded, all in *Baltimore,* and none killed in action.

The smoke eventually cleared substantially, and at 1116 the U.S. squadron headed back in to finish the fight with the enemy. They resumed the bombardment, and in less than an hour all of the Spanish ships were destroyed or put out of action. A white flag appeared over the naval station at Cavite, and the Battle of Manila Bay was over.

From *Olympia*'s main deck that night, Wayne Longnecher watched the remnants of the Spanish fleet burning across the water. "It was a beautiful sight to see; besides about 12 or 13 ships all in flames, small magazines were going up all night." He and his shipmates would never forget that night, nor the day's events that led up to it.

John Tisdale's hitch was up, and soon after the battle, he made his way halfway across the world to return home. He had left California as a young boy, still "wet behind the ears." He came home a Sailor and combat veteran, with tattoos to tell parts of his story and a newfound confidence that comes to those who have faced great challenges and prevailed.

Upon his arrival in America, Tisdale found the country ecstatic over the U.S. Navy's victory at Manila Bay. Everywhere he went, he heard songs with lyrics praising the great triumph. Banners proclaimed Dewey and his men the "saviors of the Republic," and newspaper stories spoke of a "new era of American dominance of the sea."

When the smoke finally cleared, the Spanish fleet had been utterly destroyed, and 381 Spaniards had lost their lives. The Asiatic Squadron had lost not a single man, much less a ship. As in all battles, technology, logistics, and no small amount of courage were major factors in the outcome. But it should be apparent that American tactics were clearly superior to those of the Spanish, and this played no small role in the overwhelmingly favorable outcome of the battle.

Despite this impressive victory, the U.S. strategy for winning the war with Spain was not yet complete. Another Spanish fleet remained in the Atlantic, and until it could be defeated, the war was still undecided.

Santiago

Commodore Dewey's execution of Mahan's "offensive defense" strategy was not going to work in the Atlantic. Since the outbreak of war, there had been a great deal of anxiety among the American public that the Spanish might send their Atlantic fleet under Admiral Pascual Cervera y Topete to attack cities along the East Coast of the United States. Because the U.S. Navy could not be certain of the location of Spanish forces, it could not risk going on the offensive and leaving the East Coast unguarded. There also was a logistical reason that Rear Admiral William T. Sampson, Commander of the Home Squadron, could not take his ships across the ocean in search of Cervera's fleet: his warships could not carry sufficient coal to make the voyage and then to fight a battle without replenishment. The only strategy available to Sampson was to wait for the Spanish to come to him.

Because Cuba was the root cause of the war, it seemed reasonable that Cervera would most likely take his fleet there. It made good strategic sense, therefore, for Sampson to set up his base of operations at Key West, Florida, just eighty nautical miles from Cuba. But to calm the anxieties of the nation, the Navy created the Flying Squadron under Commodore William S. Schley to remain at Hampton Roads, Virginia, in case Cervera did indeed attempt an attack somewhere along the eastern seaboard.

Cervera left Europe on 28 May 1898 with all the Spanish ships that could be spared—four cruisers and two destroyers—and headed for the Caribbean Sea. Sampson's ships had been patrolling the so-called Windward Passage along the northern coast of Cuba in hopes of intercepting the Spanish fleet, but Cervera headed farther south to replenish his coal on the northern coast of South America before heading for Cuba. Successfully eluding the U.S. Navy, Cervera's ships eventually arrived unmolested at Santiago on the southeastern side of Cuba.

With the enemy's position at last fixed, the U.S. Navy could go on the offensive and carry the fight to him. Adhering to another of Mahan's maxims—that of massing forces—every available U.S. ship now converged on the Caribbean. Schley's Flying Squadron was released from its defensive duties to join Sampson's force in the Caribbean, and even USS *Oregon* left her station in the Pacific to make a high-speed run around the treacherous Cape Horn to join the impending battle.

Because Santiago Bay was too small to allow much maneuvering—less than two nautical miles across at its widest point—and because the narrow entrance was well-defended by gun batteries on either side, going in after the Spanish fleet did not make good tactical sense. Instead, the American ships set up a blockade outside the bay, keeping Cervera's force bottled up for more than a month.

At 0930 on Sunday, 3 July 1898, with the crews of the U.S. ships all preparing for personnel inspection, the battleship *Iowa* suddenly fired a gun to get the attention of all ships. From her yardarm flew the signal flags "two-five-zero." No one needed to check the codebook. It was what everyone had been anticipating for weeks: "Enemy coming out."

The Americans were all still clad in their finest white uniforms for the inspection as they dashed to their battle stations. Within minutes, the white duck cloth worn by the stokers in the boiler rooms had been transformed to black as they shoveled coal into the gaping furnaces to build up sufficient steam for the great steel giants to get under way.

The first ship to emerge from Santiago Bay was Cervera's flagship, *Maria Teresa,* leading a column of the other Spanish ships. *Maria Teresa* seemed to be headed straight for the cruiser *Brooklyn,* Schley's flagship. Assuming that the Spanish cruiser was trying to ram, Schley made a tactical decision he would come to regret: he ordered the helm put over to starboard. Cervera did not intend to ram but was attempting to evade instead. By putting his helm over to starboard as well, he caused the two ships to diverge. Schley continued to hold his rudder over so that *Brooklyn* turned through a complete circle, which gave Cervera time to open the distance and make a dash westward along the southern coast of Cuba.

Battleship *Texas* had taken the more aggressive move of turning to port, *toward* the Spanish ships. But the turning *Brooklyn* had crossed right into her path, causing *Texas* to back her engines to avoid a collision. This initial tactical confusion had given the Spanish ships a head start, and for a time it seemed they might escape.

But the U.S. ships were faster once they got up a good head of steam. Soon they had closed to gun range and commenced firing. A running gunfight lasted for several hours.

U.S. and Spanish ships slug it out during the Battle of Santiago Bay in July 1898. *U.S. Naval Institute Photo Archive*

The crews of the U.S. ships were better trained and had their adversaries out-gunned. *Maria Teresa* was the first ship to succumb. Numerous shells struck her, one of which severed her fire mains, making it impossible for her crew to fight the spreading fires and forcing her to flood her magazines to prevent a fatal explosion. Burning and sinking, she struck her colors at 1015.

The other Spanish ships suffered similar fates. The destroyers had been the last to emerge from Santiago Bay and succumbed to the deadly fire of the gunboat *Gloucester* and the cruiser *Indiana* before they could launch their torpedoes as planned. American gunners pounded the other Spanish cruisers into submission, and, one by one, the Spanish put their rudders over to starboard and deliberately ran aground on the Cuban shore to avoid sinking.

Only *Cristóbal Colón* was able to escape the devastating onslaught—for a time. She was the fastest Spanish ship and, spurred on by frequent shots of brandy, her stokers were able to pour on coal fast enough to keep her out of range of her pursuers. But by 1300 the stokers were unquestionably exhausted (and probably drunk), and shells from *Oregon* and *Brooklyn* began to find their marks. *Cristóbal Colón* could not endure the pounding long, and soon her captain struck her colors and she too headed for the nearby shore to ground herself.

The American strategy had paid off. The Spanish threat in the Atlantic had been eliminated and, coupled with some important land actions, the war was over in little more than a month. Spanish casualties at Santiago had been in the hundreds. The U.S. Navy had lost one killed and one wounded. Victory led to the end of Spanish rule in Cuba, the Philippines, and Puerto Rico and set the stage for America's role as a world power in the coming twentieth century.

Tactics Count

As we have seen, strategy has much to do with the outcome of a war. But wars are not won without battles. And battles are not often won without superior tactics. While strategy is in the hands of a relative few—usually admirals and commodores—tactical decisions must be made by many and, therefore, must often be made by Sailors of much lesser rank. John Paul Jones, revered as the father of the U.S. Navy, was a mere lieutenant when he defeated the much superior HMS *Serapis* in his most famous battle. James Elliott Williams was a first class petty officer when he earned the Medal of Honor by defeating an entire regiment of North Vietnamese soldiers with just the two patrol craft under his command.

A Spanish ship in the aftermath of the Battle of Santiago Bay. Spanish casualties were in the hundreds; the U.S. Navy lost one killed and one wounded. *U.S. Naval Institute Photo Archive*

Tactics and courage often go hand in hand. Both Jones and Williams used superior tactics to achieve their victories, but the tactical decisions they made could not have been carried out without a great deal of courage on their part and on the part of the men fighting with them. In one of the great tactical victories of all time, known as the Battle of Samar, U.S. ships caused a powerful Japanese fleet—which included several battleships and a super battleship—to turn back without striking their intended target, the vulnerable amphibious forces on the beaches of Leyte Island. Yet the ships who accomplished this great feat were a handful of destroyers and destroyer escorts with little hope of survival, much less victory—truly a tactical triumph bought with an incredible amount of courage!

In that same 1944 campaign in Leyte Gulf, another battle had taken place the night before, and this one (described in chapter 5) was marked by superb tactics on the part of the Americans. Another Japanese force was approaching the landing area from a different direction, coming up from the south through a narrow passage among the Philippine Islands known as Surigao Strait. This force of battleships, cruisers, and destroyers came under the cover of darkness, a good tactical decision because the force had no air cover. Had they been able to penetrate Leyte Gulf from the south as planned, the Japanese could have inflicted serious damage on the U.S. landing forces arrayed there. But the Americans, commanded by Rear Admiral Jesse Oldendorf, knew the Japanese were coming and had planned their tactics masterfully.

Because the Japanese would be confined to the narrow strait as they approached, they would have to come in a column formation and would have little maneuvering room. Oldendorf capitalized on this by placing the battleships and cruisers at the north end of the strait, out in the more open waters of the gulf, where they had room to maneuver and to form a line blocking the exit from the strait. This employed a naval tactic as old as sea warfare itself, called *crossing the T*. With the Japanese column forming the base of the T, and the American force capping it, the U.S. ships would be showing their sides to the Japanese ships' bows. This meant the Americans could bring all their guns to bear by training them to one side, while the Japanese could fire only their forward mounts straight ahead. Even worse for the Japanese, when the battle commenced, only ships near the head of the column would be in range so that they alone could fire, while all of the U.S. ships could fire broadsides at once.

Taking further advantage of his geographic position, Oldendorf arrayed his destroyers along either side of the northern end of the strait in such a way as to allow them to charge down the sides of the narrow passage, using the darkness and smokescreens as cover, to launch torpedo attacks at the Japanese flanks.

The plan worked beautifully. Warned of the Japanese approach by PT boats that Oldendorf had placed at the south end of the strait, the U.S. forces at the northern end were ready when the Japanese arrived. American destroyers led the attack using just their torpedoes, knowing that muzzle flashes from their guns would reveal their positions to the enemy. These "tin cans" inflicted serious damage on the approaching enemy. Then the lead Japanese ships took another beating as they came within range of the line of battleships and cruisers blocking the northern end of the strait.

To make matters worse, the Japanese commander made a serious tactical blunder when, deciding that retreat was his best option, he used a corpen maneuver instead of a turn. The former required his ships to maintain the order of the column and turn much as a railroad train would—engine first, followed by each car in succession—which meant that each ship would move into range of the U.S. battleships and cruisers who were raining down death and destruction. Had the Japanese commander used a turn instead of a corpen, all of the Japanese ships would have turned simultaneously, reversing the order of the column and exiting much more efficiently and safely.

A Japanese destroyer was the first to be sunk. Then battleship *Fuso* was literally blown in two, each half burning furiously and lighting up the strait

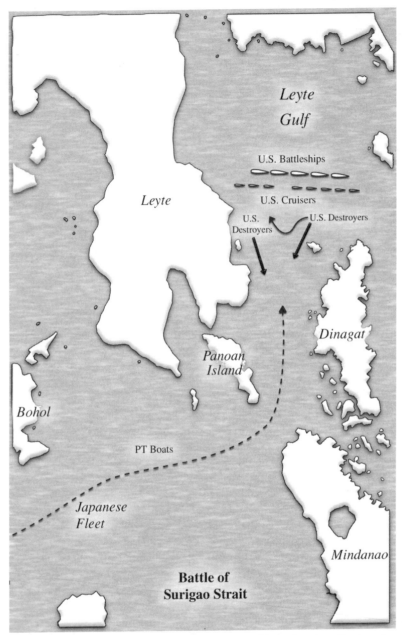

From the northern end of Surigao Strait, U.S. battleships and cruisers fired on the approaching Japanese fleet that was trying to attack the landing forces in Leyte Gulf. American destroyers charged down into the narrow waterway in the dark of night to launch their torpedoes. *U.S. Naval Institute staff*

like beacons in the night. More Japanese ships succumbed as the battle continued, until barely one badly damaged destroyer was able to escape. When dawn illuminated Surigao Strait, the remains of a powerful Japanese naval force littered the waters. It was a temporary monument to a one-sided victory for the U.S. Navy rarely equaled in history.

A Formula for Success

In the Spanish-American War, World War II, and many other times in U.S. naval history, good tactics supporting good strategy were key components in the final outcomes. But from the foregoing examples, it should be evident that there is more to the equation of victory. The war words *strategy* and *tactics* are rightfully associated with the human brain. But three other words are every bit as essential to victory in war, and they are more appropriately associated with the heart and the soul of the American Sailor—honor, courage, and commitment. These attributes—maintained as guiding principles at all times, whether the nation is at peace or at war, and coupled with the right strategy and tactics when hostilities become necessary—have resulted in a long record of achievement that has not only earned the U.S. Navy an enviable reputation, but also has played an indispensable role in preserving the freedom of this great nation.

Strange but True 9

Morgan Robertson once wrote a novel titled Futility. *It was not particularly good literature, but it did have one unusual characteristic that almost defies the imagination.*

It told the story of a fictitious ship, a cruise liner Robertson vividly fabricated, that was the very cutting edge of technology, considered unsinkable and therefore carrying too few lifeboats for her passengers and crew. In the novel, this ship gets under way for her maiden voyage and, on a cold April night, strikes an iceberg and is lost.

Many will quickly recognize the similarity between this tale and the true story of the sinking of the Titanic. *She too struck an iceberg on her maiden voyage on a cold April night. She too was considered unsinkable and carried too few lifeboats. Both ships had three screws and two masts. Both were rated to carry three thousand passengers. Both vessels struck icebergs on their starboard sides. Robertson's fictitious ship was 800 feet long, had nineteen watertight compartments, and was making 25 knots when she struck the iceberg.* Titanic *was 882.5 feet long, had sixteen watertight compartments, and was making 22.5 knots when she actually struck the iceberg.*

One might think Robertson was stealing his story line except for the amazing fact that he wrote his story in 1898 and Titanic *did not sail until 1912! And if all of those coincidences were not enough, one final fact is that Robertson had named his imaginary ship* Titan.

Sailors are known as a superstitious lot. Through the centuries, many legends have become part of nautical lore. The Flying Dutchman *is said to roam the seven seas with a ghost crew, the appearance of dolphins in a ship's bow wave when she is departing on a cruise is said to be a harbinger of good luck, and whistling aboard ship was once believed to create storms or headwinds. While these beliefs are no more real than bad luck occurring on Friday the thirteenth, there are times when occurrences are difficult to dismiss as mere coincidence. And a few of those coincidences are part of the history of the U.S. Navy.*

Collisions

During the hotly contested struggle for the Solomon Islands during World War II, when Japanese and American Soldiers and Marines were engaged in heavy fighting on Guadalcanal and some of the other islands in the chain, the Imperial Japanese Navy supported their forces ashore by making frequent sorties down a water passage among the many islands that soon became known as "The Slot." These sorties—dubbed the "Tokyo Express" by the Americans—led to frequent engagements with U.S. ships in the area and resulted in a number of major naval engagements that proved to be key components in the ongoing campaign.

On the night of 1 August 1943, fifteen U.S. torpedo boats engaged four of these Tokyo Express destroyers. Unlike many other nights, neither side suffered any losses in the fighting. Later, in another part of the passage, one of the U.S. boats—*PT 109*—was unfortunate enough to be lying in the path of *Amagiri,* one of the marauding enemy destroyers. It was a pitch-black night, and neither vessel's captain was aware of the other's presence in the darkened Slot.

A U.S. PT boat, similar to the one on patrol in The Slot on the night of 1 August 1943. *U.S. Naval Institute Photo Archive*

The fast-moving Japanese ship crashed into the PT boat with great force. The smaller vessel never stood a chance; she was cut in two and her fuel tanks exploded. Two of the American Sailors were killed in the collision and resulting explosion, and several others were badly injured.

The Japanese destroyer continued on down The Slot, and the survivors were left in the dark waters to fend for themselves. Fend they did. With the fitter men helping the more seriously injured, these PT Sailors swam to one of the many islands that make up the Solomons archipelago.

They guessed correctly that no one knew they were there. The crews of the other boats out in The Slot that night had seen the explosion and assumed all hands had been lost. Knowing that they—particularly the injured—could survive for just a limited time in the inhospitable jungle on the island, *PT 109*'s captain devised several plans to try to get them rescued, including swimming out into The Slot in hopes of getting the attention of U.S. vessels on patrol.

The plan that ultimately worked, causing them to be rescued after a week, was a message carved on a coconut shell and delivered to the U.S. forces by friendly natives in the area.

The captain, a young lieutenant from a wealthy family in Boston, was awarded the Navy and Marine Corps Medal for heroism, and little more than fifteen years later he was elected president of the United States. On his desk in the Oval Office, he kept a small plaque that quoted a Breton fisherman's prayer: "O God, thy sea is so great, and my boat is so small."

John F. Kennedy and ten of his crew escaped death that dark night in the Solomons, but he could not escape it in the glaring daylight in Dallas when he was assassinated on 22 November 1963.

To honor the felled president and former Sailor, an aircraft carrier was named USS *John F. Kennedy* and commissioned on 7 September 1968. Seven years later, in an ironic event similar to the collision of the PT boat and the destroyer, the aircraft carrier bearing Kennedy's name was involved in a terrible collision with the cruiser *Belknap*. Reminiscent of the ensuing conflagration in The Slot in 1943, aviation fuel poured down from the carrier's flight-deck refueling stations into the cruiser's superstructure, causing a horrific fire that burned most of the night and melted *Belknap*'s superstructure. Heroic efforts saved the ship, but six *Belknap* Sailors and one from *Kennedy* died, and many others were seriously injured.

The coincidence of collision was bizarre in its own right, but even more amazing was that out of 365 possible days in a year that the collision between USS *Belknap* and USS *John F. Kennedy* could have occurred, this disaster took place on the night of 22 November 1975—*the twelfth anniversary of the assassination of President John F. Kennedy*. Strange, but true.

USS *Belknap* after her collision with USS *John F. Kennedy. U.S. Naval Institute Photo Archive*

The Triangle

There is an area of the Atlantic Ocean off the southeastern United States popularly known as the "Bermuda Triangle," or sometimes the "Devil's Triangle." These waters have a long-standing reputation for mysterious happenings, not the least of which are unexplained disasters. No nautical charts show this area under either popular name, and the U.S. Board of Geographic Names does not officially recognize it, but the apexes of this triangle are generally accepted to be Bermuda, Florida, and Puerto Rico. The U.S. Coast Guard is "not impressed with supernatural explanations of disasters at sea," explaining that "the combined forces of nature and unpredictability of mankind outdo even the most far-fetched science fiction many times each year." Yet "strange but true" is an apt description for this part of the world, where many vessels and aircraft have been lost without explanation and often without a trace.

While no one has ever been able to prove any direct correlation, some characteristics of the Bermuda Triangle may be worth noting. The unpredictable Caribbean-Atlantic weather pattern in this area might well play a role; sudden local thunderstorms and waterspouts frequently occur in this area. The topography of the ocean floor varies from extensive shoals around the islands to some of the deepest marine trenches in the world. With the interaction of strong currents over the triangle's many reefs, the topography is in a state of constant flux, and new navigational hazards can develop rather quickly.

One of the most interesting facts about this triangle is that it is one of only two places on Earth where there is no compass variation—both gyro and magnetic compasses are perfectly aligned in this area. The other region where this occurs is just off the east coast of Japan. Japanese and Filipino seamen call it the "Devil's Sea" because it too is known for the mysterious disappearances in its waters. As most mariners know, compass variation in the rest of the world is a factor that must be reckoned with constantly and can sometimes amount to as much as 20 degrees' difference between true and magnetic north. What, if anything, this lack of variation—a seemingly good thing—might have to do with the strange occurrences in the area is anyone's guess, but it is a fact that adds to the region's mysteriousness.

Whether there are scientific explanations for these strange events or they are merely the kind of coincidence that myths are made of, the Bermuda Triangle was the scene of two incidents involving the U.S. Navy that have served to enhance the legendary stature of this area.

One of those incidents occurred during World War I and involved a Navy ship with the mythological name *Cyclops*. The U.S. Navy played a number of important roles in that conflict, known at the time as the "Great War." Escorted by destroyers, the Cruiser Transportation Force and the Naval Overseas Transportation Service carried more than two million Soldiers and 6.5 million tons of cargo to Europe, dramatically reducing the number of Allied ships lost to German submarines in the process. Naval aircraft, flying from European bases, aided U.S. destroyers in the antisubmarine effort, including the bombing of German bases at Zeebrugge and Ostend. Large U.S. Navy minelayers sowed some sixty thousand mines in the great North Sea mine barrier, which was designed to deny German submarines access to open waters. A division of U.S. battleships joined the British Grand Fleet in the North Sea to contain the German High Seas Fleet; in the Mediterranean, U.S. subchasers distinguished themselves by protecting Allied ships from submarine attack. And, in an unusual development, U.S. naval elements fought ashore in France using huge 14-inch guns that were mounted on railroad cars and served by seaman gunners. In the final analysis, control of the sea approaches to Europe made victory for the Allies possible. Sailors in the U.S. Navy, together with their allies in the Royal Navy, were the instruments of that control.

Because this was the age when many ships were coal-fired, Navy colliers (coal carriers—forerunners to today's oilers) played an essential role by ensuring that adequate supplies of coal were available where needed. USS *Cyclops* was one such collier and, soon after the United States entered the war in 1917, she was tasked with fueling British ships operating in South American waters.

Returning to U.S. waters early in 1918, *Cyclops* was in Norfolk, Virginia, when she received orders to carry coal to Brazil and then return to Baltimore with a load of manganese ore. Having safely delivered her coal to Rio de Janiero, she departed Brazil for the return trip on 16 February. After a short stop at Barbados on 3 and 4 March, she was under way again, headed through the Bermuda Triangle en route to a scheduled arrival in Baltimore on 13 March. On board were 306 people, including her crew, an

American consul general, and 72 other passengers, mostly Sailors on leave, changing duty stations, or headed home to muster out of the Navy.

Cyclops never arrived. In those days of limited communications and rather primitive tracking systems, it took a while before anyone realized the ship was overdue. On 23 March, the Navy launched a search operation to find the missing ship. All the ships that could be spared fanned out over the Bermuda Triangle looking for the missing collier. The search continued until 1 June, when Assistant Secretary of the Navy Franklin Roosevelt at last declared *Cyclops* officially lost and all embarked personnel legally deceased.

Not a single trace of the 542-foot long, more than twenty-thousand-ton ship and her 306 passengers and crew was ever found. The Navy followed up with an investigation that spanned a decade and is recorded in some fifteen hundred pages of interviews and testimony in the National Archives. Because the nation was at war at the time, an obvious possible explanation for the ship's disappearance was that a German submarine sank her, but after the war, German records were searched and nothing was found that indicated any such attack took place. Many other theories were officially investigated and many more have been offered, but to this day, the mystery of the disappearance of USS *Cyclops* has never been solved.

The Navy again found itself faced with a mysterious disappearance in the infamous Bermuda Triangle shortly after the end of World War II. At about 1400 on the afternoon of 5 December 1945, Flight 19—consisting of five

The collier (coal ship) USS *Cyclops. U.S. Naval Institute Photo Archive*

Avenger torpedo bombers—departed from the U.S. Naval Air Station, Fort Lauderdale, Florida, on an advanced overwater navigational training flight. The pilots and their crews were to execute "Navigation Problem No. 1," which was described thus: "(1) depart 26 degrees 03 minutes north and 80 degrees 07 minutes west and fly 091°T, distance 56 miles, to Hen and Chickens Shoals to conduct low level bombing; after bombing, continue on course 091°T for 67 miles; (2) fly course 346°T, distance 73 miles, and (3) fly course 241°T, distance 120 miles; then return to U.S. Naval Station, Fort Lauderdale, Florida."

In charge of the flight and piloting one of the aircraft was a senior qualified flight instructor. The other planes were piloted by qualified pilots with between 350 and 400 hours' flight time, at least 55 of which were in this type of aircraft. The weather conditions over the area covered by the track of the navigational problem were considered average for training flights of this nature, though there were a few thunderstorms in the area.

At about 1600, a shore-based radio station intercepted a radio message between the flight leader and another pilot. The message indicated that the aircraft were apparently experiencing some kind of compass malfunction and that the instructor was uncertain of his position and could not determine the direction of the Florida coast. Attempts to establish further communications on the training frequency were unsatisfactory because of interference from Cuban radio stations and a great deal of static caused by atmospheric conditions. All radio contact was lost before the exact nature of the trouble or the location of the flight could be determined.

All available facilities in the immediate area were called upon to locate the missing aircraft and help them return to base. These efforts were not successful. No trace of the missing airplanes or their crews was found even though an extensive search operation was launched and continued for five days. On the evening of 10 December weather conditions deteriorated to the point that further efforts became unduly hazardous.

To further compound the mysteriousness of the situation and add to the legend of the "Devil's Triangle," a Navy patrol plane, which was launched at approximately 1930 on 5 December to search for the missing torpedo bombers, also was neither seen nor heard from after takeoff. No trace of that plane or its crew was ever found.

In a twist of fate, in 1991 a salvage ship found five Avengers in six hundred feet of water off the coast of Florida. It appeared that Flight 19 had at last been located. But examination of the planes showed that they were not the same aircraft that had taken off as Flight 19, so the final resting place of the planes and their crews is still one of the many secrets of the Bermuda Triangle.

In 1977, the now-classic movie *Close Encounters of the Third Kind* offered an explanation for the disappearance of Flight 19 that is not likely to find its way into official Navy records. It is likely, however, that reasoned theories and fanciful explanations of the strange happenings in the Bermuda Triangle will continue as long as there are unanswered questions and odd coincidences. Such strange but true occurrences have always added to the mystery of the sea.

Jinx?

When the frigate USS *United States* was commissioned in 1797, she was the first American warship to be launched under the naval provisions of the Constitution of the new nation that had won its independence from Great Britain just a few years before. Built in time to participate in the Quasi-War with France, she captured a number of French privateers and recaptured several American ships that had been taken by the French.

In 1812, a new threat arose when Britain challenged the sovereignty of the new nation, and the United States again went to war for its independence and its honor. At the time, Britain's Royal Navy was unquestionably the most powerful one in the world; the fledgling U.S. Navy did not seem to have any chance against so formidable a force. Even though a fleet engagement between the two navies was out of the question, that did not stop courageous American Sailors from engaging the British in ship-to-ship actions—and winning! A series of victories—USS *Essex* captured HMS *Alert,* frigate *Constitution* defeated the British frigate *Guerrière,* and USS *Wasp* took HMS *Frolic*—stunned the British public and drove up insurance rates at Lloyd's of London. The next victory belonged to USS *United States*; she not only defeated the frigate HMS *Macedonian* but also actually brought her back to New York City to ultimately serve in the American Navy. The capture of a British warship created a huge sensation, raising American spirits at a time when the war was not going well on other fronts.

Such a celebrated beginning seemed to promise a glorious career for the ship bearing the name of her country. But her luck changed. Never again would she fight a major battle. No more would she be the subject of newspaper headlines and the talk of the social circuit. She was destined for an ignominious end.

After the damage from her glorious battle had been repaired, *United States* left New York to rejoin the war, accompanied by USS *Hornet* and her former adversary—HMS *Macedonian*—who had also been repaired and was now christened USS *Macedonian.* Within a week, however, the three ships were chased into New London, Connecticut, by a powerful

The frigate USS *United States* battling the British frigate HMS *Macedonian*. *U.S. Naval Institute Photo Archive*

British squadron, and there they were forced to remain until the end of the war.

A chance to get back into action seemed imminent when America declared war on Algiers in February 1815 and *United States* was assigned to a squadron preparing to head for the Mediterranean to fight the so-called Barbary pirates of North Africa. But *United States* was in a state of bad repair from her long stay in New London under blockade, and she was unable to leave with the rest of the squadron. When she at last got to the Mediterranean, she remained there until 1819 but never participated in anything other than patrols. While her presence in North African waters was important, it was a bit of an inglorious comedown for the famous frigate that had once prevailed against the Royal Navy.

In the years that followed, *United States* would go into and out of service, periodically deploying to various parts of the world, participating in antislavery patrols, but never doing anything like the action of her early days. Herman Melville—later the renowned author of *Moby Dick* and other classic novels—sailed in her for a time. Whether it was more a reflection of him or the ship he served in is a matter of conjecture, but he had little of a positive nature to report when he chronicled his experiences in *White-Jacket*.

From 1849 until 1861, *United States* rotted away in Norfolk, Virginia, and might well have ended her days that way except for the outbreak of the American Civil War. On 20 April 1861, the Navy Yard at Norfolk was captured by Confederate troops. Before leaving the yard, Union Sailors burned the ships that could not be gotten under way. But they failed to torch *United States,* believing it unnecessary to destroy the decayed relic. The Confederates, pressed for vessels in any kind of condition, repaired the ship and commissioned her CSS *United States.* "Confederate States Ship *United States*" seemed a bit odd to many, so she was often referred to as CSS *Confederate States.* Beyond her seaworthy days, she nonetheless was fitted out with a deck battery of nineteen guns for harbor defense and served as a receiving ship for newly reporting Sailors of the rebel navy.

In this role, she served her new owners well, but when the Confederates were forced to abandon the Navy Yard in May 1862, they decided to sink her in the middle of the Elizabeth River to form an obstruction to oncoming Union vessels. Surprisingly, the old girl did not give up without a fight. The ancient timbers of the frigate were found to be so strong and well preserved that the men trying to scuttle her ruined a whole box of axes in the attempt. Ultimately, they had to bore through her hull from inside before she would settle to the muddy bottom of the river.

Once Norfolk was again under Federal control, she was raised and towed to the Navy Yard. There she remained until December 1865, when the Bureau of Construction and Repair's earlier order—that she be broken up and her wood sold—was at last carried out.

It was a sad ending for a ship whose beginnings had been so promising. It was also somehow unsettling for a ship with so important a name to have gone the way she had. But no one seemed to have given much thought to the matter at the time and for a long time after.

Then, on 25 September 1920, the keel was laid for a new *Lexington*-class battle cruiser in the Philadelphia Navy Yard, and the new ship was given the name *United States.* It seemed for a while that the old meaningful name was to be resurrected, and hopefully the glorious heritage of her predecessor would pass on to this new powerful ship now under construction.

But it was not to be. World politics intervened, and on 8 February 1922, with the ship barely 12 percent complete, construction was halted in compliance with the Treaty for the Limitation of Naval Armaments. This treaty had been signed by the United States and other world naval powers in an attempt at arms limitation with the hope of preventing future war. The unfinished hulk of the would-be *United States* was sold for scrap in October of the following year. (Ironically, the treaty also ultimately ended up as a meaningless scrap of paper when some years later the world's greatest sea war was fought on all the seven seas.)

In the spring of 1949 the keel was laid for another *United States.* This one was to be a "super carrier," designed to meet the challenges of the developing superpower confrontation with the Soviet Union by her ability to launch long-range aircraft equipped with atomic weapons.

This time internal politics intervened. Just five days after her keel-laying, work was terminated at the order of the secretary of defense, who had decided that aircraft carriers were no longer needed because U.S. Air Force bombers alone were capable of fighting the Soviet Union should war come. This tipped off a major battle between the two services, provoking Secretary of the Navy John L. Sullivan to resign in protest and causing what has come to be known as the "revolt of the admirals," when senior officers in the Navy put their careers on the line to express their serious concerns before Congress. It was not a happy time for the nation or its defense establishment. Chief of Naval Operations Louis Denfield was relieved of his command as a result of the "revolt," and the war of words between the Navy and Air Force continued for some time. The debate was finally ended when North Korea invaded South Korea, and U.S. aircraft carriers played a

An artist's sketch of what was supposed to be the "super carrier" USS *United States. U.S. Naval Institute Photo Archive*

vital role in holding off the enemy onslaught until more forces could arrive to launch a successful counterstrike at Inchon.

All of this started when the name *United States* was once again assigned to a Navy ship! Talk of a jinx began to circulate.

These superstitious rumblings had not yet quieted when again, in November 1993, another *United States* was laid down. This one was to be an even bigger, more capable ship—a *Nimitz*-class nuclear-powered aircraft carrier. But fourteen months after construction was begun, the decision was made to rename the ship USS *Harry S. Truman,* to honor the thirty-third president of the United States. While few debated the wisdom of naming a ship after the commander in chief who had first gone to war against Communism—and there was nothing sinister or deliberate in thwarting plans for another *United States*—for those who subscribe to such things, it was not a great leap to imagine that a jinx was at work.

To this day, there has never been another ship in the U.S. Navy named USS *United States.* Blaming a jinx may not be logical, but it certainly seems to fit this situation.

There is nothing new here. Far from it. Among the most prevalent legends of the sea is the idea of a jinxed or cursed ship, a vessel that is destined for bad luck, either by chance or from some supernatural cause. Tales from the biblical story of Jonah to Samuel Taylor Coleridge's classic poem "The Rime of the Ancient Mariner" reinforce the idea in our culture. Some Sailors of the day tried to explain the disappearance of *Cyclops* as the inevitable outcome for a "jinxed ship," pointing out that the ship had experienced other problems, including an accident in which a Sailor had been killed by the ship's propellers. More modern Sailors point to an imagined Kennedy-family jinx as the cause behind the *Kennedy-Belknap* collision.

In fact, seasoned Sailors know better. They know that jinxes can be explained in two ways. First is the luck factor. One does not have to be very old and wise to realize that life is not always fair and equitable. As the saying goes, "Bad things happen to good people"; likewise, bad things can happen to good ships. Despite her great reputation, USS *Watertight* might be caught in an unpredicted storm and lose her search radar antenna—even though the shipyard did a flawless job of installing it and the ship's electronics technicians were meticulous about maintaining it.

Bad things also can happen to "bad" ships. The other factor that contributes to the jinx idea is almost as difficult to measure or quantify in any scientific way, yet "salty" Sailors will swear by it. The "personality factor" of ships has much to do with how they are perceived by others and something to do with how much good or bad "luck" comes their way. Any experienced teacher will insist that different classes have different "personalities." "My ten o'clock class is reserved and studious, while the one at eleven-thirty has more discipline problems but is also livelier during class discussions."

Just as classrooms full of students take on composite personalities, so do ships. The word on the waterfront might be that USS *Watertight* is a "can-do" ship, always ready to carry out any assigned mission speedily and efficiently, while USS *Neversink* is always a "little behind the power curve." These "personalities"—actually reflections of leadership, morale, and other factors—have a lot more to do with what happens to a ship than does anything supernatural. *Neversink* is more likely to run aground or lose a man overboard than is *Watertight* because the latter is better run, with a well-trained crew and better leaders who keep morale high.

While jinxes are no more real than are bogeymen and hobgoblins, there is something in our nature that makes the possibility of such things attractive. Most likely it is the need for explanations and order. There is something more satisfying in knowing there is a reason—however unscientific—for an occurrence or series of occurrences than in having to accept that it is just random, meaningless coincidence, beyond any laws or control.

As long as strange but true things continue to occur, however, there will be legends and myths, whispers of jinxes, and tales of the supernatural. In truth, it is not altogether surprising in light of one final factor. Anyone who has been to sea and peered into its mysterious depths cannot help but wonder what lies below. Any Sailor who has watched the changing moods of the sea, or seen the dancing stars of luminescence in a ship's wake, or heard the ominous wail of the wind in a squall, will be tempted to think of powers beyond those of simple physics. The Sailor's realm is a hauntingly beautiful and sometimes ominous place to live and work and dream and wonder.

Lucky Bag

10

Maintaining good order, discipline, and cleanliness aboard ship has been a high priority in the U.S. Navy from its earliest days. One method for achieving these things was the tradition of the "lucky bag." As the tradition goes, any personal items left out in the berthing compartment ("gear adrift") were confiscated by the master at arms and placed in a special bag. These items were later auctioned off—the funds used for the general welfare of the crew—thereby making those Sailors fortunate enough to obtain new items for relatively little money "lucky."

This practice, of course, led to a varied assortment of unrelated items in the bag. Together, as representations of the personal lives of the Sailors who once owned them, these items might tell something about a ship's crew. Here, too, in this chapter are a variety of items unrelated except that they are all parts of the heritage of the U.S. Navy. Together, they tell some important and interesting things about this Navy.

They Also Serve

It was several minutes past midnight on 15 July 1967. A quarter moon had earlier slipped behind heavy clouds gathering over the South China Sea. The resulting darkness was welcomed by the crew of trawler number 459, making their way along the coast of South Vietnam near Cape Batangan; the darker it was, the less chance they would be spotted by American or South Vietnamese coastal patrol units. The Communist vessel was laden with ninety tons of arms, ammunition, and various other supplies, enough to keep a Vietcong regiment going for several months.

What these infiltrators did not know was that the destroyer escort USS *Wilhoite* had been lurking just beyond the horizon, keeping track of the North Vietnamese trawler by radar ever since a Navy P-2 aircraft had discovered her four days earlier. Because the trawler had no radar of her own, her master had no way of knowing that he was being stalked.

Trawler 459 had been moving up and down the South Vietnamese coast for days, carefully staying out in international waters, waiting for the right moment to run to shore undetected. Her crew had placed fishing nets on her decks to disguise her real purpose.

Unaware of her stalker and under the cover of the darkness, the trawler made her move, turning toward the shore and heading for the mouth of the Sa Ky River. At first, all was quiet, and the Communist infiltrators must have been feeling optimistic. Their hopes were soon shattered, however, when out of the shadows emerged the ominous shapes of several vessels of varying size. The Americans had sprung a trap. A Swift boat, the patrol gunboat USS *Gallup,* and the Coast Guard cutter *Point Orient* joined *Wilhoite.* All were elements assigned to the Coastal Surveillance Force (dubbed "Operation Market Time").

Illumination flares suddenly glared out of the darkness, bathing the sea in a ghostly light, and a loudspeaker blared out a call for the intruder to heave to and surrender. But the trawler maintained course and speed in a desperate run for the shore. Two of the U.S. vessels opened fire, sending hyphenated tracers across the Communist ship's bow. This warning too was ignored. The on-scene commander gave the order to engage, and six .50-caliber machine guns, two mortars, and a 3-inch/50-caliber gun opened fire on the North Vietnamese trawler. The intruder returned fire with her 12.7-mm deck guns and a 57-mm recoilless rifle. The fight was on.

The trawler was soon taking the worst of it. The incessant fire of the American vessels chewed mercilessly at her hull and superstructure. When two helicopter gunships arrived, the enemy's fate was sealed. Soon, fires raged from stem to stern on the hapless ship.

U.S. Navy Swift boats were an important element of Operation Market Time during the Vietnam War. *U.S. Naval Institute Photo Archive*

The trawler ran aground near the mouth of the Sa Ky River and continued to burn throughout the night, the flames reflecting off the clouds of the tropical night sky in an eerie pyrotechnic dance. In the morning, when the Americans were able to board the enemy ship, they were amazed to find that several tons of ammunition had not ignited and were still intact.

It had been a successful operation by any standard. By waiting until the enemy vessel had moved into the territorial waters of South Vietnam, the Americans had adapted to the restrictions placed upon them by international law. By remaining over the horizon while stalking the enemy, the U.S. Sailors had put their technological advantage to good tactical use. By ferociously engaging the intruder when the time came, they ensured that the mission was successfully accomplished and that important supplies would not be delivered to enemy units ashore.

But there was another—less glamorous, but no less important—aspect to this story. In an article published in the U.S. Naval Institute's *Proceedings* magazine in September 1968, the commander of the operation, Charles Stephan, described what happened and gave appropriate credit to the warriors who fought the battle and prevailed. He also noted that maintaining the Market Time barrier against other possible infiltrators was extremely important. In that light, he added: "But a special word of praise is in order for the *Pledge* [a U.S. minesweeper on patrol nearby] and those Swift boats that patrolled within eye and earshot of the action, and, overcoming with exemplary discipline, an almost irrepressible urge to join the battle, maintained the integrity of their patrols. They also serve."

Commander Stephan's words illustrate an easily overlooked aspect of the U.S. Navy's heritage. This book and many others focus a great deal of attention on heroism in battle and exemplary performance in stressful situations. While this is appropriate—the Navy exists to be ready for those moments when defending the nation requires extraordinary feats—it does not properly acknowledge that many Sailors, through no fault of their own, are never confronted with those extraordinary situations that we love to read about. Yet without those who day in and day out do the *ordinary,* there would be no *extraordinary* to celebrate.

As Commander Stephan pointed out, they also serve who maintain uneventful patrols when, not far away, a major battle is raging. They also serve who run the oilers and the ammunition ships all over the world to keep the warships supplied with what they need. They also serve who fly the CODs out to the carriers, delivering mail from home and aircraft maintenance parts. They also serve who provide medical care, cook meals, repair showers, keep pay records, update software, swab decks, lay down fixes, build runways in jungles, gather intelligence, man lecterns, lubricate machinery, splice lines, prepare correspondence, contribute to charity events, drive vehicles ashore, and steer the ship at sea.

Still others serve the Navy and the nation—sometimes the well-being of all mankind—by stepping outside the bounds of routine; their actions are noncombatant in nature but are nonetheless bold or daring. These are Sailors who have gone where others had feared to go or simply had not thought of going. It was Sailors who first went to the North Pole in 1909 and later made the first flight over it in 1926. The Wilkes expedition was a nineteenth-century Navy-sponsored exploration of the Pacific that traveled more than eighty thousand miles, surveyed 280 islands, made the first sighting of the continent of Antarctica, and brought back huge amounts of data that advanced the world's knowledge in the fields of hydrography, geology, meteorology, botany, zoology, and ethnography. Sailors explored the Dead Sea, the Amazon River, the Isthmus of Panama, and many other parts of the world. As of this writing, the number of Sailors who have gone into outer space approaches one hundred, a point of great pride within the Navy. And every one of the astronauts who flew the Mercury, Gemini, and Apollo missions that led to the landing on the Moon was retrieved from the sea upon their return to Earth by naval task forces manned by thousands of Sailors.

All Sailors, whether they do the usual or the unusual, whether they labor ashore, ply the world's seas, penetrate an ocean's depths, soar the blue skies, or venture into the blackness of space, serve the nation with every watch they stand, every duty they carry out, every moment they stand ready to do what is required. And even though danger, boredom, exhaustion, and sacrifice are often their shipmates, Sailors have the satisfaction of knowing that their "job" is more than an occupation. They know that they do more than simply earn a paycheck. They also *serve.*

Circumnavigations

Most schoolchildren know that Ferdinand Magellan was the commander of the first voyage to go around the world. Like Columbus, this Portuguese mariner believed he could get to the lucrative Spice Islands to the east by sailing west and circling the globe. Like Columbus, he believed the world was much smaller than it actually is. Also like Columbus, he sailed under a Spanish flag, setting out in September 1519 with five ships (*Trinidad, San Antonio, Concepción, Victoria,* and *Santiago*) and 270 men under his command.

The fleet made its way across the Atlantic and then southward along the coast of South America until they eventually found the straits that led to the

Pacific Ocean and today bear his name. The passage through these treacherous Straits of Magellan took thirty-eight days, during which the crews saw many fires from Indian camps burning on the nearby shores and so named the land *Tierra del Fuego* ("Land of Fire").

Emerging from the straits, Magellan thought the Spice Islands were just a few days' sail away. He soon learned what every Sailor who has crossed the Pacific knows—it is one big ocean! Four months later, suffering from starvation, thirst, and disease, the explorers reached the Philippines. Unfortunately for Magellan, his voyage ended there; on 27 April 1521, he was killed by the natives in the midst of a tribal war.

Sebastian del Cano took command of what was left of the expedition; he eventually made it back to Spain with one ship (*Victoria*) and eighteen crew members. It was a momentous achievement, but accomplished at great cost.

More than four hundred years later, the feat was repeated, but this time under different circumstances. In February 1960, USS *Triton* put to sea for her shakedown cruise. She was the fifth U.S. Navy ship to bear the name of the Greek demigod of the sea who was the son of Poseidon and who used his conch-shell trumpet alternately to summon storms and to still the sea. It was an appropriate name for a ship who, like her namesake, had harnessed

USS *Triton*, one of the Navy's earliest nuclear submarines, was destined to make history on her shakedown cruise. *U.S. Naval Institute Photo Archive*

the forces of nature: powering this modern warship was a nuclear reactor that gave her great speed and virtually unlimited sea-keeping ability.

To prove her capabilities, *Triton* sailed completely around the world, following the same track that Magellan had used. What was markedly different this time, however, was that she made the voyage nonstop in sixty days and twenty-one hours, and she made it *under the water*!

Triton was one of the first generation of nuclear-powered submarines. Her epic circumnavigation proved the great capabilities of this new kind of ship and greatly enhanced the nation's prestige at a time when image was

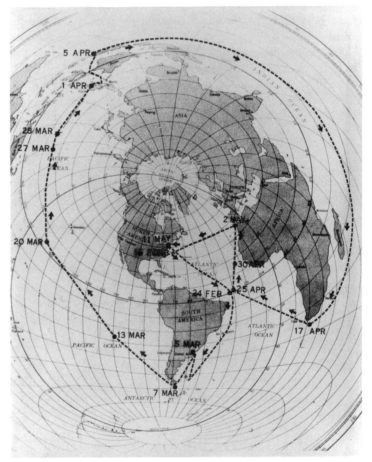

Triton's track as she made her historic underwater circumnavigation. *U.S. Naval Institute Photo Archive*

one of the weapons of the Cold War with the Soviet Union. Her crew received the Presidential Unit Citation and her skipper, Captain Edward L. Beach, was awarded the Legion of Merit. Today, *Triton*'s dive stick resides in the lobby of the Naval Academy's Beach Hall, headquarters of the U.S. Naval Institute.

Amazing Grace

As a young girl, Grace Brewster Murray had an unusually inquisitive mind. When she was seven years old and wondered how her alarm clock worked, she disassembled it. When she was unable to get it back together, she got another and took it apart to see if she could figure it out. When that failed, she got another, and another. By the time she finished her quest, all seven of the household alarm clocks lay in pieces.

But Grace Murray Hopper (she married Vincent Foster Hopper in 1930) put her inquisitiveness to good use. She earned a bachelor's degree in mathematics and physics from Vassar College and went on to earn both a master's degree and a PhD in mathematics from Yale University (she was the first woman to earn the latter). When she joined the Navy in 1943 in the midst of World War II, a wise detailer decided she might be a good person to assign to the Bureau of Ordnance in a special program known as the Computation Project. In those days, computers were just beginning to make their debut, and this made Hopper one of the pioneers.

The Computation Project was a joint effort of the Navy, the IBM Corporation, and Harvard University. Grace Hopper became one of the programmers of the world's first large-scale computer, the Mark I. This early machine was no desktop personal computer. Describing it as "an impressive beast," Hopper remembered it as "51 feet long, 8 feet high, and 5 feet deep." She mastered the Mark I and its improved versions, the Mark II and Mark III.

One day while diagnosing a problem in one of these temperamental machines, she found that the cause was a moth trapped in one of the relays. Extracting it with a pair of tweezers, she then taped the expired moth into the computer's logbook, with an explanation that the problem had been a "bug" and told her supervisor that the computer had been "debugged." To this day, Grace Hopper is credited with coining the term that has endured as part of the computer lexicon.

After the war, she remained in the Naval Reserve while continuing her career in computing. Graduating from the highly mechanized Mark series computers, she began work on a newcomer called UNIVAC (Universal Automatic Computer). With its arrays of vacuum tubes and magnetic drums, this was the first computer that could rightfully be called "electronic."

In the years that followed, Hopper's reputation grew as she worked to make computers better and better. Among her many achievements was her contribution to creating the first language that allowed programmers to speak to computers with words rather than numbers.

In 1966 Grace Hopper retired from the Naval Reserve, but the Navy soon realized the importance of computers and recalled her to active duty for six months. That half-year turned into nearly two decades of additional service!

While serving in the Naval Automation Data Command, she also traveled the world, speaking to thousands about the future of computers. Sometimes these speaking engagements earned her honoraria, which she turned over to Navy Relief (more than thirty-four thousand dollars). One of her constant themes was that change could be good. She was often frustrated when she would hear yet another Sailor say, "But that's how we've always done it." With a wry smile on her wizened face she was heard to reply, "Someday I'm going to shoot somebody for saying that." To prove her point that convention is not always necessary, she kept a clock on her wall that kept perfect time but ran counterclockwise. She also always carried a one-foot piece of wire with her—because one foot is the distance light travels in a nanosecond. She would brandish it before listeners and explain why programmers should not waste time, not even a nanosecond.

Grace Hopper at her *second* retirement ceremony with Secretary of the Navy John Lehman. *U.S. Navy*

Grace Hopper, then a rear admiral, eventually retired from the Navy a second time—this time for good—in 1986. She had earned an array of awards, both military and civilian, too numerous to list. Her retirement ceremony was held onboard USS *Constitution*; thus the oldest active duty naval officer in service ended her long career on the decks of the Navy's oldest commissioned warship.

Grace Murray Hopper died on New Year's Day 1992. Just five years later, an *Arleigh Burke*–class guided missile destroyer was commissioned bearing her name. Officially USS *Hopper,* the ship is better known throughout the fleet by the nickname Rear Admiral Hopper had earned during her long and extraordinary career: "Amazing Grace."

Can Do

On 10 June 1965, a reinforced Vietcong regiment attacked the compound of Detachment A-432, 5th Special Forces Group, at Dong Xoai, fifty-five miles northeast of Saigon in South Vietnam. Facing the enemy onslaught along with the eleven Army Green Berets were nine Sailors.

One of the Sailors was Construction Mechanic Third Class Marvin Shields. The young petty officer had joined the Navy primarily to build things, but on this particular day, he and his shipmates were going to have to fight alongside the Army commandos.

Early in the battle Shields was wounded, but he continued to supply his fellow Americans with needed ammunition for the next three hours. When the enemy forces launched a massive attack at close range with flamethrowers, hand grenades, and small-arms fire, Shields stood his ground alongside his shipmates and the Soldiers. Wounded a second time in this assault, Shields nevertheless ignored the mortal danger and helped a more critically injured Soldier to safety while under intense enemy fire.

For four more hours, Shields and the others maintained a barrage of fire that kept the enemy at bay. When the compound commander, Second Lieutenant Charles Q. Williams, asked for a volunteer to help him take out an enemy machine-gun emplacement that was endangering the lives of all the Army and Navy personnel in the compound, Shields volunteered. Armed with a 3.5-inch rocket launcher, Shields and the Green Beret commander advanced on the enemy emplacement despite heavy fire from several enemy positions. The two men succeeded in taking out the enemy machine-gun nest and then attempted to return to the relative safety of the compound. The young Sailor's luck had at last run out. Struck a third time, this wound would prove fatal.

Construction Mechanic Third Class Marvin Shields had joined the Navy to build things, but in Vietnam he stood alongside Army Green Berets in a vicious firefight. *Naval Historical Center*

For his courageous actions, Marvin Shields was posthumously awarded the Medal of Honor, the first Sailor to win the nation's highest honor for action in Vietnam.

In April 1971, to further honor this intrepid Sailor who fought so ferociously alongside some of the Army's fiercest Soldiers, the fifteenth *Knox*-class destroyer escort was commissioned into the Navy as USS *Marvin Shields*.

This seemingly strange situation, with Sailors fighting ashore like soldiers, was actually not so unusual. Marvin Shields and the other Sailors were part of a special Navy unit: SeaBee Team 1104. They were there in the jungles of Southeast Asia to build a base, just as they had in many other parts of the world during earlier wars.

The "SeaBees" came into existence shortly after the beginning of World War II, when the use of civilian workers to build naval bases in war zones proved impractical. Under international law, civilians were not permitted to resist enemy military attack; participating in combat actions, even defensive ones, could result in summary execution as guerrillas. To counter this problem, skilled workers were recruited into the Navy directly from the construction trades to form "Construction Battalions." In typical Navy fashion, these were soon referred to as "CBs," and that evolved into the now-famous term SeaBees.

During World War II, the SeaBees performed now-legendary deeds in both the Atlantic and Pacific Theaters of operation. Earning thirty-three Silver Stars and five Navy Crosses, they built more than a hundred major airstrips, nearly five hundred piers, several thousand ammunition magazines, hundreds of square blocks of warehouses, hospitals to serve more than seventy thousand patients, tanks for the storage of a hundred million gallons of gasoline, and housing for one and a half million people. They suffered more than two hundred combat deaths, earned more than two thousand Purple Hearts, and served on four continents and on more than three hundred islands.

When the Marines invaded Guadalcanal early in the war, the men of the 6th Naval Construction Battalion followed them ashore and thus became the first SeaBees to build under combat conditions. The airfield there was vital, and the SeaBees kept it open by continuously repairing the damage despite almost constant bombardment by the enemy. The first decorated SeaBee hero of the war, Seaman Second Class Lawrence C. "Bucky" Meyer, was among the SeaBees working on that airfield. In those precious few hours of off time, when others were grabbing catnaps or dashing off a quick letter home, Seaman Meyer worked on an abandoned machine gun until he had it in working order. On 3 October 1942, during an air attack, he used his salvaged machine gun to do battle with a Japanese Zero fighter that was strafing the field. His courage in facing and defeating the enemy aircraft earned him the Silver Star.

During the landing on Treasury Island in the Solomons in late 1943, Fireman First Class Aurelio Tassone of the 87th Naval Construction Battalion was driving his bulldozer ashore when it became evident that a Japanese pillbox was holding up the advance from the beach. Tassone headed straight for the pillbox, using the bulldozer blade as a shield against the enemy fire, while Lieutenant Charles Turnbull provided covering fire with his carbine. Despite the continuous heavy fire, Tassone crushed the pillbox with the bulldozer, killing all twelve of its occupants. Tassone's courageous action earned him a Silver Star and inspired the now legendary image of the SeaBee astride his bulldozer rolling over enemy positions.

Yet another milestone in SeaBee history occurred in Hollywood rather than in the South Pacific. The release of the motion picture *The Fighting SeaBees* in 1944, starring John Wayne and Susan Hayward, made SeaBee a household word. (Interestingly, John Wayne's last motion picture was *Home for the SeaBees,* a Navy documentary filmed in 1977.)

During the Normandy invasion, 6 June 1944—known more popularly as "D-Day"—the SeaBees were among the first to go ashore as members of naval combat demolition units. Working with U.S. Army Engineers, their crucial task was to destroy the steel and concrete barriers that the Germans had built in the water and on the beaches to forestall amphibious landings. When dawn betrayed their presence, they came under murderous German fire. Whole teams were wiped out when shells prematurely detonated their explosives, but the survivors pressed on, planting their explosive charges to blow huge holes in the enemy's defenses.

The SeaBees remained with the armies battling their way into Europe, providing vital assistance in overcoming natural and man-made obstacles as the great invasion continued. The final great SeaBee effort in the European Theater took place during the crossing of the Rhine River in March 1945. The U.S. Army, concerned about the river's swift and tricky currents, called upon the SeaBees to help transport General George Patton's armored forces across the Rhine at Oppenheim in a frontal assault that swept away the German defenders. The SeaBees operated more than three hundred craft to shuttle thousands of troops into the heart of Germany, playing a major role in the defeat of Hitler's forces and the liberation of Europe from Nazi tyranny.

Following the victories in Europe and Asia, the SeaBees helped war-ravaged nations to rebuild while also building and maintaining advanced bases important to the Cold War. Cubi Point Naval Air Station in the Philippines and a huge floating dock at Holy Loch, Scotland, for the repair and service of the Polaris missile submarines are both SeaBee projects.

At the landing in Inchon that changed the course of the Korean War, the SeaBees positioned vitally needed causeways while battling enormous thirty-foot tides, swift currents, and continuous enemy fire. In an incident that came to be known as the "Great SeaBee Train Robbery," the need to break the equipment bottleneck at the harbor inspired a group of SeaBees to go behind enemy lines and capture some abandoned locomotives. Despite enemy mortar fire, they succeeded in bringing back the engines and turning them over to the Army Transportation Corps. For the rest of the Korean War, the SeaBees built and maintained air bases, aided in evacuations, and helped keep vital seaports functioning.

In Vietnam, the SeaBees built remote bases, roads, airfields, cantonments, warehouses, hospitals, storage facilities, bunkers, and other facilities that were critically needed to support the combatant forces. In addition to the many SeaBee team activities in remote locations, such as when Marvin Shields fought alongside the Green Berets in Dong Xoai, construction battalions built large coastal strongholds in the northernmost provinces and huge port facilities at Da Nang, Chu Lai, and Phu Bai.

Since the Vietnam War, the SeaBees have carried on their unique naval functions in such far-flung places as Bosnia, Haiti, and the Saudi Arabian desert. Virtual miracle workers when it comes to quickly building naval bases and airfields in remote locations, they are unlike most other construction workers because these men and women must sometimes take a break from pouring concrete and laying cables to pick up their weapons and do battle. For more than half a century these largely landlocked Sailors have upheld the highest traditions of the U.S. Navy, providing vital services without which the operating fleets could not function, often under difficult and dangerous circumstances, and always guided by the principle embodied in their simple but meaningful motto: "Can do."

Bathyscaphe

In 1960, Navy Lieutenant Don Walsh and Swiss scientist Jacques Piccard left the destroyer escort USS *Lewis* and climbed into a strange vessel that had been named *Trieste*. Less than sixty feet long and known technically as a "bathyscaphe," this oddity was a submarine of sorts that used a combination of iron pellets (nine tons of them) for ballast and gasoline (twenty-eight thousand gallons) for buoyancy. The two men were crammed into a sphere on *Trieste*'s underside that was made of an alloy of nickel, chromium, and molybdenum and had an interior diameter of just six and one-half feet.

Casting off from *Lewis,* Walsh and Piccard headed down toward their destination—the bottom of the Marianas Trench, at the time believed to be the deepest point in all the world's oceans at 35,800 feet, or nearly seven miles. At about 800 feet, all light was gone, and they continued down into inky darkness, where no man had ever gone before. At about 6,000 feet, it became so cold they had to put on warmer clothing. As they continued their descent, they suddenly felt the vessel shake violently as though an explosion had taken place; one of the windows in the entrance shaft to the vessel had cracked from the tremendous pressure that was building as the vessel went deeper into the ocean. This was not a venture for the fainthearted.

After four hours and forty-eight minutes, the two men felt a soft bump, and they knew they had arrived at the deepest point in the world's oceans. The pressure at this depth was more than one hundred thousand tons, and Walsh and Piccard were astonished to see a flounderlike fish and some shrimp on the bottom as they peered out through their eight-inch-thick glass window.

Their ascent to the surface took three hours and seventeen minutes, and when Walsh emerged from the confines of the bathyscaphe, he tossed a weighted American flag over the side so that it would go to the bottom and mark the spot of the record-setting dive. To this day, that record has not been broken.

Friday the Thirteenth

Meeting in Philadelphia on Friday, 13 October 1775, the delegates to the Second Continental Congress voted to fit out two sailing vessels with ten carriage guns and eighty-man crews and sent them out on a cruise of three months to intercept transports carrying munitions and stores to the British army in America. This was an audacious move, considering that it would be nearly nine months before that same Congress would produce the Declaration of Independence proclaiming the new United States of America. One might argue that it was also a move bordering on the irrational, considering the size and incredible power of the Royal Navy. One might also note that Friday the thirteenth was not the ideal date to make such a move. But undaunted by such things, men like John Adams, who understood the importance of sea power, got the resolution passed, little realizing that they had signed the "birth certificate" of what would eventually become the most powerful navy in the history of the world.

In 1972, the CNO issued a long-overdue decree, officially authorizing recognition of 13 October as the appropriate date for celebrating the Navy's birthday. Since that time, each CNO has encouraged a Navy-wide celebration of this occasion "to enhance a greater appreciation of our Navy heritage, and to provide a positive influence toward pride and professionalism in the naval service." On that date every year, Sailors the world over gather for formal parties ashore, or have a piece of cake specially prepared by the cooks in the ship's galley, or simply pause for a moment before assuming their next watch to reflect on what it means to be part of an organization that is hundreds of years old, has changed in countless ways, and yet carries with it the same bold spirit that was present at its birth.

Remembrance

Herman Wouk is one of the greatest writers of naval fiction and was once a Sailor himself. Countless Sailors have read Wouk's Pulitzer Prize–winning *The Caine Mutiny,* which has often been used as a textbook at the Naval Academy for its insights into a portion of the Navy's heritage and for its lessons on leadership. And Wouk's two books chronicling the history of World War II, *The Winds of War* and *War and Remembrance,* stand as monuments to the Navy's great struggles in the victory at sea in the Pacific.

Although his works are technically fiction, they are filled with historical facts and, more importantly, they provide a deeper understanding of the human experience of war than any straight history can ever do. It is noteworthy, then, that this great writer stepped out of his role as anonymous narrator only once to make an overt comment about what he was writing.

He had been describing the sacrificial attack of the torpedo bombers at the Battle of Midway, telling how these aircraft, manned by an assortment of young men representing most of the states that are combined to make up the United States, charged headlong into battle and certain death, and in so doing turned the tide of battle and altered the course of the world's history. He had been relating how, in just a very few minutes, thirty-three pilots and thirty-five radioman gunners were killed as they distracted enemy fighter aircraft long enough for their fellow Sailors in the dive-bombers to strike a fatal blow into the very heart of the Japanese navy, the same aircraft carriers that had struck at Pearl Harbor on the first day of the war. Describing this incredible moment as "the soul of the United States of America in action," Wouk wrote that "the memory of these three American torpedo plane squadrons should not die." He then halted the telling of his story, pausing for several pages to list the names and the birthplaces of each of the sixty-eight men who paid the ultimate price that day.

This unusual tribute to real people in the midst of a work of fiction tells us that there is something truly extraordinary about the Battle of Midway. On its Web site, the Naval Historical Center describes the battle as "the decisive battle of the war in the Pacific," and few historians dispute that. It was a battle that was won by the courage and sacrifice of those pilots and gunners who took to the air knowing that the odds were stacked against them. It was also won through some exceptional intelligence work by a handful of cryptanalysts working long hours for weeks on end to decipher the enemy's intentions. And by hundreds of shipyard workers who performed maintenance miracles to ensure that three instead of just two American aircraft carriers were available to fight. And by several admirals who made key decisions at the right times. And by those anonymous others who muscled the bombs onto aircraft, found the winds for the launch, kept the steam flowing and the electrons streaming, prepared the meals, kept the records, and cleaned, lubricated, repaired, and performed countless other duties to ensure that this outnumbered and outclassed fleet was ready to do battle, to do what U.S. Sailors are meant to do.

Recognizing the particular significance of this battle and, more importantly, what it represents, the CNO sent out a message to the entire Navy on the fifty-eighth anniversary of the battle, saying: "Midway was won, not by superior numbers or daunting technology, but by the courage and tenacity of Sailors who fought a vicious air and sea battle against overwhelming odds. Their victory helped win us the world we have today, and it is appropriate that we remember it and those who participated in it." In that same message, the CNO then decreed:

> The two most significant dates in our Navy's history are **13 October 1775, the birth of our Navy**, and **4 June 1942, the Battle of Midway**. These two prominent days will henceforth be celebrated annually as the centerpieces of our heritage. Twice a year, we will pause as a Navy, to reflect upon our proud heritage and to build in all hands a renewed awareness of our tradition and history. Through such reflection, we will help define the significance of our service today in defense of our country's freedom. We are the caretakers of a torch passed on by nearly two hundred and twenty five years of naval heroes. Honoring their contributions will enrich each of us. I believe it is appropriate that we take time to pause and reflect formally upon our proud naval heritage.

And, ever since, the Navy has heeded that CNO's words. In the spring of every year, no matter where they are stationed, American Sailors come together to remember a moment in our Navy's history when the extraordinary was accomplished by the ordinary, to reflect on what that represents to each man and woman who wears or has worn a Navy uniform, to hope that they too will be ready should the day come when they will have to meet similar challenges and find the strength to carry on the finest ideals of the United States of America, just as those at Midway once did.

Bravo Zulu

It is appropriate to close the final chapter of this book with a discussion of two words, strange to the rest of the world but very meaningful to the men and women who serve in today's Navy. Every Sailor knows (and aspires to) the two words "Bravo Zulu." It is the Navy's unique way of praising someone, of saying, "Well done." While everyone in the Navy knows what it means, not everyone knows how it came to be. "Why not Whiskey Delta?" one might ask.

The origins of the term can be found in the practice of using codes to convey information or orders at sea. Before radio was invented, ships needed some means of communicating with each other. A set of signal flags representing letters and numbers was produced so that messages could be created and hoisted by one ship and read by other ships within visual range. But trying to spell out a message of very many words would require a lot of halyard space, so signal books were devised with simple codes that assigned longer meanings to short combinations of letters. For example, if all ships in a squadron had the same signal book that assigned the code letters "DCV" to mean, "Engage the nearest enemy from windward," the squadron commodore could order that for all his ships at once, simply by hoisting those three flags. This system had an added advantage: if the enemy did not have the same signal book, he would not know what the commodore was intending.

When radio was invented, the same codes could still be used to convey longer messages in shorter terms (over longer distances), simply by broadcasting the code letters by voice or Morse code. The problem with voice radio is that letters such as *t, d, e,* and *p* sound too much alike. A commodore intending to tell his ships to "engage the enemy" (DCV) might accidentally tell them to "return to port" (TCE) if they misheard the letters. To counter that problem, a "phonetic alphabet" was devised, where each letter has a word assigned to it so that there will be no confusion. In the first such alphabet, created in 1913, "DCV" became "Dog Cast Vice" and "TCE" became "Tare Cast Easy."

Over the years, for various reasons, the phonetic alphabet was changed (once in 1927, again in 1938, and yet again in World War II). The final change, resulting in the phonetic alphabet in use today, occurred in 1957, altering the phonetic words to make them more easily pronounceable by America's NATO allies. The only words to remain the same since 1913 are "Mike" and "X-ray."

The signal books, assigning specific meanings to different combinations of letters and numbers, have also changed to reflect advances in technology and to keep enemy forces from becoming familiar with the codes. The codes have also grown, incorporating administrative as well as tactical information. One of the signals included along the way was that which allowed a commander to send his approval for a successful evolution, to say, "Well done." During World War II "Tare Victor George" was listed in the codebook with that meaning.

A new codebook, called the *Allied Naval Signal Book* (ACP 175), was adopted after NATO was created in 1949. Until then, each navy had used its own signal code and operational manuals. World War II experience had shown that it was difficult, or even impossible, for ships of different navies to operate together unless they could readily communicate, and ACP 175 was designed to remedy this problem.

ACP 175 was organized in the general manner of other signal books, that is, starting with one-flag signals, then two-flag signals, and so on. The two-flag signals were organized by general subject, starting with AA, AB, AC . . . AZ, BA, BB, BC . . . BZ, and so on. The B signals were the "administrative" signals, and the last signal on the administrative page was "BZ," standing for "well done" (thus replacing the old "TVG"). This was spoken as "Baker Zebra" until 1957, when the phonetic alphabet was changed to the "Alfa, Bravo, Charlie, Delta" one still in use today. With that change, "BZ" became "Bravo Zulu," the code familiar to, and coveted by, Sailors today.

Theodore Roscoe's informal history, *This Is Your Navy,* written specifically for Sailors, was the inspiration for this book in a number of ways. The cover for that earlier book was simple in design, yet so very appropriate. Featuring simply the title, the author's name, and three Navy signal flags, it was Roscoe's way of summing up the content of his book, which unashamedly sang the praises of the U.S. Navy. The three flags were Tango, Victor, and Charlie, forerunner to Bravo Zulu: "Well done."

Appendix

Battle Streamers

Since 1971, the U.S. Navy has observed the practice during ceremonial occasions of adding a cluster of multicolored streamers adorned with silver and bronze stars to the top of its flag. These streamers and stars symbolize the dedicated and heroic service that Sailors have demonstrated for more than two hundred years.

All streamers are three feet long and two and three-quarters inches wide, but each one is unique in its combination of colors and represents an individual war, campaign, or theater of operations. The embroidered stars further represent individual battles or specific operations that rate special recognition. One battle or operation is represented by one bronze star. To save space, five battles or operations are represented by one silver star. The three battles of the Quasi-War with France, for example, are recognized by a streamer with three bronze stars, while the fourteen separate battles of the War of 1812 are represented by two silver stars and four bronze stars.

Some battle streamers represent wars (such as the Revolutionary War and the Spanish-American War), while others represent a period or campaign (such as operations against West Indian pirates and the China relief expedition). World War II was such a vast war that it is represented by a series of streamers, each one standing for a different theater of operations (Asiatic-Pacific Theater, European–African–Middle Eastern Campaign, and so on).

Taken together, these battle streamers provide a summary operational history of the U.S. Navy. Each battle streamer is listed below, followed by a brief description of the war, campaign, or theater of operations it represents. Also listed are the individual battles or special operations recognized by the stars on each streamer.

Note: The stars on three banners pictured in this appendix—Revolutionary War, Armed Forces Expeditionary Service, and Vietnam Service—do not correspond to the paragraphs that describe them. At the time we went to press, copies of the updated streamers were not available to reproduce here.

Revolutionary War, 1775–83

Beginning with actions in coastal waters in early 1775, followed by Commodore Esek Hopkins's 1776 amphibious assault to capture military stores at New Providence in the Bahamas, and reaching a climax in 1781 when French fleet action off the Virginia Capes led to victory at Yorktown, the war at sea played a vital role in the nation's struggle for independence. Small, fragmented American naval forces lacked the capabilities for major fleet engagements, but their contributions were crucial to failure or success.

The Continental Navy was aided by various state navies, privateers, and a fleet of schooners sent to sea by General George Washington. With these various seagoing forces, the Americans captured nearly two hundred enemy merchant ships to provide vitally needed supplies for the hard-pressed Army, periodically transported Washington's troops, and joined in the defense of important port cities—New York, Philadelphia, and Charleston. Despite overwhelming odds, American Sailors carried the patriotic cause to sea against the overwhelming strength of Britain's Royal Navy. Operations in European waters, especially when John Paul Jones and his men in *Bonhomme Richard* defeated HMS *Serapis* in battle, brought the war to England's shores.

★★ Stars

Two silver stars are included on the Revolutionary War battle streamer, representing ten different battles, campaigns, and operations.

1. New Providence, Bahamas, operation (3 March 1776). In the first Continental Navy operation of the war, a squadron of ships commanded by Esek Hopkins landed shore parties in the Bahamas and captured a British fort at New Providence, bringing back much-needed ammunition and weapons to General George Washington's Army.

2. Inland waters and amphibious operations. An outclassed American force at Lake Champlain was able to slow the British advance from Canada and set up the vital American strategic victory at Saratoga in 1777. Eleven of the thirteen states (New Jersey and Delaware were the exceptions) created navies for the defense of their seaports, and some participated in commerce-raiding operations. On several occasions, Washington relied upon local vessels to effect some of his most important operations: his escape from New York, in which nine thousand men were ferried across the East River in nine hours, and his assault across the Delaware River to capture Trenton are notable examples.

3. West Indies and European convoy operations. Although not part of the rebellious colonies, the West Indies were an important component of the economy in the New World, as well as a source of great distraction for the Royal Navy as it defended both its holdings there and its convoys carrying goods to and from the region.

4. Operations in European waters. Various American ships under the command of Lambert Wickes, Gustavus Conyngham, and John Paul Jones operated in the waters near Britain and France, seizing British ships and conducting raids ashore. This caused a great deal of alarm in England and further resulted in British merchants demanding naval escorts for their ships.

5. Commerce raiding operations. Unable to stand up against the powerful Royal Navy in direct conflict except on rare occasions, American Sailors waged a kind of guerrilla war at sea by capturing British merchant ships. Washington sent six schooners to sea on commerce raids in the fall of 1775 to capture thirty-eight British prizes. In the nine years of war, nearly two hundred British ships were captured.

6. *Randolph* versus *Yarmouth* (7 March 1778). The U.S. frigate *Randolph* engaged the far more powerful British ship of the line *Yarmouth* in a heroic night action that ended when *Randolph* exploded, killing all but 4 of her 315-man crew.

7. *Ranger* versus *Drake* (24 April 1778). In a "warm, close, and obstinate" action, American Sailors in *Ranger* (commanded by John Paul Jones) captured the British sloop of war *Drake*.

8. *Bonhomme Richard* versus *Serapis* (23 September 1779). American Sailors in *Bonhomme Richard* defeated the more powerful HMS *Serapis* in the most famous sea battle of the war. Captain John Paul Jones is said to have uttered his famous words "I have not yet begun to fight" in response to the British captain asking if he wished to surrender.

9. Other single-ship actions. *Lexington* captured HMS *Edward*. Sloop of war *Providence* captured brig *Diligent*. *Alliance* simultaneously defeated two enemy brigs (*Atalanta* and *Trepassy*). And the list goes on.

10. Transport and packet operations. Ships were the single means of transport and communication across the Atlantic, performing such important duties as transporting Benjamin Franklin, John Adams, and others to Europe to arrange for a French alliance that proved vital to the American cause.

Quasi-War with France, 1798–1801

With independence won, the last ship of the Continental Navy was sold in 1785, and the nation soon thereafter experienced the consequences of neglecting sea power. In 1794, the actions of Mediterranean pirates caused Congress to provide a Navy for the protection of commerce. Subsequently, French privateers began seizing American merchant ships, provoking an undeclared war fought entirely at sea.

In this quasi-war the new U.S. Navy received its baptism of fire. Captain Thomas Truxtun's insistence on the highest standards of crew training paid handsome dividends as Sailors in the frigate *Constellation* won two complete victories over French men-of-war. U.S. naval squadrons, operating principally in West Indian waters, sought out and attacked enemy privateers until France agreed to an honorable settlement.

Stars★★★

Three bronze stars represent the two ship-to-ship engagements and one series of operations during the Quasi-War with France.

1. *Constellation* **versus** *l'Insurgente* **(9 February 1799).** The American frigate soundly defeated her French counterpart because of superior ship handling and excellent crew discipline. The captured French ship remained in the U.S. Navy as USS *Insurgent.*

2. *Constellation* **versus** *la Vengeance* **(1–2 February 1800).** Although the French ship's broadside was considerably heavier, *Constellation's* crew inflicted heavy damage and casualties, causing the French captain to strike his colors twice before ultimately escaping.

3. Anti-privateering operations. Nearly eighty French privateers were captured during the Quasi-War. Most notable among the American ships conducting these operations were the schooners *Experiment* and *Enterprise.*

Barbary Wars, 1801–05, 1815

The Barbary States of North Africa (Tripoli [current-day Libya], Tunis, Algiers, and Morocco) had plundered seaborne commerce for centuries. They demanded tribute money, seized ships, and held crews for ransom or sold them into slavery. While the more powerful nations of Europe chose to pay the tribute money, the fledgling United States refused and instead sent naval squadrons into the Mediterranean to oppose these piratical practices. Under the leadership of Commodores Richard Dale and Edward Preble, the U.S. Navy blockaded the enemy coast, bombarded its shore fortresses, and engaged in close, bitterly contested gunboat actions.

The relatively small U.S. Navy amazed its European counterparts in these early operations and accomplished far more than could be expected of such a newly formed service. Several incidents, including the burning of the captured *Philadelphia* and the sailing of *Intrepid* alone into the harbor at Tripoli, loaded with explosives to blow up enemy vessels moored there, set valorous examples for the young naval service.

After gradual withdrawal of the U.S. Navy led the Barbary powers to renew their age-old piratical practices, two naval squadrons under Commodores Stephen Decatur and William Bainbridge returned to the Mediterranean in 1815. Diplomacy backed by resolute force soon brought the rulers of Barbary to terms and gained widespread respect for the new American nation.

Stars ★ ★ ★ ★

Four bronze stars represent the various actions during the Barbary Wars.

1. Actions in the harbor at Tripoli. During the first of several attacks on the port city of Tripoli, U.S. Sailors in boarding parties captured several enemy vessels in fierce hand-to-hand fighting. On 3 September 1804, in an act of great courage and sacrifice, a group of volunteer U.S. Sailors sailed the appropriately named ketch *Intrepid* into Tripoli's harbor. The *Intrepid* was loaded with explosives; the Sailors intended to head the vessel for a

Tripolitan flotilla, detonate the explosives, set the *Intrepid* on fire, and escape into small boats. By great misfortune, the explosives detonated in a huge explosion before they were intended, costing the lives of the entire crew.

2. Blockade of Tripolitan coast. During blockade operations, U.S. ships not only maintained an effective blockade but also captured or destroyed a number of Tripolitan vessels, including *Meshuda* by frigate *John Adams, Mirboha* by frigate *Philadelphia,* and *Mastico* by schooner *Enterprise.*

3. Destruction of the captured USS *Philadelphia* (16 February 1804). When misfortune caused the U.S. frigate *Philadelphia* to fall into enemy hands, American Sailors, led by the courageous Lieutenant Stephen Decatur, sailed *Intrepid* into the harbor at Tripoli, destroyed the captured ship, and escaped, causing Britain's great naval hero Lord Horatio Nelson to call the exploit "the most daring act of the age."

4. Operations against Algiers (1815). When Algerian vessels renewed attacks on American merchant shipping, Congress declared war on Algiers (eight days after peace was signed with Great Britain, concluding the War of 1812) on 4 March. The war was short (four months), with the Algerians suffering all the losses and the dey of Algiers signing a peace treaty dictated "at the mouths of cannons," in Commodore Stephen Decatur's words.

War of 1812

Interference with the United States' commerce and its rights to sail the seas without hindrance led to war with Great Britain. Surprising the world, Sailors of the U.S. Navy proved their ability to stand up to the powerful Royal Navy, winning several courageous victories in ship-to-ship actions; the most memorable of these was that by Captain Isaac Hull in USS *Constitution* ("Old Ironsides") over HMS *Guerrière.* Despite the Royal Navy's close blockade of the American coast, a number of U.S. warships were able to slip through the blockaders to take their toll of enemy naval and merchant ships.

Commodore Oliver Hazard Perry's brilliant success in the Battle of Lake Erie placed the Northwest Territory firmly under American control and sent the nation's morale soaring. Another fleet victory by Commodore Thomas Macdonough on Lake Champlain turned back a British invasion from Canada.

Commodore Joshua Barney and his Sailors and Marines made a heroic stand in the land fighting at the Battle of Bladensburg outside Washington. In the final contest of the war, Commodore Daniel Patterson correctly predicted that an enemy blow would come at New Orleans rather than Mobile. Patterson's small naval squadron so delayed and harassed the advancing British with ship gunfire that General Andrew Jackson was enabled to prepare his defenses and gain the historic New Orleans victory.

 Stars

Two silver and four bronze stars represent the fourteen actions during the War of 1812 (which actually lasted until 1814).

1. *Constitution* versus *Guerrière* (19 August 1812). In the first action of the war between two frigates, USS *Constitution* sank HMS *Guerrière,* lifting national morale at a time when the land war was going badly for the Americans. Time and again during the engagement, British cannon shot failed to penetrate the U.S. frigate's hull, earning her the nickname "Old Ironsides." In his after-action report, Captain Isaac Hull cited the courage and fighting skill of the black Sailors in the crew, writing that he "never had any better fighters" and that they "stripped to the waist, and fought like devils . . . utterly insensible to danger."

2. *United States* versus *Macedonian* (28 October 1812). In a second frigate action, U.S. Sailors were again victorious over the Royal Navy. This time, the British vessel was captured and ultimately served in the U.S. Navy for many decades to come.

3. *Constitution* versus *Java* (29 December 1812). In a hard-fought battle—the third consecutive meeting of frigates—American Sailors again defeated the British. HMS *Java* was so badly damaged that she had to be scuttled.

4. *Chesapeake* versus *Shannon* (1 June 1813). The string of U.S. victories in frigate engagements ended when HMS *Shannon* defeated USS *Chesapeake,* but the words of Captain James Lawrence as he lay dying— "Don't give up the ship"—set an important U.S. naval tradition that continues to this day.

5. *Essex* versus *Phoebe* and *Cherub* (28 March 1814). Ending an extraordinarily successful commerce-raiding expedition into the Pacific that crippled Britain's whaling industry, the frigate *Essex* was defeated by two British ships (frigate *Phoebe* and sloop of war *Cherub*) when the British ships violated neutral waters to attack her. Despite the loss, *Essex*'s captain and crew exhibited the same courage and daring that had characterized their exploits for a full year prior.

6. *Constitution* versus *Cyane* and *Levant* (20 February 1815). Frigate *Constitution* defeated two British ships (frigate *Cyane* and sloop of war *Levant*).

7. Sloop of war and brig single-ship actions. While the frigate-to-frigate engagements were capturing the attention and the imagination of the world, the smaller ships were likewise doing battle in the far corners of the earth. The various actions included, among others: on 18 October 1812, U.S. sloop *Wasp* captured sloop HMS *Frolic* five days out of Philadelphia; sloop *Hornet* sank British brig *Peacock* in early 1813 off British Guiana; sloop *Enterprise* captured the brig *Boxer* off the coast of Florida in August; and on 29 April 1814, sloop *Peacock* captured the British brig *Epervier*.

8. Commerce raiding in the Atlantic. By keeping the pressure on British merchant shipping, some of the advantages enjoyed by the more powerful Royal Navy were offset.

9. Operations against whaling fleets in the Pacific. The frigate *Essex* was the most famous of the American ships attacking this vital British industry, virtually destroying it for a time by taking twelve prizes around the Galapagos Islands from April through July 1813.

10. Battle of Lake Erie (10 September 1813). One of the most important naval actions of the war occurred when an American squadron of nine ships (flying a flag with the words "Don't Give Up the Ship") under the command of Oliver Hazard Perry defeated a more heavily armed squadron of British ships, capturing them all and allowing an American Army to launch an offensive to recapture Detroit.

11. Battle of Lake Champlain (11 September 1814). In a battle credited with causing the British to come to the peace table, an American squadron under Thomas Macdonough defeated a British squadron, causing an advancing British army to retreat into Canada.

12. Defense of Washington (July–August 1814). Although unable to stop the British advance, Commodore Joshua Barney and his naval brigade showed great courage in resisting superior British forces.

13. Defense of Baltimore (September 1814). Defenders at Fort McHenry were able to prevent the British advance on Baltimore, inspiring Francis Scott Key to write the words to what later became the American national anthem.

14. Battle of New Orleans (December 1814–January 1815). Slow communications of the day did not prevent this battle from taking place even though the war had officially ended earlier. Supported by naval forces, including a heroic stand by a naval battery on the west bank of the Mississippi River, the American Army under General Andrew Jackson was able to withstand the British assault and save New Orleans from capture.

African Slave Trade Patrol, 1820–61

In 1819, Congress declared the long illegal, infamous slave trade to be piracy and, as such, punishable by death. The Navy's African Slave Trade Patrol was established to search for and bring to justice these dealers in human misery. The patrol, which from time to time included USS *Constitution,* USS *Constellation,* USS *Saratoga,* and USS *Yorktown,* relentlessly plied the waters off West Africa, South America, and the Cuban coast, all principal areas for the slave trade. They captured more than a hundred suspected slavers before the patrols ended with the coming of the Civil War.

Operations against West Indian Pirates, 1822–30s

During the decade between 1810 and 1820, pirates increasingly infested the Caribbean and the Gulf of Mexico, and by the early 1820s, nearly three thousand attacks had been made on merchant ships. Financial loss was great; murder and torture were common.

In 1822 the Navy created the West India Squadron to combat the problem. Under the leadership of Commodores James Biddle, David Porter, and Lewis Warrington, Sailors of the American Navy crushed the pirates and ended their previously unchallenged crimes.

Sailors manning open boats for extended periods through storms and intense heat relentlessly ferreted out the outlaws from uncharted bays and lagoons. Added to the danger of close-quarter combat was the constant exposure to yellow fever and malaria in the arduous tropical duty.

The Navy's persistent and aggressive assault against the freebooters achieved the desired results. Within ten years, Caribbean piracy was all but extinguished, and an invaluable service had been rendered to humanity and the shipping interests of all nations.

Indian Wars, 1835–42

The boggy maze of the Florida Everglades long provided a fortress of refuge for the resourceful Seminole Indians. In 1835 the massacre of an Army detachment by the Indians caused the Navy to send Sailors and Marines into the watery environment.

Landing parties from the West India Squadron commanded by Commodore Alexander Dallas relieved Army garrisons, enabling them to move into the interior. In 1836, involvement of the Creek Indians extended the war to southern Alabama and Georgia. Small Navy steamers plying the Chattahoochee and other rivers supplied army troops, reinforced by nearly the entire Marine Corps, to keep U.S. lines of communication open and secure.

American Sailors also operated a brown-water "mosquito fleet" composed of small sailing craft, flat-bottomed barges, and shallow dugouts that could penetrate hundreds of miles into swamps and twisting tributaries to find and help defeat the elusive enemy.

Mexican War, 1846–48

Friction between the United States and Mexico, aggravated by an ever-increasing American population in the southwest and the admission of the Texas Republic into the Union, resulted in war. A variety of operations not only served to assure an American victory but also prepared U.S. forces for the great challenges of the coming Civil War.

Stars★★★★

Four bronze stars represent the actions during the Mexican War.

1. Veracruz landing (9 March 1847). Veracruz, key to ultimate victory on the Gulf of Mexico, fell before a brilliantly executed amphibious assault planned by Commodore David Conner. More than twelve thousand troops were put ashore with their equipment in a single day, and, at the request of General Winfield Scott, naval gunners and their heavy cannon went ashore to help the Army artillery pound the enemy into submission, opening the way for the capture of Mexico City.

2. Riverine operations. From the Gulf of Mexico, Sailors under the command of Commodore Matthew C. Perry, navigating small side-wheel steamers and schooners, fought their way up tortuous rivers to capture Frontera, San Juan Bautista, and other enemy strongholds and supply sources.

3. East coast blockade. The Navy's Home Squadron was sent south to successfully blockade Mexico's east coast, exerting important economic and international pressure on the enemy.

4. West coast blockade and operations in California. Sailors from the Pacific Squadron under Commodores John Stoat and Robert Stockton blockaded Mexico's west coast and conducted successful amphibious operations, landing at Monterey, San Francisco, and San Diego.

Civil War, 1861–65

In a war so dominated by massive land battles, it is easy to overlook the role of naval warfare, but as a result of operations on the high seas, on rivers, and in bays and harbors, the Navy was a decisive factor in the Civil War's outcome. One of the major contributing factors to Union victory was the Navy's ability to effectively blockade Confederate ports, thereby bringing about economic pressure and seriously limiting Southern maneuverability. The Navy also joined with the Army to launch a series of major amphibious assaults, which resulted in the capture of a number of key strategic positions.

Armored ships proved more effective than their wooden predecessors, ushering in a new era of naval warfare and maritime technology. The indecisive battle between the USS *Monitor* and CSS *Virginia* (former USS *Merrimack*), the first ever between armored vessels, caught the attention of the world and proved to be a turning point in naval history.

Although Confederate naval forces fought valiantly throughout the war, control of the sea by the Union Navy isolated the South and gave the North's military forces the added dimension of mobility that sea power provides.

★ ★ ★ Stars

Three silver stars on the Civil War battle streamer represent the fifteen battles and operations of the Civil War.

1. Blockade operations. The Union Navy blockaded some three thousand miles of Confederate coast—from Virginia to Texas—in a mammoth effort to cut off supplies, destroy the Southern economy, and discourage foreign intervention.

2. Capture of Hatteras Inlet, North Carolina (29 August 1861). In the first amphibious operation of the war, Union Army and Navy forces captured Forts Hatteras and Clark, closing off the entrance to Pamlico Sound in North Carolina to Confederate blockade runners and providing the Union blockading squadron with an advanced base for their operations.

3. Capture of Port Royal Sound, South Carolina (7 November 1861). The largest fleet (seventy-seven vessels) ever assembled under the U.S. flag up to that time attacked and captured Forts Walker and Beauregard, providing the Union Navy an advance base in South Carolina. A small Confederate squadron was able to successfully evacuate the troops from the forts before they fell to the Union forces.

4. Capture of Fort Henry, Tennessee River (6 February 1862). Gunfire from Union ships under the command of Andrew Foote was so effective that Sailors were able to capture this key fort without the assistance of Army troops. After the devastating fire from the mixed fleet of wooden and ironclad gunboats disabled all but four of the fort's guns, the fort's commander surrendered.

5. Capture of Roanoke Island (7–8 February 1862). A joint Army-Navy expedition captured the strategically important Roanoke Island in North Carolina's Albemarle Sound, completing the Union's hold on the Carolina islands.

6. USS *Monitor* versus CSS *Virginia* (former USS *Merrimack*) (9 March 1862). In the first-ever battle between ironclads, USS *Monitor* and CSS *Virginia* fought to a draw. Tactically, neither ship was able to defeat the other; strategically, the Union blockade was not broken and the James River was denied to Union forces.

7. Battle of New Orleans (24 April 1862). Led by Flag Officer David Farragut, Union Sailors in a fleet of wooden ships bravely endured a gauntlet of heavy fire from fortifications on both sides of the Mississippi River and then soundly defeated a Confederate flotilla, ultimately leading to the surrender of New Orleans, a tremendous strategic and psychological blow to the Confederacy.

8. Capture of Vicksburg (4 July 1863). A combined Army-Navy siege resulted in the fall of this key Mississippi city. Coupled with the Union victory at Gettysburg, this signaled the beginning of the end of the Confederacy.

9. USS *Kearsarge* versus CSS *Alabama* (19 June 1864). Hundreds watched from French coastal cliffs as Confederate cruiser *Alabama* was sunk in a ship-to-ship battle with the screw sloop *Kearsarge,* ending *Alabama*'s long and successful worldwide commerce raiding campaign that covered more than seventy-five thousand miles and took sixty-four prizes.

10. Battle of Mobile Bay (5 August 1864). The last major port on the Confederacy's Gulf coast was closed by Union forces after a naval squadron led by Rear Admiral David Farragut defied gun batteries and mines (called "torpedoes" in those days) to enter the Alabama Bay and defeat a Confederate squadron in a pitched battle. At a critical moment, Farragut made an important tactical decision and uttered the now-famous words: "Damn the torpedoes! Full speed ahead."

11. Destruction of CSS *Albemarle* (27–28 October 1864). In an act of great courage, William B. Cushing and thirteen other Sailors destroyed a Confederate ironclad by ramming her with a spar torpedo under the cover of darkness while the ship was at her mooring in the Roanoke River.

12. Capture of Fort Fisher, Wilmington, North Carolina (13–15 January 1865). In a large joint operation that involved sixty Union ships, eighty-five hundred Army troops, a naval brigade of sixteen hundred Sailors, and four hundred Marines, the fort guarding the entrance to the Cape Fear River in North Carolina was seized. The Soldiers were able to capture the fort from the rear while the defenders were preoccupied by a courageous and costly frontal assault by the Sailors and Marines.

13. Operations on the Mississippi and tributaries. In a giant pincers campaign, river gunboats moved north and south along the Mississippi River and its tributaries, seizing key points and contributing to the economic and military strangulation of the Confederacy.

14. Campaigns in the Chesapeake and tributaries. Because the Chesapeake Bay lay in close proximity to both the Union capital at Washington, D.C., and the Confederate capital at Richmond, Virginia, this bay and its many tributaries served as both a "highway" and a barrier as the two sides maneuvered and periodically engaged in one of the major theaters of the war.

15. Atlantic operations against commerce raiders and blockade runners. The Union blockade of Confederate ports led to an ongoing struggle between the two navies to gain some military advantage at sea. The weaker Confederate Navy resorted to sporadic commerce raiding, and the South's continual attempts to evade the blockading ships caused the Union Navy to expend a great deal of effort in suppressing both of these activities.

Spanish-American War, 1898

On the night of 15 February 1898, the battleship USS *Maine* was shattered by an explosion that sent the ship and two-thirds of her crew to the bottom of Havana harbor. Bolstered by widespread sympathy for those who were seeking Cuban independence from Spain's colonial rule, the emotionally charged *Maine* tragedy forced the already strained Spanish-American relations to the breaking point, precipitating a short war rapidly decided by two major naval engagements.

On 1 May the U.S. Pacific Squadron under Commodore George Dewey steamed into Manila Bay, Philippine Islands, and destroyed the Spanish fleet. Two months later, Admiral William Sampson won an equally annihilating victory over the Spanish in a running battle off Santiago, Cuba.

In addition to Sampson's and Dewey's crushing victories, naval operations included a blockade of the Cuban coast; bombardment of Spanish fortifications at San Juan, Puerto Rico, by battleship USS *Iowa,* armored cruiser USS *New York,* and other ships; and gunfire support of Marine and Army landings in Cuba and Puerto Rico.

The United States emerged from the Spanish-American War as a major naval power.

Stars★★★★

Four bronze stars represent the two major battles and two campaigns of the Spanish-American War.

1. Battle of Manila Bay (1 May 1898). Already deployed to the western Pacific, the Asiatic Squadron under the command of Commodore George Dewey engaged a Spanish fleet at Manila Bay in the Philippines. Despite enemy reliance upon the additional firepower of Spanish shore batteries to supplement those of the fleet, the battle proved to be a one-sided affair. The Spanish fleet was destroyed, with six ships sunk and the rest disabled, while U.S. ships were merely lightly damaged. American Sailors suffered only 8 men slightly wounded; Spanish casualties were 91 killed and 280 wounded.

2. Pacific Ocean operations. Following the Battle of Manila Bay, naval forces supported Army operations in the Philippines, and the cruiser *Charleston* captured the island of Guam on 21 June 1898.

3. Battle of Santiago (3 July 1898). A major naval battle off the southern coast of Cuba ended in another lopsided victory for the U.S. Navy, with an entire Spanish fleet destroyed and just minimal damage to the U.S. ships involved. One American Sailor was killed and another seriously wounded, while the Spanish suffered 323 dead and 151 wounded.

4. Atlantic/Caribbean operations. Besides the victory at Santiago, U.S. naval forces conducted various operations in the Atlantic Ocean and Caribbean Sea. The first shots of the war were fired in the Atlantic when the gunboat *Nashville* captured the Spanish freighter *Buenaventura*. Dozens more Spanish merchant ships were taken as the short war progressed. Other operations included blockade, reconnaissance, and homeland security patrols; troop support operations in Cuba and Puerto Rico; and several daring raids into Spanish-controlled harbors.

Philippine Insurrection Campaign, 1899–1902

With the close of the Spanish-American War, the United States acquired the Philippine Islands, long torn by strife. Military action was necessary to bring stability to the troubled area. Landing parties of Sailors and Marines went ashore at various points to quell disturbances and maintain order. Naval ships supported Army operations with gunfire, provided mobility to deploy forces rapidly, and patrolled the waters of the archipelago to prevent supplies reaching the insurgents.

China Relief Expedition, 1900–1901

The United States had maintained an American naval presence in East Asian waters from 1835, protecting lives and property during the many unrests that shook Imperial China. Chinese dissidents—called "Boxers" by outsiders, from their self-proclaimed name of "Righteous Society of Heavenly Fists"— revolted in the spring of 1900, and in June they surrounded the foreign legations in Peking (present-day Beijing) and began a two-month siege. An international relief force, including U.S. Sailors and Marines, slowly fought its way inland to rescue the beleaguered legations. USS *Newark* and USS *Monocacy* landed Marines and Bluejackets to help reclaim the walled city of Tientsin from the Boxers and to provide logistic support to the multinational force fighting to relieve Peking. By late August the uprising was spent and the siege was lifted.

Latin American Campaigns, 1906–20

In response to internal upheaval and European threats of intervention relating to international debts, the U.S. Navy was called upon to help establish political and economic stability in Latin America during the first two decades of the twentieth century.

★ Stars

One silver star represents the five campaigns in Latin America during the early decades of the twentieth century.

1. Cuban pacification campaign (1906–09). Following the elections of 1906, a revolution broke out in Cuba. Sailors and Marines from the cruiser *Denver* went ashore to help restore order in the capital city of Havana in September. A large contingent of Marines was subsequently landed at various locations in Cuba to protect Americans there and to help maintain order. Marines remained there until 1909.

2. First Nicaraguan campaign (1912). After several previous interventions, Sailors and Marines landed in Nicaragua to assist the government, which was besieged by rebel forces. American forces disarmed the rebels surrounding the government at Granada, defeated another rebel force at Coyotope, and recaptured the rebel-held city of Leon, effectively ending the revolution.

3. Mexican service campaign (1914). U.S. warships stationed off the coast to protect Americans in Mexico during a revolution ultimately landed a force of Sailors and Marines at Veracruz to prevent a German arms shipment from being off-loaded. A naval brigade fought defenders there to capture the city. Fifty-five Medals of Honor were awarded to Sailors and Marines as a result of that action, the largest number ever awarded for a single engagement.

4. Haitian campaign (1915, 1919–20). Revolutionary chaos in Haiti in 1915 led to U.S. intervention. After several engagements with various forces, U.S. Sailors and Marines were able to quell the fighting and establish a U.S. occupation of the country that would continue for several years. Rebellious forces plunged the country into chaos again in 1919, causing U.S. forces there to fight numerous actions until order was restored in 1920.

5. Dominican campaign (1916). U.S. Sailors and Marines fought a series of actions in the Dominican Republic to restore order there.

World War I, 1917–18

Recognizing the dependence of Great Britain on ocean communications, Germany launched an intense submarine campaign to bring the British to terms, and they very nearly succeeded. Indiscriminate attacks on American ships, with accompanying loss of life, led the United States into war.

After America entered the war, the outcome hinged upon a steady flow of troops and supplies across the ocean to the battlefields of France. A vast convoy system of merchant ships, destroyers, and cruisers went into operation and dramatically reduced ship losses. Naval aircraft flying from European bases aided in the antisubmarine effort, including the bombing of Zeebrugge and Ostend. Large U.S. Navy minelayers laid some sixty thousand mines in the great North Sea mine barrier designed to deny German submarines access to the open sea.

Various craft were mobilized in opposition to U-boats, which had deployed to the U.S. Atlantic coast. Escorted by destroyers, the Cruiser Transportation Force and the Naval Overseas Transportation Service participated in carrying more than two million Soldiers and 6.5 million tons of cargo to Europe.

Not one American Soldier on his way to France was lost to submarine action. A division of U.S. battleships joined the British Grand Fleet in the North Sea to contain the German High Seas Fleet and thus prevent its contesting the control of the sea. In the Mediterranean, U.S. subchasers distinguished themselves in protecting Allied ships from submarine attack. And U.S. naval elements fought ashore in France when 14-inch guns, mounted on railroad cars and served by seaman gunners, effectively bombarded enemy concentrations at long range.

In the final analysis, control of the sea approaches to Europe made victory possible.

★ Stars

One silver star represents the five operations in World War I.

1. Atlantic convoy operations. The U.S. Navy Cruiser and Transport Force moved nearly a million Soldiers across the submarine-infested Atlantic without a single loss of life as a result of enemy action. Convoys continued resupply operations throughout the war, losing merely 8 ships out of 450 by war's end.

2. Western Atlantic operations. While many naval assets were committed to trans-Atlantic convoys and combat operations in European waters, other American naval vessels (many of them subchasers and other small antisubmarine units) and aircraft (including dirigibles) carried out U.S. coastal patrols and convoy escort operations between New York and Norfolk, Virginia. The destroyer *Jouett* and six subchasers were also formed into an on-call "naval hunt squadron" operating out of Norfolk.

3. Operations in northern European waters. U.S. battleships, destroyers, subchasers, minesweepers, tenders, armed yachts, and others conducted various operations in northern European waters, including attacking

German U-boats, supplementing the British Grand Fleet, and escorting local convoys.

4. Mediterranean operations. American ships provided vital protection of the western entrance to the Mediterranean Sea, and subchasers organized into a submarine hunting group nicknamed "the splinter fleet" conducted antisubmarine operations in the Mediterranean itself.

5. Operations on the European continent. Large-caliber naval guns were mounted onto railway cars and deployed to France to take part in combat operations on the Western Front; naval aviators joined the battle in the skies over Europe, conducting both fighter and attack missions in this emerging form of warfare; and naval vessels participated in landing operations, including the insertion of troops at Murmansk after Russia fell to the Communist revolution and dropped out of the war.

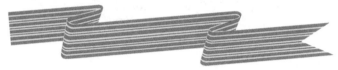

Second Nicaraguan Campaign, 1926–33

Civil war broke out in Nicaragua during the first months of 1926, and U.S. naval landing parties went ashore to establish a neutral zone for the protection of American citizens.

As the fighting intensified and spread, additional coastal enclaves were formed by the Navy to shelter refugees. By January 1927, two light cruisers and seven destroyers had reinforced the U.S. Special Service Squadron.

When the danger points moved inland, three thousand U.S. Marines, supported by planes from Navy Observation Squadron 3, landed at the request of the Nicaraguan government. Once order was restored, Sailors and Marines monitored free elections and organized and trained an efficient National Guard.

Yangtze Service, 1926–27, 1930–32

Shallow-draft gunboats of the U.S. Navy sailed China's largest river for more than fifty years before being officially organized as the Yangtze Patrol Force in August 1921.

These ships protected U.S. citizens against bandits and warlord forces in a turbulent China. In the mid-1920s, the internal struggle for power was accompanied by many acts of violence against foreigners. Units of the Yangtze Patrol Force, reinforced by destroyers and light cruisers from the U.S. Asiatic Fleet, steamed upriver to protect Americans and national interests.

Numerous confrontations occurred. When the situation stabilized, an uneasy peace returned to the Yangtze valley, and the gunboats resumed anti-bandit activities. In the early 1930s, severe floods along the entire river valley brought the gunboats and additional ships of the Asiatic Fleet into action again, this time in the humanitarian cause of aiding the millions of Chinese left homeless by the catastrophe.

China Service, 1937–39, 1945–57

Japanese aggression against China, verified by the move into Manchuria in 1931 and subsequent incidents in Shanghai, surfaced anew in 1937 when a minor clash near Peking erupted into a full-scale invasion.

The area of hostilities spread quickly, and units of the U.S. Asiatic Fleet evacuated American citizens and protected national interests, standing firm against Japan's increasingly belligerent actions toward neutrals. At Shanghai, U.S. ships were endangered by Japanese aerial bombings and artillery fire. On 12 December 1937, Japanese naval aircraft attacked and sank the river gunboat USS *Panay.*

After World War II, the U.S. Navy returned to China to repatriate Japanese soldiers and to assist the Chinese central government in enforcing the surrender terms. Seventh Fleet Amphibious Forces provided transport for Chinese Nationalist troops and carried food supplies from Shanghai up the Yangtze to fight near-famine conditions in the interior.

American Defense Service, 1939–41

Two days after the start of World War II in Europe, but before the United States was formally involved, President Franklin D. Roosevelt ordered the

Navy to organize a neutrality patrol to report and track any belligerent air, surface, or underwater forces approaching the United States or the West Indies.

With the fall of France in June 1940, Germany gained valuable U-boat bases to press the attack against British lifelines, and possibilities were raised of German occupation of French territories in the Western Hemisphere. Assigned additional responsibilities in defense of this hemisphere, the U.S. Navy began the escort of convoys to Iceland. U-boat attacks on these convoys brought American destroyers into combat. On 31 October 1941, more than a month before the Japanese attack on Pearl Harbor, USS *Reuben James* was torpedoed and sunk by a German U-boat, becoming the first U.S. naval vessel destroyed by enemy action in World War II.

These operations were a precursor to the Battle of the Atlantic, fought during World War II, on which the survival of Great Britain and the projection of American power overseas depended.

World War II: American Theater, 1941–46

In the first six months following the entry of the United States into the war, the vast majority of merchant ship sinkings were in the western Atlantic. Consequently, the U.S. Navy's role in convoy protection increased markedly once the United States entered the war.

In addition to the increasing requirements for added protection of the trans-Atlantic convoys, the Navy had to protect ships moving fuel and other critical materials and supplies along the eastern seaboard of the United States. Numerous sinkings along the East Coast during the first half of 1942 seriously reduced available shipping and gravely threatened American productivity, making homeland security a high priority. To coordinate the convoy protection activities and to counter these homeland threats, the Navy created the Tenth Fleet.

Coastal convoys were initiated as escorts became available. Escort carriers, destroyers, and destroyer escorts were formed into Hunter-Killer groups to carry the offensive against the U-boats wherever they might be found. In the South Atlantic, the Fourth Fleet waged relentless war against raiders, blockade runners, and submarines.

Through such actions the U-boat campaign in the Atlantic was defeated.

Stars ★

One bronze star appears on the American Theater streamer.

1. Escort, antisubmarine, armed guard, and special operations. With America's ability to support the war in jeopardy, all available means were brought to bear to defeat the U-boats, including the use of patrol aircraft and blimps, Naval Armed Guard crews, defensive minefield harbor entrance nets, and even the mobilization of yachts for escort duty.

World War II: Asiatic-Pacific Theater, 1941–46

The war in the Pacific was essentially a maritime war. It was on the sea that Japan depended for materials to sustain it and via the sea it launched its aggressions. In fact, its first attack was intended to destroy the nucleus of the U.S. Fleet at Pearl Harbor. The vital core of the American military effort was the contest for control of the seas, from which all other operations—sea, amphibious, land, and air—branched and received their support.

When the Japanese conducted a surprise attack on the main U.S. base in the Pacific at Pearl Harbor on 7 December 1941, America was unprepared for war. For the next several months, the Japanese achieved victory after victory, taking the Dutch East Indies, the British bastion at Singapore, Hong Kong, the Philippines, and various other islands in the Pacific. The few U.S. and Allied warships available offered valiant resistance against overwhelming odds, but for a time they were unable to stop the Japanese onslaught.

In April 1942, American morale was lifted and Japanese confidence shaken when a U.S. carrier task force steamed into the very heart of Japanese waters and launched Army aircraft on a first strike against the home islands.

At last the tide began to turn in May when carrier actions in the Battle of the Coral Sea caused a Japanese invasion force to turn back from its advance on Australia. A month later, the decisive Battle of Midway provided the turning point in the war when U.S. naval forces sank four Japanese carriers and prevented the invasion of Midway Island.

In the amphibious assault and defense of Guadalcanal, at sea and ashore, the advance of Japan into the South Pacific was halted. Step-by-step amphibious operations were launched from the South Pacific area and westward through the mid-Pacific by Admiral Chester Nimitz, and northward from the southwest Pacific by joint forces under General Douglas MacArthur.

New concepts and techniques in mobile logistic support and underway replenishment made a high tempo of sustained operations possible. U.S. submarines took a heavy toll of Japan's warships and devastated the merchant marine, thereby severing its economic lifeline.

The capture of the Marianas, and later Iwo Jima, provided fixed bases for air attacks against Japan, and the Fifth Fleet drastically reduced the power of Japanese aviation in the Battle of the Philippine Sea. Operations around Leyte destroyed much of the remaining enemy surface fleet as the recapture of the Philippines began.

At Okinawa the fleet faced and survived the fanatic attacks of kamikazes. The isolation of Japan from the sea was made complete by an intense mining campaign and the final attacks on the remnants of the Japanese fleet.

The end came quickly after the atomic bomb attacks on Hiroshima and Nagasaki. Japan surrendered on board USS *Missouri* in Tokyo Bay, 2 September 1945.

 Stars ★★★

Eight silver and three bronze stars represent the forty-three different battles and operations in the Pacific during World War II.

1. Pearl Harbor–Midway (7 December 1941). The Japanese surprise attack on the Pacific Fleet at Pearl Harbor was a disaster of great proportions, offset only by the individual heroism of Sailors, Marines, and Soldiers and by the absence of U.S. carriers, allowing them to carry on the fight until the U.S. Navy could recover from the devastating attack. Midway was also bombarded by Japanese surface ships, but with less effect.

2. Wake Island (8–23 December 1941). American defenders of Wake Island put up a valiant resistance against a Japanese invasion force—holding off the invaders for several weeks, sinking two destroyers and a transport, as well as seriously damaging a cruiser, two destroyers, and a freighter—before eventually succumbing.

3. Philippine Islands operation (8 December 1941–6 May 1942). While American and Filipino defenders were under siege by a Japanese invasion force, U.S. submarines and PT boats served as transports, evacuating key personnel (including the president of the Philippines and General Douglas MacArthur), money, weapons, and other important items, before the islands fell to the Japanese. During this same period, Guam also fell to the Japanese.

4. Netherlands East Indies engagements (23 January–27 February 1942). With its British, Dutch, and Australian allies, the greatly outclassed U.S. Asiatic Fleet fought a valiant but hopeless holding action in the western Pacific. In a series of battles (Makassar Strait, Badoeng Strait, and Java Sea) the Allied forces operated without air cover and with antiquated ships and were able to inhibit but not stop Japanese advances in the area.

5. Pacific raids (1942). U.S. aircraft carriers were not at Pearl Harbor on 7 December, so they were able to carry out a series of raids on various Japanese bases in the Pacific while the U.S. Navy began its recovery and prepared for the long offensive campaign ahead. Roaming the vast reaches of the Pacific in the early months of 1942, they struck various islands held by the Japanese, including the Gilberts and Marshalls, Wake Island, Marcus Island, and New Guinea. A planned raid on the great Japanese bastion on Rabaul was thwarted but resulted in the biggest air battle in the war to date in which Lieutenant Edward "Butch" O'Hare became the Navy's first ace of the war, shooting down five of the eighteen enemy planes lost. The most spectacular raid occurred in April, when Army planes launched from the flight deck of USS *Hornet* attacked Tokyo and other Japanese cities.

6. Coral Sea (4–8 May 1942). The first naval battle in history in which neither side's ships could see one another was fought between Japanese and American carrier forces north of Australia. The battle was a tactical victory for the Japanese but a strategic victory for the Americans. For the first time in the war, the Japanese were stopped and turned back as they abandoned their advance on southeastern New Guinea and northern Australia.

7. Midway (3–6 June 1942). Arguably the most spectacular naval victory of the war, the Battle of Midway was a major turning point. Although the Japanese force was far superior to the U.S. (eight aircraft carriers to three; seven battleships to none; eleven cruisers to eight; and fifty-five destroyers to thirty-three), the Americans used better intelligence, excellent tactics, a great deal of courage, and a measure of good luck to defeat the Japanese armada, sinking four aircraft carriers and causing the Japanese to abandon their invasion of the strategically significant Midway Island.

8. Guadalcanal-Tulagi landings (7–9 August 1942). In an operation code-named "Watchtower," the Navy and Marine Corps went on the offensive by landing on two islands in the Solomons chain where the Japanese had been building an airfield and a seaplane base that threatened the sea lines of communication between the United States and Australia. Although the landings were initially unopposed, the Japanese scored a stunning victory in a night naval battle (known as the Battle of Savo Island) in which a force of cruisers and destroyers surprised the Americans and sank four U.S. heavy cruisers without significant damage to the attacking force. The Americans remained determined despite this setback, and so began a six-month struggle for control of Guadalcanal that was marked by the most concentrated and drawn-out air, land, and naval battles of the war.

9. Capture and defense of Guadalcanal (10 August 1942–8 February 1943). Despite the early setback at Savo Island, the long campaign for control of Guadalcanal eventually ended in victory for U.S. forces. During the most intense months of the campaign, U.S. forces controlled the waters around Guadalcanal by day and the Japanese controlled them by night. Japanese naval units repeatedly came down the passage (called "The Slot") among the Solomon Islands to reinforce and resupply their troops on Guadalcanal; Americans dubbed this repeated operation the "Tokyo Express." A series of air, land, and sea battles raged on and around the Solomons until the Japanese finally withdrew their remaining forces in February 1943.

10. Makin raid (17–18 August 1942). In a daring and morale-boosting operation, a Marine battalion was landed by submarine on Makin Island in the Gilberts, destroyed the Japanese garrison there, and then reembarked on the submarines.

11. Eastern Solomons (23–25 August 1942). A large Japanese force attempted to land fifteen hundred troops in the Solomons, but a U.S. force was able to turn back the attempted reinforcement and to sink a Japanese light aircraft carrier. The U.S. carrier *Enterprise* was damaged and temporarily knocked out of the war for the first time.

12. Buin-Faisi-Tonolai raid (5 October 1942). U.S. carrier aircraft from USS *Hornet* bombed these Japanese bases in the Bougainville area of the Solomons. These bases were staging areas for the infamous Tokyo Express.

13. Cape Esperance (11–12 October 1942). In a hard-fought night surface action between U.S. and Japanese cruisers and destroyers (dubbed "Second Savo"), the Japanese lost a heavy cruiser and a destroyer, while the Americans lost one destroyer.

14. Santa Cruz Islands (26 October 1942). A large Japanese force of four carriers, four battleships, fourteen cruisers, and forty-four destroyers, intent upon destroying the U.S. naval forces (two carriers, one battleship, six cruisers, and fourteen destroyers) supporting the forces ashore at Guadalcanal, scored a tactical victory by sinking the carrier *Hornet* and the destroyer *Porter* while suffering only heavy damage to two of their carriers. But the battle was a strategic defeat for the Japanese because the U.S. naval forces remained.

15. Naval Battle of Guadalcanal (12–15 November 1942). On the night of 12–13 November, a short but bloody surface engagement (dubbed "Third Savo") turned back a larger Japanese force at a cost of several ships lost on both sides and two U.S. admirals killed. On the fourteenth, U.S. aircraft sank six of eleven troop transports on their way to reinforce Guadalcanal; another was heavily damaged and turned back, while the remaining four were destroyed the next morning by artillery fire after landing just two thousand of the ten thousand troops intended for the reinforcement. And on the night of 14–15 November, a battle between U.S. and Japanese battleships caused the Japanese force to retire before it could carry out its mission of shelling the airfield on Guadalcanal.

16. Tassafaronga (30 November 1942). A surface engagement (dubbed "Fourth Savo") resulted in greater damage to the U.S. force, but once again, the Japanese were thwarted from delivering supplies and reinforcements to their troops on Guadalcanal. Soon after, the Japanese abandoned their long struggle to keep Guadalcanal. Some historians see this as the true turning point in the Pacific War.

17. Eastern New Guinea operation. From 17 December 1942 until 24 July 1944, naval operations conducted by the U.S. Seventh Fleet supported General Douglas MacArthur's southwest Pacific campaign as his Army forces recaptured key positions along the northern New Guinea coast. U.S. naval elements supported the occupation of Saidor (2 January–1 March 1944) and Wewak-Aitape operations (14–24 July 1944).

18. Rennel Island (29–30 January 1943). One of the last naval engagements of the Guadalcanal campaign took place off Rennel Island in the Solomons. In an outstanding display of seamanship, the cruiser *Louisville* took the damaged cruiser *Chicago* under tow in complete darkness.

19. Consolidation of the Solomon Islands (8 February 1943–15 March 1945). The Navy played a crucial role in defeating remnant Japanese forces in the Solomons and pushing northeastward through the archipelago, gradually wresting control of the entire area.

20. Aleutians operation (26 March–2 June 1943). American forces recaptured the Alaskan islands of Attu and Kiska from the Japanese, who had taken them earlier in the war. Not only was American territory regained but also a route for staging aircraft into Siberia was secured. The campaign resulted in the Battle of the Komandorski Islands (26 March 1943), a classic daylight surface engagement between a U.S. cruiser-destroyer force and a superior Japanese flotilla.

21. New Georgia group operation (20 June–16 October 1943). The Third Amphibious Force, supported by the growing power of the Third Fleet, captured New Georgia and the strategically important airfield at Munda Point in a hard-fought campaign that included a series of related battles at Kula Gulf, Kolombangara, Vella Gulf, Vella Lavella, among others.

22. Bismarck Archipelago operation (25 June 1943–1 May 1944). Because of its connecting position between the Solomons and New Guinea, the neutralization of the Bismarck archipelago was a key consideration in southwest Pacific strategy. Coordinated operations of the various American forces in the area effectively implemented this component of U.S. strategy by running extensive PT boat operations, landing in the Admiralty and Green Islands and conducting air and surface bombardments of Japanese bases in Rabaul, New Ireland, Kavieng, Cape Gloucester, and other locations.

23. Pacific raids (1943). An important component of American strategy were the various raids into Japanese-controlled waters, which kept the enemy off balance and in a reactionary mode, preventing them from concentrating their forces at key positions. In 1943, U.S. forces raided Marcus Island, the Tarawa atoll, and Wake Island.

24. Treasury-Bougainville operation (27 October–15 December 1943). U.S. forces first seized two islands in the Treasury group in preparation for a seizure of Bougainville, at the northern end of the Solomons. A key battle of the struggle for Bougainville took place at Empress Augusta Bay (2 November 43), on the western side of the island, when U.S. forces turned back a superior Japanese force that had sortied from Rabaul.

25. Gilbert Islands operation (13 November–8 December 1943). Although suffering a high number of casualties, U.S. forces successfully captured Betio, Makin, and Apamama of the Tarawa atoll in the Gilberts, confirming much of the previously developed amphibious doctrine and providing many new lessons that would contribute significantly to ultimate victory in the Pacific.

26. Marshall Islands operation (26 November 1943–2 March 1944). Forces of the Fifth Fleet captured first Kwajalein, then the Eniwetok atoll, as U.S. forces under Admiral Chester Nimitz moved westward across the central Pacific at the same time that forces under Army General Douglas MacArthur moved through the southwest Pacific toward Japan.

27. Asiatic-Pacific raids (1944). While major U.S. forces advanced across the central Pacific, taking Japanese strongholds at key points and bypassing others to "wither on the vine," naval forces continued to strike at various targets (such as Truk, Yap, Ulithi, and others) to keep the Japanese off balance and to prepare the way for the advancing amphibious forces.

28. Kurile Islands operation (1 February 1944–11 August 1945). As U.S. forces converged on Japan, American naval unit forces struck at an ever-growing list of targets—Matsuwa, Suribachi Bay, the Okhotsk Sea, for example—among the islands in and around Japanese home waters.

29. Hollandia operation (21 April–1 June 1944). In a successful flanking movement, U.S. forces landed near the border of Dutch New Guinea, bypassing a large Japanese army and catching it in a pincer between American and Australian forces. Hollandia became a major naval and air base used in the ongoing New Guinea campaign.

30. Western New Guinea operations (21 April 1944–9 January 1945). In the southwest Pacific, naval operations continued to support the advance along the coast of New Guinea, second largest island in the world, with operations at Toem, Wakde, Sarni, Biak, Noemfoor, and Sansapor.

31. Marianas operation (10 June–27 August 1944). U.S. forces effectively neutralized Japanese bases in the Bonins and Marianas, capturing and occupying Saipan and Guam. The Japanese responded by sending their main battle fleet, which resulted in the one-sided Battle of the Philippine Sea. So many Japanese aircraft were shot down that the battle became known as "The Marianas Turkey Shoot."

32. Tinian capture and occupation (24 July–1 August 1944). Described as the best-executed amphibious operation of the war, U.S. forces captured and occupied Tinian in the Marianas.

33. Western Caroline Islands operation (31 August–14 October 1944). U.S. forces captured and occupied the southern Palau Islands and struck targets at Yap, the Bonins, and the Philippines.

34. Leyte operation (10 October–16 December 1944). Combined forces of the Third and Seventh Fleets landed at Leyte Island in the Philippines. The Japanese responded with a large and elaborate operation, resulting in a series of battles (Surigao Strait, Samar, Engaño, and others) that ended in the virtual destruction of the Japanese battle fleet. In an act of desperation, the Japanese introduced the suicide bomber (kamikaze), hitting four U.S. carriers and sinking one.

35. Luzon operation (12 December 1944–1 April 1945). In the ongoing campaign to reoccupy the Philippines, American forces landed at Mindoro and Lingayen Gulf while conducting various supporting operations against targets in Formosa, the China coast, and the Nansei Shoto in Japan.

36. Manila Bay–Bicol operations (29 January–16 April 1945). Essential to the retaking of the Philippines was the seizure of Manila, the capital city. Naval forces participated in multiple ways, including minesweeping and landing troops at Corregidor, Subic Bay, and other locations.

37. Iwo Jima operation (15 February–16 March 1945). In a very hard-fought battle involving three days of the heaviest naval bombardment of the war and a siege that would last more than two months, U.S. forces captured the island of Iwo Jima, making Japan vulnerable to land-based air attack by B-29 bombers.

38. Consolidation of the southern Philippines (28 February–20 July 1945). Operations such as those in Palawan, Visayan, Mindanao, among others, completed the reconquest of the Philippines.

39. Okinawa Gunto operation (17 March–30 June 1945). The U.S. assault on Okinawa, though ultimately successful, was met by tenacious resistance on land and a massed air attack—largely by kamikazes—that sank and damaged many U.S. vessels, making it one of the costliest operations of the war. The kamikaze (in some ways, a forerunner of the guided missile) proved to be the most effective antiship weapon of the war.

40. Borneo operations (27 April–20 July 1945). Operations were conducted at Tarakan Island, Brunei Bay, and Balikpapan.

41. Third Fleet operations against Japan (10 July–15 August 1945). American carrier aircraft and surface vessels struck many targets in the homeland of Japan itself.

42. Escort, antisubmarine, armed guard, and special operations. Naval Group China, Task Group 30.4, Task Group 12.2, and special salvage teams contributed to the victory at sea in the Pacific.

43. Submarine war patrols (Pacific) (7 December 1941–2 September 1945). One of the major contributing factors to victory in the Pacific was the war-long submarine campaign that devastated the Japanese economy and slowly strangled the Japanese navy and merchant marine.

World War II: European–African–Middle Eastern Campaign, 1942–45

The Battle of the Atlantic was a life-and-death struggle against the German submarine offensive to choke off the sea passage between the United States and Europe. Had the U-boats succeeded in halting the waterborne movement of men and materials, Nazi Germany might well have emerged victorious.

The United States and Great Britain instituted a highly effective convoy control and routing system. The ever-versatile destroyer was joined by mass-produced destroyer escorts, a new ship type designed specifically for convoy duty. Naval aircraft flying from the nineteen small escort carriers in Hunter-Killer groups added long-range offensive operations to the convoys' protective coverage, and Naval Armed Guard crews on merchant ships discouraged attack by surfaced U-boats.

Convoys laboring through rough waters of the North Atlantic were stalked by submarine "wolf packs," and those making the extremely hazardous run to northern Russian ports were subjected to attack from German land-based aircraft and surface ships as well. As courageous seamen continued to bring through the troop-carrying and supply-filled ships, the U-boat campaign was defeated.

Landings in Morocco, Sicily, Italy, and Normandy were instrumental in wresting control of continental Europe from the Nazis and Fascists. Essential to these operations were naval bombardment, the clearing of obstacles, and minesweeping. At Normandy, naval vessels provided covering fire for establishing and securing the beachheads in France while shells from the battleships USS *Texas,* USS *Nevada,* and USS *Arkansas* destroyed targets far inland to block the movement of German reinforcements. With the beachhead secured, LSTs and a variety of amphibious types assured an uninterrupted flow of logistic support.

Two months after Normandy came the perfectly executed landings in southern France, the last major amphibious action in the European war. Marseille was seized, and through this excellent Mediterranean port, troops were funneled for the final push on Germany.

After the crossing of the Rhine with the help of naval landing craft, the Third Reich collapsed and surrender came 7 May 1945. The Allied victory in Europe had hinged on preventing enemy submarines from cutting the sea-lanes, on the amphibious capability to project powerful armies onto enemy-held territory, and on the ability to sustain them by sea once ashore.

★ Stars ★★★★

One silver and four bronze stars represent nine operations and campaigns in Europe, Africa, and the Middle East during World War II.

1. North African occupation (8 November 1942–9 July 1943). Not yet ready to assault Nazi-controlled Europe, U.S. and British forces opened a front in North Africa by landing troops on the French-controlled coast. French resistance resulted in a naval battle off Casablanca in which several French ships were destroyed.

2. Sicilian occupation (9 July–17 August 1943). In a huge amphibious landing, British and American forces landed along a beachfront more than one hundred miles long, ultimately leading to the conquest of the island that was defended by large Italian and German armies.

3. Salerno landings (9–21 September 1943). With the assistance of excellent naval gunfire support, Allied forces were able to hold the beachhead at Salerno on "the ankle of the Italian boot."

4. West coast of Italy operations (1944). Landings at Anzio and other sites along the west coast of Italy contributed to the ultimate conquest of Fascist Italy.

5. Invasion of Normandy (6–25 June 1944). Dubbed "Operation Overlord" and popularly known as "D-Day," Allied forces returned to the European continent in a gigantic amphibious operation across the English Channel. Naval forces played key roles in transport and gunfire support.

6. Northeast Greenland operation (10 July–17 November 1944). Naval operations in the northeast Greenland area contributed to the victory in the Battle of the Atlantic.

7. Invasion of southern France (15 August–25 September 1944). Originally scheduled to coincide with the Normandy landings, the amphibious landing of three U.S. and two French divisions was delayed because of a shortage of landing craft. The landing (dubbed "Operation Dragoon") secured Allied use of the port of Marseille to support the western advance on Nazi Germany.

8. Reinforcement of Malta (14 April–16 May 1942). Malta's central position in the Mediterranean made it a key strategic island in the European war.

9. Escort, antisubmarine, armed guard, and special operations. Many convoys kept the flow of troops and supplies moving across the Atlantic, without which the war in Europe could not have been won. Minesweeping and other operations were also vital to the war effort.

Korean Service, 1950–54

On 25 June 1950, Communist North Korean forces invaded South Korea. The United States, within the framework of a UN resolution, responded to the invasion. As the defenders were pushed down the Korean peninsula by superior Communist forces, U.S. naval forces played a key role in slowing the advance of the invaders by launching air strikes and firing gun missions at the enemy's flanks.

In one of the greatest counterstrokes of history, the U.S. launched a highly doubtful amphibious invasion well behind enemy lines at Inchon on the west coast of Korea near the capital city of Seoul, turning the tide and driving the enemy back up the Korean peninsula in full retreat. Only intervention by the Chinese Communists prevented a complete UN victory and brought the war back roughly to the seventeenth parallel, where it had begun.

The remainder of the war was a virtual stalemate, with each side making small gains at various times while both sides attempted to negotiate a truce. During the entire war, U.S. sea power kept the sea lines of communication open to prevent a Communist takeover of South Korea. Ships of the Military Sea Transportation Service carried the fighting men and millions of tons of dry cargo, ammunition, and petroleum products to Korea across the Pacific, thousands of miles from the United States. Gradually, as strength built up, the U.S. and Allied naval vessels tightly blockaded both coasts of the long Korean peninsula to deny the enemy supply by sea. Battleships, including USS *Missouri,* cruisers, and destroyers delivered sustained and accurate fire on enemy troop concentrations, lines of communication, and installations.

Carrier planes ranged deep into North Korea to strike at bridges, transportation centers, and other facilities, and they provided close air support for American and Korean forces along the fighting front. Mines posed the most serious and persistent threat to the UN's entry into coastal waters and to amphibious operations. U.S. Navy minesweepers met the challenge as they carried out the hazardous clearing of heavily mined harbors at Wonson, Chinnampo, and elsewhere.

Eventually, the war was brought to a close by a negotiated truce. Communist aggression had been stopped, and the Republic of South Korea remained free to pursue a democratic form of government.

Stars

Two silver stars represent ten campaigns and operations during the Korean War.

1. North Korean aggression (27 June–2 November 1950). During the opening ten days of hostilities, destroyers covered the evacuation of American citizens as well as the movement of critically needed ammunition into the combat area. The antiaircraft cruiser USS *Juneau* conducted the first bombardment of the war, and aircraft from the carrier USS *Valley Forge* blunted the enemy air effort by blasting airfields in the north. On the ground, outnumbered defenders fell back into a perimeter pivoted on the port city of Pusan. Vessels poured men and materials into Pusan and Pohang. Warships off the coast provided gunfire. Carrier planes added their close support to planes of the U.S. Air Force, thus enabling the embattled troops to maintain their foothold.

2. Inchon landing (13–17 September 1950). In a bold counterstroke, the Navy's amphibious capability was brought into play with telling effect. A naval task force of the Seventh Fleet made an "end run" by landing the First Marine Division and Army troops at Inchon, outflanking the invaders and sending them reeling northward.

3. Communist China aggression (3 November 1950–24 January 1951). Following up on the masterstroke at Inchon, UN forces pushed the invaders northward, back into North Korean territory. Naval forces supported the northward advance with gun and air strikes. As the Communist North Korean forces were driven farther north, approaching the Chinese border, their Communist Chinese allies entered the war, crossing the Yalu River and hurling back UN forces. In the early dark days of the reversal, U.S. sea power once again played a vital role. In mid-December. American amphibious ships successfully withdrew more than one hundred thousand military personnel, ninety-one thousand refugees, three hundred fifty thousand tons of cargo, and seventeen thousand vehicles from the port of Hungnam, while Chinese Communist forces were held at bay by heavy ship fire and carrier aircraft.

4. First UN counteroffensive (25 January–21 April 1951). As the UN mounted its counteroffensive against the Communist forces, U.S. naval forces supported the land campaign by conducting air and gunfire missions against enemy lines of communication (railways, roads, bridges, for example), mounting an effective siege of the North Korea's principal port at Wonsan, inserting commando teams at key locations, conducting minesweeping operations, launching search and rescue missions, and providing close air support to troops.

5. Communist China, spring offensive (22 April–8 July 1951). As the land war continued, naval forces continued to provide vital support. On 20 May, USS *New Jersey,* one of several battleships recommissioned for service in the Korean War, fired her first bombardment mission at Kangsong.

6. UN summer–fall offensive (9 July–27 November 1951). Although truce talks had begun, the fighting raged on as each side vied for advantage, supported by U.S. Navy carrier and surface forces.

7. Second Korean winter (28 November 1951–30 April 1952). The Navy continued the struggle under the arduous conditions of the Korean winter; Sailors frequently had to chop away large accumulations of ice from ships' topsides to prevent them from becoming dangerously top heavy. Flight deck crews also had to struggle with ice, snow, frigid winds, and temperatures that froze lubricating oils.

8. Korean defense, summer–fall 1952 (1 May–30 November 1952). This period was marked by extensive carrier operations against North Korean targets, including the capital city of Pyongyang and many power plants.

9. Third Korean winter (1 December 1952–30 April 1953). U.S. sea power continued to keep the pressure on Communist adversaries while negotiations continued for a truce.

10. Korea, summer–fall 1953 (1 May–27 July 1953). In the final months of the war, U.S. Navy ships and aircraft kept sea lines of communication open and maintained pressure on the Communists in the hot war in Korea while containing the Communist threat elsewhere as part of the Cold War.

Armed Forces Expeditionary Service, 1958–

Since the Korean War, the flexibility of the U.S. Navy has never been more evident. Various naval elements have been involved in numerous and varied operations, including direct intervention, forward presence, peacekeeping, retaliatory attacks, emergency evacuation, sea control, and humanitarian aid. These operations included the amphibious and other actions of the Sixth Fleet in response to the appeal of the Lebanese government in 1958; Seventh Fleet operations off Quemoy and Matsu and in the Taiwan Straits between August 1958 and June 1963; the Berlin crisis of 1961; support of UN operations in the Congo between July 1960 and September 1962 and again in November 1964; the Cuban missile crisis in 1962 and the "quarantine" enforced by the Second Fleet; Dominican operations in 1965 and 1966; certain actions in the Korean area during 1966 through 1974; varied operations in Southeast Asia; operations in Lebanon between 1983 and 1987; landings in Grenada, Panama, Somalia, and Haiti; strikes against Libya in 1986; various operations in the Persian Gulf from 1987 to the present; and peacekeeping operations in the Balkans.

While other major operations (such as the Vietnam War and the first Persian Gulf War) have been recognized by their own individual battle streamers, the various operations listed here have been recognized under the generic battle streamer for Armed Forces Expeditionary Service. It is anticipated that other operations will be recognized and added to this battle streamer as time goes on.

 Stars ★★★

Five silver and three bronze stars represent twenty-eight different expeditions to date that are recognized by this battle streamer.

1. Lebanon (1958). Supported by naval units offshore, U.S. troops were sent into the small Middle Eastern nation that was threatened by civil war and invasion.

2. Taiwan Straits (1958–59). To send a strong deterrent message to the Communist Chinese who seemed intent upon attacking the Chinese Nationalists, a six-carrier task force positioned itself in the straits of Taiwan.

3. Quemoy and Matsu Islands (1958–63). When these two Nationalist Chinese islands were bombarded and threatened with invasion by the Communists on the Chinese mainland, President Dwight D. Eisenhower ordered elements of the U.S. Seventh Fleet to intervene. The presence of this U.S. fleet caused the Communists to halt their bombardments and prevented them from seizing the islands.

4. Vietnam (1958–65). After the French withdrew from Indochina and before direct U.S. involvement with massive military power, American advisors lent support and provided large amounts of money to the South Vietnamese government's struggle against insurgent Communist (Vietcong) forces. U.S. naval advisors became involved in the so-called brown-water operations on the rivers and littorals of Vietnam, eventually leading to active involvement through the River Patrol Force, the Coastal Surveillance Force, and the Mobile Riverine Force. U.S. Navy ships ran surveillance operations off the coast of North Vietnam, and special forces conducted raids against enemy facilities along the Communist coast. In the "Tonkin Gulf Incident," U.S. surface ships and carrier aircraft battled with North Vietnamese naval units and subsequently launched retaliatory air strikes.

5. Congo (1960–62). The U.S. Navy helped the UN prevent disorders in the newly independent states in the African Congo region.

6. Laos (1961–62). U.S. forces were involved in the fighting in Laos between the U.S.-backed government and the Communist Pathet Lao.

7. Berlin (1961–63). In the Cold War, the city of Berlin, Germany, became a focal point of the clash between Communism and the West, particularly with the construction of the Berlin Wall that prevented Germans from fleeing the Communist regime. Tensions ran high, and, although the confrontations never led to direct conflict, U.S. military presence and support was a major factor in the struggle.

8. Cuba (1962). The discovery of offensive nuclear missiles in Cuba led to a confrontation between the United States and the Union of Soviet Socialist Republics. The U.S. Navy played the most overt and visible role in the crisis by forming a quarantine around the island that prevented Soviet ships from bringing in more missiles.

9. Congo (1964). U.S. naval units moved into this troubled African region in support of a rescue mission in which Belgian paratroopers were dropped from U.S. Air Force planes into the Democratic Congo Republic to extract seventeen hundred prisoners from the recent civil war who were threatened with massacre.

10. Dominican Republic (1965–66). A revolution in the Central American nation endangered American citizens there, causing the United States to send in troops, which were supported by Navy units offshore.

11. Korea (1966–74). The truce ending the fighting in the Korean War did not end the tension. Continual U.S. presence and periodic maneuvers by U.S. naval forces contributed to the maintenance of the status quo in this Far Eastern "tinderbox."

12. Cambodia (29 March–15 August 1973). After the withdrawal of U.S. forces from Vietnam, Americans continued to be involved in the Cambodian struggle until the country fell to the Communist Khmer Rouge.

13. Thailand (29 March–15 August 1973). U.S. operations were conducted in and from Thailand in support of the operations in Cambodia.

14. Cambodia evacuation (Operation Eagle Pull) (11–13 April 1975). U.S. personnel conducted a massive evacuation to save many from the advancing Communist forces, who eventually took power and began a reign of terror.

15. Vietnam evacuation (Operation Frequent Wind) (29–30 April 1975). This massive evacuation saved Americans and many South Vietnamese from being captured or killed by advancing Communist forces.

16. *Mayaguez* operation (15 May 1975). After Communist Cambodian forces seized the U.S. containership *Mayaguez,* U.S. naval and Marine elements mounted a rescue operation at Koh Tang Island, where the ship had been taken. U.S. carrier forces simultaneously struck at air and naval bases in Cambodia.

17. El Salvador (1 January 1981–1 February 1992). As part of the Cold War struggle to keep third-world nations from falling under Communist influence and control, U.S. forces were involved in various operations for more than a decade in this Central American nation.

18. Lebanon (1 June 1983–1 December 1987). U.S. involvement in this troubled Middle Eastern nation included naval presence at times of crisis, the insertion of Marines as peacekeepers, air and fire support missions (including some fired by battleship), and evacuation operations.

19. Grenada (Operation Urgent Fury) (23 October–21 November 1983). In response to a Marxist coup and the threat of the establishment of a Communist military base on this Caribbean island, a U.S. twelve-ship task force, in conjunction with five hundred Marines, five hundred Army Rangers, five thousand Army paratroopers, and several SEAL units, assaulted the island. In three days, the island was occupied, government officials and American citizens were rescued, and more than six hundred Cubans were captured.

20. Libya (Operation Eldorado Canyon) (12–17 April 1986). In response to a Libyan-sponsored terrorist attack, U.S. Navy and Air Force aircraft attacked numerous targets in Libya, including known terrorist training camps, air defense positions, military aircraft and airfields, a naval base, and key government positions.

21. Persian Gulf (Operation Earnest Will) (24 July 1987–1 August 1990). In response to attacks on shipping in the Persian Gulf as a result of the ongoing Iran-Iraq War, U.S. naval ships escorted Kuwaiti oil tankers (which had been reflagged as U.S. merchant vessels). This action led to numerous naval operations and engagements, including air and surface strikes on selected Iranian targets, minesweeping operations, air and surface reconnaissance operations, and Operation Praying Mantis (retaliatory surface and air strikes against Iranian naval ships and bases and several oil platforms in the Persian Gulf). Ultimately, a total of 270 merchant vessels were escorted in 136 convoys, with just one merchant vessel and one naval ship damaged (both by mines).

22. Panama (Operation Just Cause) (20 December 1989–31 January 1990). After a series of provocations that convinced President George H. W. Bush that American interests (the Panama Canal) and U.S. citizens (some thirty-five thousand were in the country at the time) were threatened, he ordered U.S. forces into Panama. They effectively took control of the situation, captured General Manuel Noriega (source of much of the problem), and restored order to the strategically important nation.

23. Somalia (Operation Restore Hope) (3 December 1992–31 March 1995). In an attempt to safeguard the delivery of much-needed food and medical supplies to war-torn Somalia, U.S. Navy SEALs and Recon Marines led the way, landing at Mogadishu. Followed by some 12,500 American and 6,000 international troops from other nations, the situation caused the mission to change from one of humanitarian aid to actual combat. When all international forces were eventually withdrawn, a U.S. task force provided protection for the evacuation.

24. Persian Gulf/Iraq (Operation Southern Watch) (1 December 1993–19 March 2003). U.S. aircraft maintained reconnaissance patrols and flew frequent combat response missions in established zones over Iraq (these were "no-fly" zones for the Iraqis) as part of a containment strategy against Iraqi leader Saddam Hussein, who continually defied UN restrictions placed upon him in the aftermath of the Persian Gulf War.

25. Haiti (Operation Uphold Democracy) (16 September 1994–31 March 1995). To ensure the restoration of Haitian President Jean-Bertrand Aristide and to maintain order in the strife-torn nation, a U.S. task force landed Marines at Cap Haitien, leading the way for the establishment of a UN task force on the troubled island.

26. Operation Joint Endeavor (20 November 1995–16 December 1996). U.S. and allied nations deployed peacekeeping forces to Bosnia to implement the military elements of the Dayton Peace Accords. Working with U.S. Army and Air Force units as well as elements from NATO, Sailors and Marines helped to ensure stability in this war-torn region.

27. Operation Joint Guard (20 December 1996–20 June 1998). U.S. forces continued to ensure peace in Bosnia-Herzegovina as Operation Joint Endeavor transitioned into Operation Joint Guard.

28. Operation Joint Forge (21 June 1998–). Despite a reduction in forces, U.S. forces (including U.S. Navy SeaBees) remain in Bosnia-Herzegovina to maintain peace and stability.

Vietnam Service, 1962–73

From the time that American assistance to the Republic of South Vietnam was confined to an advisory status through the period of major combat actions, the varied and extensive roles of the U.S. Navy were crucial to the overall military effort in Southeast Asia.

The early participation of the U.S. Seventh Fleet allowed it to detect the infiltration of Communists by sea from the north, after which the Coastal Surveillance Force (Operation Market Time) conducted inshore operations as well as offshore patrols to augment the efforts of the Vietnamese Navy.

Mobility and the endurance sustained by underway replenishment forces resulted in maximum use of Seventh Fleet carriers for retaliatory raids, for strikes in support of troops ashore, and for attacks against the enemy lines of communication. Naval air operations were of particular importance in the days before adequate airfields could be built ashore, and the ability of task forces to operate in the nearby Tonkin Gulf permitted effective and efficient air operations against targets in North Vietnam.

The Amphibious Force of the Seventh Fleet projected ashore the first organized ground forces—U.S. Marines at Danang in March 1965—and carried out many later landings. Destroyers, cruisers, and the battleship *New Jersey* added the weight of their gunfire in support of forces ashore and conducted operations against the logistics lines of the enemy along the coast of North Vietnam.

The Amphibious Command drew upon its Underwater Demolition Team capability to develop SEAL teams, which conducted operations against Vietcong guerrillas. The River Patrol Force (Operation Game Warden) extended the control of waterways in the Mekong Delta and other areas of the Republic of South Vietnam. The joint Navy-Army operations of the Mobile Riverine Force captured base areas and defeated enemy concentrations.

Elements of the Coastal Surveillance, River Patrol, and Mobile Riverine Forces were eventually combined into Operation SEALORDS to interdict infiltration routes from Cambodia into the Mekong Delta, to control vital Mekong Delta waterways, and to harass the enemy in his base areas. The Navy's Service Force and the SeaBees provided essential support to in-country forces.

Sea lines of communication were a key to the prosecution of the war. From across the seas came the vast quantity of supplies required to fight this major war. Ships under the Navy's Military Sealift Command delivered all but a small percentage of the tonnage, and the Navy's sea power ensured that these capabilities remained unchallenged throughout the war.

Naval medical personnel serving valiantly in the field with the Marines, as well as in hospitals and in hospital ships, saved lives and healed the wounded with unprecedented success. Salvage forces provided similar services for ships and craft, rescuing vessels in distress and recovering those lost in combat or to disastrous weather.

After years of negotiations (from 1968 to 1973), the Paris Agreement of January 1973 between the United States, South Vietnam, North Vietnam, and the National Liberation Front finally ended the war, leaving the South Vietnamese with the responsibility for defending their own nation.

 Stars ★★

Three silver and two bronze stars represent the seventeen different campaigns and operations of the Vietnam War.

1. Vietnam advisory campaign (15 March 1962–7 March 1965). In the early days of U.S. involvement in Vietnam, Sailors worked with the developing VNN as advisors, helping them with such things as logistical support, vessel construction techniques, and so forth. As the Communist insurgency increased, the Americans became more and more involved in combat operations. During this phase, Seventh Fleet ships fought a battle with Vietnamese patrol craft in the Gulf of Tonkin and launched a retaliatory air strike into North Vietnam. A sustained bombing campaign of the North (dubbed "Rolling Thunder") began on 2 March 1965.

2. Vietnam defense campaign (8 March–24 December 1965). As Communist efforts in South Vietnam increased, U.S. carriers continued bombing North Vietnam while U.S. Marines landed from Seventh Fleet ships at Danang, marking the beginning of major combat involvement in Vietnam. The Navy established the Coastal Surveillance Force (dubbed "Operation Market Time"), using its own Swift boats and Coast Guard WPBs to stop Communist infiltration from the sea. On 18 December, the U.S. Navy began patrolling the rivers of South Vietnam in an operation named Game Warden.

3. Vietnamese counteroffensive, phase 1 (25 December 1965–30 June 1966). As the war continued, the Navy continued to patrol the coasts and rivers in brown-water operations. Minesweeping craft began patrolling the Long Tau River leading to Saigon to keep that vital waterway open to merchant traffic. Naval patrol craft worked to keep Vietnamese harbors open and safe in Operation Stable Door. Navy helicopters called "Seawolves" began supporting the newly arrived Navy PBRs in Game Warden missions.

4. Vietnamese counteroffensive, phase 2 (1 July 1966–31 May 1967). To support U.S. Army operations in the strategically vital Mekong Delta and RSSZ, the Navy created the Mobile Riverine Force, using altered landing craft as river assault vessels to carry Soldiers into the many waterways of the region and to provide fire and blocking support during these operations. Boatswain Mate First Class James Elliott Williams earned the Medal of Honor when he took his PBR patrol in harm's way and destroyed sixty-five enemy vessels and killed or captured hundreds of enemy soldiers that were infiltrating the Mekong Delta. Naval air operations continued from "Yankee Station" off North Vietnam and "Dixie Station" off South Vietnam.

5. Vietnamese counteroffensive, phase 3 (1 June 1967–29 January 1968). PBR patrols were extended into the northern provinces of South Vietnam (so-called I-Corps tactical zone) during Operation Green Wave, while the Mobile Riverine Force conducted several large operations in the Mekong Delta and RSSZ. SeaBee units continued the massive buildup of combat support facilities all over South Vietnam.

6. Tet counteroffensive (30 January–1 April 1968). Enemy attacks erupted all over South Vietnam during the holiday period known as Tet. After some initial setbacks in the early hours of the surprise offensive, U.S. and South Vietnamese forces responded by soundly defeating enemy elements. General William Westmoreland, overall commander of U.S. forces in South Vietnam, credited the Mobile Riverine Force with "saving the [Mekong] Delta" during this period.

7. Vietnamese counteroffensive, phase 4 (2 April–30 June 1968). In the aftermath of the Tet Offensive, naval forces continued to patrol the rivers and coastlines and to provide direct air support for various operations in South Vietnam. Air operations against the North continued in the panhandle region.

8. Vietnamese counteroffensive, phase 5 (1 July–1 November 1968). Combat and support operations continued, but the strategy began to shift to the "Vietnamization" of the war (turning over patrol and combat operations to the South Vietnamese). As a first step, the VNN began minesweeping operations on the Long Tau River.

9. Vietnamese counteroffensive, phase 6 (2 November 1968–22 February 1969). Bombing of North Vietnam was halted as a peace gesture, but reconnaissance flights continued. Air operations in the South continued, and the U.S. Navy initiated the Operation SEALORDS interdiction strategy that led to increased fighting on the waterways. The Navy also implemented its ACTOV in December 1968.

10. Tet 1969/counteroffensive (23 February–8 June 1969). Fighting continued in the Mekong Delta as the U.S. Navy launched several offensives (Operation Giant Slingshot, Operation Barrier Reef, among others). The Navy also conducted raids into the rivers in the I-Corps tactical zone.

11. Vietnam summer–fall 1969 (9 June–31 October 1969). Turnover to the VNN picked up speed while American Sailors kept the pressure on enemy forces through continued offensive operations.

12. Vietnam winter–spring 1970 (1 November 1969–30 April 1970). Several operations were conducted during this period (Sea Float, Breezy Cove, Ready Deck, and the like) to maintain pressure on enemy forces while ACTOV continued.

13. Sanctuary counteroffensive (1 May–30 June 1970). Naval air provided support for an incursion into Cambodia. Operation Blue Shark replaced the Operation Market Time raider program.

14. Vietnamese counteroffensive, phase 7 (1 July 1970–30 June 1971). American naval advisors played an increasingly central role in South Vietnam as Vietnamization continued. U.S. naval air supported the South Vietnamese incursion into the Laotian sanctuary.

15. Consolidation I (1 July–30 November 1971). U.S. Sailors remained in Vietnam, performing advisory roles while air reconnaissance and occasional retaliatory strikes were conducted against North Vietnam.

16. Consolidation II (1 December 1971–29 March 1972). Air operations against North Vietnam intensified as it became clear that a major military buildup was under way.

17. Vietnam ceasefire campaign (30 March 1972–28 January 1973). In April 1972, the last naval bases were turned over to the South Vietnamese; in that same month, the North Vietnamese launched a major invasion of the south. U.S. airpower played a key role in repelling the invaders as American advisors fought alongside their Vietnamese counterparts in the largest series of battles since the Tet Offensive of 1968. In January 1973, the Paris Peace Accords were signed, ending U.S. involvement in the war.

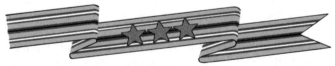

Southwest Asia Service, 1991–95

This medal was authorized on 12 March 1991 for participation in or support of military operations in Southwest Asia or in the surrounding areas between 2 August 1990 and 30 November 1995, including Operations Desert Shield and Desert Storm.

Stars ★ ★ ★

Three bronze stars represent the three different campaigns of the Southwest Asia Service battle streamer.

1. Defense of Saudi Arabia (2 August 1990–16 January 1991). When Iraq invaded Kuwait, President George H. W. Bush ordered two U.S. aircraft carriers into the area to join other naval forces already on station as a visible deterrent to further Iraqi aggression against the strategic vital nation of Saudi Arabia. A massive buildup of U.S. forces in the region (dubbed "Operation Desert Shield") prepared to go to war with the Iraqi forces to drive them out of Kuwait.

2. Liberation and defense of Kuwait (17 January–11 April 1991). In a massive attack involving air, naval, and ground forces (dubbed "Operation Desert Storm"), the United States led a coalition of forces to liberate Kuwait. Air strikes, missile attacks, and naval gunfire missions led the attack, carrying out such missions for more than a month before ground troops began the final assault that defeated the Iraqi forces and liberated Kuwait.

3. Southwest Asia ceasefire campaign (12 April 1991–30 November 1995). In the aftermath of Operation Desert Storm, U.S. forces remained in the area, carrying out various missions (among them, reconnaissance, air strikes, and humanitarian aid) to contain Iraq and prevent further destabilization in the region.